Medicare Now and in the Future

MARILYN MOON

Medicare Now and in the Future

THE URBAN INSTITUTE PRESS
Washington, D.C.

THE URBAN INSTITUTE PRESS
2100 M Street, N.W.
Washington, D.C. 20037

Editorial Advisory Board
William Gorham
Demetra S. Nightingale
Craig G. Coelen   George E. Peterson
Adele V. Harrell   Felicity Skidmore
Ronald B. Mincy   Raymond J. Struyk
Marilyn Moon

Library of Congress Cataloging in Publication Data

Medicare Now and in the Future/Marilyn Moon.

1. Medicare. 2. Medicare—Forecasting. 3. Medicare—Cost control.
4. Forecasting. 5. Medicare—trends. I. Title.

HD7102.U4M666   1993   92-38302
368.4'26'00973—dc20   CIP

ISBN 0-87766-591-5 (alk. paper)
ISBN 0-87766-590-7 (alk. paper; casebound)

Urban Institute books are printed on acid-free paper whenever possible.

Printed in the United States of America.

Distributed by:
          University Press of America
4720 Boston Way   3 Henrietta Street
Lanham, MD 20706   London   WC2E 8LU   ENGLAND

THE URBAN INSTITUTE is a nonprofit policy research and educational organization established in Washington, D.C., in 1968. Its staff investigates the social and economic problems confronting the nation and government policies and programs designed to alleviate such problems. The Institute disseminates significant findings of its research through the publications program of its Press. The Institute has two goals for work in each of its research areas: to help shape thinking about societal problems and efforts to solve them, and to improve government decisions and performance by providing better information and analytic tools.

Through work that ranges from broad conceptual studies to administrative and technical assistance, Institute researchers contribute to the stock of knowledge available to public officials and private individuals and groups concerned with formulating and implementing more efficient and effective government policy.

Conclusions or opinions expressed in Institute publications are those of the authors and do not necessarily reflect the views of staff members, officers or trustees of the Institute, advisory groups, or any organizations that provide financial support to the Institute.

CONTENTS

Tables

Figures

Reining in the growth of entitlement programs, particularly curtailing the healthcare costs that contribute so much to this growth, will clearly be high on the agenda of the Clinton administration. Medicare will be at the heart of these efforts. In her book, Marilyn Moon draws on research done on the Medicare program at the Urban Institute and elsewhere to describe both the possibilities and the pitfalls that await those who wish to make major cuts in the program. This volume is less oriented to a particular research project than are many of the Institute's books, but it is certainly consistent with the goal of the Urban Institute to inform policy debate on important domestic programs.

The book begins by providing an excellent history of the development of Medicare. Moon provides a very clear discussion of the most important policy changes in recent years. She describes, for example, the development of Medicare's prospective payment system for hospitals and its fee schedule for physicians. She highlights the accomplishments of these policies as well as the problems that still face them. The discussion makes it clear that further cutbacks in hospital and physician payments will be difficult to achieve without linkage of those policies to payments for care provided to the rest of the population. It is clear that Medicare has achieved a great deal in payment policy, but for the program to go further on its own will pose serious risks for access to care for the nation's elderly. President Clinton has articulated a similar view.

But Moon also points to many problems that have not yet been resolved by the Medicare program. Coverage of prescription drugs is a major one. Moon argues that it will be difficult to expand coverage of prescription drugs to the younger population and not at the same time similarly expand coverage to the elderly. Thus, all of the attention to Medicare will not be simply to reduce its scope or benefits.

Many observers argue that the benefits to the elderly from Medicare far outweigh their contributions and that therefore they should bear more of the burden of financing of the program. But Moon makes a compelling case that many of the elderly have limited income and assets. Broad-based expansions of financial responsibility could place significant burdens on large numbers of elderly Americans. Moon provides a detailed analysis of the kinds of increased financial burdens that the elderly can reasonably be expected to bear and those that they cannot.

Because Medicare will be at the heart of healthcare policy deliberations in the coming years, this book will be extremely important. But Medicare has now come to be only part of the healthcare debate. Moon makes a major contribution by providing the information necessary for readers to understand the role of Medicare in broader healthcare system reform.

William Gorham
President

PREFACE

Medicare is a fascinating and complex healthcare program. But it is often not well understood. I have been interested in writing a book on Medicare since I first started work on the program in earnest in 1981. I discovered that it was difficult to find information on how the program worked and to understand its arcane rules and regulations. Through the years I have sometimes been asked to steer people to material that could explain the program and have found it difficult to offer up suggestions. Beyond a number of early books about Medicare's beginnings, there is surprisingly little in the literature that provides an overview of the program. Thus, this was the first motivation for my efforts.

It has also become increasingly clear that Medicare needs to change over time to face the competing realities of federal budget stringency, a changing elderly population, and pressures to reform the overall healthcare system. No easy path suggests itself in Medicare. The program is very expensive and has gobbled up an increasingly large share of the federal budget at the same time that unmet needs for elderly and disabled persons remain. Further, Medicare is sometimes the goat and sometimes the shining example used by those who argue for other reforms. The second half of this book offers a number of options for change that are often put forward and concludes with a set of recommendations that I hope balance the competing influences seeking to change Medicare.

Finally, my interest in writing about Medicare was further stimulated by observing, at close range, the rise and fall of the Medicare Catastrophic Coverage Act. At the time, I was serving as Director of the Public Policy Institute of the American Association of Retired Persons. That organization was heavily involved in lobbying for the legislation, and while not directly involved, I was keenly aware of the issues and histrionics. I am unsure whether to characterize the activity surrounding catastrophic coverage as viewing the "inside of the sausage," or as watching a Greek tragedy unfold. Policy is certainly a messy process in the best of circumstances and many of the activities surrounding the legislation were not the finest hours of intelligent policymaking. But it is also the case that the first foray in changing the nature of Medicare to one that differentiated among the beneficiaries was likely doomed to failure. Whatever history's final judgement on the Catastrophic legislation, it will likely have many short term ramifications on policy for health programs and entitlement programs in the U.S. Consequently, I devote a whole chapter to what happened to that legislation and what we might learn from that period.

No project of this sort has any hope of success without the generous help of colleagues and friends, and this book is certainly no exception. Along the way, many people read and critiqued at least parts of the manuscript. I am most indebted to Douglas Gomery who succeeds in being simultaneously unfailingly supportive and a tough critic. My work is always better for his crucial eye.

Judith Feder read the manuscript at a stage when I would not have trusted anyone else to see my failings and helped me rethink issues and reorganize a number of portions of the manuscript. Her interest and enthusiasm are contagious. John Holahan carefully read the full manuscript at an early stage and helped identify other relevant research . I deeply appreciate the time and care he devoted. Steve Zuckerman, Korbin Liu, and Kathy Swartz read parts of the manuscript and saved me from some embarrassing errors. In the final stages, Pete Welch, Marianna Diggs, Diana Verrilli, and Ed Howard helped me track down missing references. Chad Abrams produced many of the graphs and tables for the volume. Molly Ruzicka expertly copyedited the volume and caught a number of inconsistencies and fuzzy language. Felicity Skidmore strongly encouraged me to keep at the project when I thought I might never finish.

And I must not forget to acknowledge the funding for this project. When I returned to the Institute in late 1989, I indicated that I wanted to be able to write a book on Medicare. John Holahan, Steve Hitchner, Bill Gorham, and Craig Coelen have all been supportive of the project and provided me with the funds to do much of the book. In addition, a grant from the Retirement Research Foundation allowed me to spend more time on developing and simulating some of the options for change that appear here.

Chapter One

PLACING MEDICARE IN CONTEXT

Medicare has contributed substantially to the well-being of America's oldest and most disabled citizens. It is the largest public healthcare program in the United States, providing the major source of insurance for acute care for the elderly and disabled populations. For many, Medicare represents a model of what national health insurance could be in the United States. Its administrative costs are low, and it is popular with both its beneficiaries and the general population. At the same time, Medicare is the fastest growing program in the federal budget, gobbling up new resources at the rate of nearly 16 percent each year during its first 25 years. Critics assail the program as being out of sync with the needs of many senior citizens through its failure to provide long-term care coverage. It is the subject of endless criticism and debate by physicians and hospital administrators, who nonetheless rely upon it for a substantial share of their revenues. Medicare is all these things and more.

In 1992, Medicare consumed $132 billion in federal outlays. Each year since 1980, it has been a major focus of budget reduction efforts. The controversy over the appropriate size and funding for the program will continue for the foreseeable future. This book examines the current status of Medicare and offers options for the future: What is Medicare, how does it work, and where is it headed? What are the problems facing Medicare, and how can they be resolved? What options for the future hold the most promise? How does Medicare relate to the growing national debate about healthcare?

WHY EXAMINE MEDICARE NOW?

The portion of the federal budget devoted to healthcare has been expanding rapidly since 1965, when Medicare was introduced as a program to help meet the healthcare needs of the aged in the United

States. Critics pointed out early on that Medicare spending was likely to grow rapidly; and grow it did. For example, in 1970, spending on Medicare totaled $6.8 billion, or about 3.5 percent of the total federal budget. Twenty years later, that share had more than doubled as Medicare accounted for 8.6 percent of the federal budget and about $107 billion in outlays (U.S. Congress, House Committee on Ways and Means [henceforth, Ways and Means] 1991) (see figure 1.1).

This rapid increase is outstripping the growth in dedicated revenues to support the hospital portion of Medicare. The Federal Hospital Insurance Trust Fund is projected to be exhausted shortly after the turn of the century if policies remain the same.[1] After postponing the

Figure 1.1 MEDICARE AS SHARE OF FEDERAL BUDGET, 1965–95

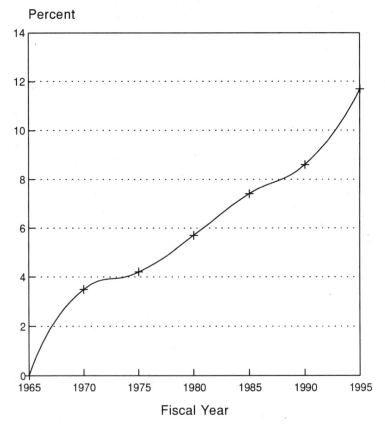

Source: U.S. Congress, House Committee on Ways and Means (henceforth, Ways and Means) (1991).

date of reckoning consistently for the past decade—by major cost-cutting efforts and increasing the wage base subject to taxation—the latest Medicare trustees report accelerated the date of exhaustion to 2002 (Board of Trustees, Federal Hospital Insurance Trust Fund [henceforth, HI Trustees] 1992). The 1993 trustees report is likely to formally recommend ways to restore the projected long-term balances in the trust fund.

Because of its size and rapid growth, Medicare also became a target in the budget reduction exercises, beginning in earnest with the administration of Ronald Reagan. Every budget submission by Presidents Reagan and George Bush has contained proposals for substantial cuts in Medicare. Many of those cost-containment changes, particularly in the area of provider reimbursement, were enacted by the U.S. Congress in the 1980s. Nonetheless, Medicare has continued to expand; its growth each year has exceeded the size of any spending cuts. Projections produced in 1992 indicated that Medicare would consume almost 16 percent of the federal budget by 2002 (Ways and Means 1992), despite cuts in the 1990 budget summit agreement of $43 billion over the five years between 1990 and 1995. These reductions, even if fully "successful," will change the overall trend line in Medicare growth very little (see figure 1.2). In Medicare, "cuts" of even billions of dollars do not mean declines in spending—just a slower rate of increase.

Thus, despite the deficit reduction package that was introduced with much fanfare in fall 1990, further budget cuts or revenue increases are likely to be sought over time. And because Medicare is such a large component of the federal budget, it is liable to receive particular scrutiny for further sources of budget reductions. Most of its enrollees are over age 65. In the last several years, the growing share of the budget devoted to older Americans has been noted with alarm by conservatives and liberals alike, some claiming that more resources should be freed up for children, and others contending that too much public money is spent on the elderly. All three presidential candidates in 1992 singled out Medicare as a program for further scrutiny and cutbacks.[2]

At the same time that much of the focus in Medicare has been on reducing spending, critics argue that the program inadequately meets the needs of the aged and disabled. Medicare's coverage is less generous than that offered many younger families and individuals through employer-subsidized insurance. The ill-fated Medicare Catastrophic Coverage Act of 1988 sought to fill in some of those gaps, but that legislation was repealed just 18 months after passage. Further,

Figure 1.2 ANNUAL FEDERAL OUTLAY FOR MEDICARE, 1970–95

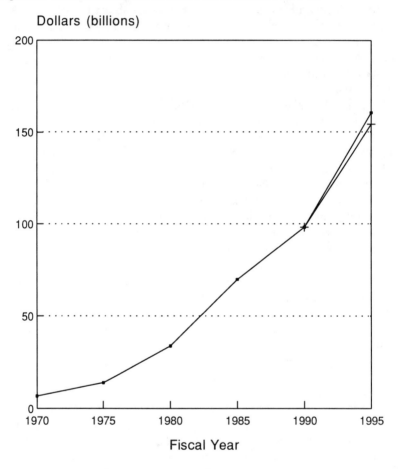

Dollars (billions)

Fiscal Year

— Before 1992 Cuts + After 1992 Cuts

Source: Congressional Budget Office (1991).

long-term care needs for elderly and disabled persons threaten many middle-class families; supporters of expanded long-term care benefits often seek to add such coverage to Medicare.[3]

In many ways, Medicare has been of only secondary concern in the debate over broader reform. Some would leave Medicare intact and mold the rest of the healthcare system around it. As a popular and successful program, it is often viewed as "untouchable" even by those advocating sweeping changes elsewhere.[4] Others would fold Medicare into a fully public system, or "privatize" it to conform to a similar market-based reform plan for younger families. Whatever the approach ultimately taken, healthcare reform will need to confront the Medicare program. Conformity of the benefit package and consistent treatment of healthcare providers between Medicare and the rest of the system is essential. If the health plan for younger families is more generous, Medicare might need to be expanded, for example. It is foolish to consider any substantial reforms in Medicare outside the context of the more general debate on health reform.

Three areas of pressure will shape the future of Medicare. First, Medicare was established to help the elderly, and then disabled persons, to afford medical care. Thus, the economic status of these two groups—and particularly the elderly—is a critical factor in assessing how the system ought to change. Second, what happens in the healthcare system overall clearly affects Medicare. In many ways, the problems facing Medicare are but a reflection of the broader problems facing healthcare in the United States. At least some of the solutions to Medicare's problems should apply systemwide. Finally, Medicare's future as a public program is tied to the financing problems facing the federal government during a period of fiscal restraint. So long as budget deficits continue at the federal level, changes in Medicare will be caught up in the pressure to limit all types of federal spending.

ECONOMIC STATUS OF OLDER AMERICANS

By every measure of economic well-being, the situation for older Americans has improved substantially over the past three decades. For example, incomes for those 65 and older have risen steadily, from a median per capita income of $3,408 in 1975 to $10,174 in 1990 (U.S. Bureau of the Census 1991). After controlling for inflation, this represents a gain of 22.9 percent in the purchasing power of this age group. Moreover, in the 1980s, the elderly's income growth outstripped increases in income for younger subgroups of the population. Although average before-tax incomes for elderly families still lag behind those of younger families, after adjusting for differences in family size and tax liabilities, the disposable (posttax) per capita incomes of older Americans do not differ substantially from those of their younger counterparts (Danziger et al. 1984; Smeeding 1986).

But to fully comprehend the ability of elderly individuals to meet their needs, it is crucial to look beyond averages and to understand the diversity of the resources available to this group. Although the elderly have shown impressive gains, not every elderly individual has experienced such increases. For example, some of the increase in well-being associated with comparisons of incomes across time reflects the changing composition of the elderly. Each year individuals turning age 65 join the elderly "category," and the incomes of new cohorts of 65-year-olds tend, on average, to be higher each year. As a result, individuals within the elderly population display much slower rates of income growth than does the group as a whole. For example, as shown in table 1.1, growth in median incomes for persons 65 and over averaged 7.1 percent for men and 4.9 percent for women between 1985 and 1990 (after controlling for inflation). But if, instead, we followed the cohort of persons aged 65 to 69 in 1985 (and aged 70 to 74 in 1990), incomes for that group rose much more slowly, and actually declined for men.

On a more positive note, elderly poverty has declined. The share of the elderly in poverty dropped from 25 percent in 1968 to 12.2 percent in 1990 (U.S. Bureau of the Census 1991b). In 1982, for the first time, the official rate of poverty among the elderly was lower than that for the rest of the population. The largest declines in poverty rates for the elderly occurred before 1975, however, and the rates have remained relatively flat since 1984 (see figure 1.3).

In addition, in recent years, the validity of the poverty measures generally used has come under increasing scrutiny. We underestimate poverty for the elderly in the United States. In her recent book on problems with the measurement of poverty, Patricia Ruggles (1990) has argued that the measures we use understate the true number of poor, and that those for the elderly are particularly misleading. That is, the standard measures use lower poverty lines for households headed by someone over age 65—an outdated concept. Ruggles esti-

Table 1.1 GROWTH IN MEDIAN INCOME FOR ALL ELDERLY AND FOR SPECIFIC COHORT IN THE UNITED STATES, 1985–90

	Median Income, 1990 ($)	Real Income Growth, 1985–90 (%)
Men		
All 65 and older	14,183	7.1
Aged 65–69 in 1985	14,665	−4.1
Women		
All 65 and older	8,044	4.9
Aged 65–69 in 1985	8,160	2.9

Source: U.S. Bureau of the Census (1986, 1991).

Figure 1.3 POVERTY RATES IN THE UNITED STATES FOR PERSONS AGED 65
AND OLDER, 1966–89

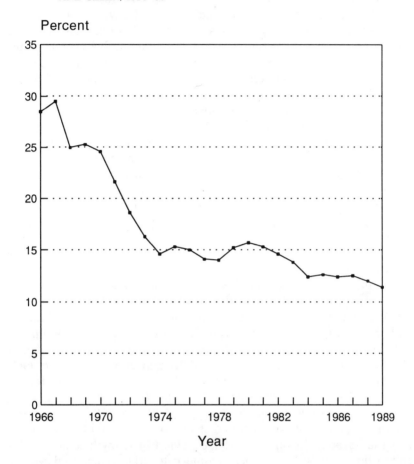

Source: U.S. Bureau of the Census, 1991b.

mated that, in 1986, eliminating this distinction would have raised
the rate of poverty among the elderly from 12.4 to 15.3 percent, well
above that for the population as a whole.

For all age groups, changing living standards are not well factored
into poverty measures. A reestimation for this reason would also
result in a disproportionate increase in the number of elderly desig-
nated as poor. If both problems are corrected, between one-fourth and
one-third of those aged 65 or more would be counted as poor.

The share of the elderly in poverty is sensitive because of the large number of older persons now clustered just above the official poverty lines. In 1990, 3.7 million individuals 65 or older were listed as poor. Another 2.1 million have incomes of no more than 25 percent above the poverty threshold. When we count the total number with incomes below 150 percent of the poverty threshold, 26.3 percent of the elderly—about 7.9 million persons—had very limited incomes (U.S. Bureau of the Census 1991b).

In 1990, virtually the same number of persons over 65 had incomes below 150 percent of poverty as the number in 1983 (Ruggles and Cullinan 1985). Even if we do not formally designate these individuals as poor, many elderly remain in the near-poor category; they have not "escaped" very far above the poverty level. People with incomes above the poverty level are generally ineligible for means-tested programs and are particularly vulnerable to any economic hardships. A severe illness could wipe out the fragile economic base of these older Americans.

It is true that the elderly do hold more assets, on average, than other families with low and moderate incomes, but even if these assets are taken into account, relatively few of today's low-income elderly would be counted as well-off. More than half of the elderly with incomes below 150 percent of the poverty threshold also had less than $10,000 in total asset holdings, for example (Ruggles and Williams 1989).

In recent years the pattern of income growth has increased this dispersion rather than lessened it. Although growth between 1967 and 1979 was disproportionately greater for the lowest-income groups, the opposite was true between 1979 and 1984 (Radner 1987). More recent studies indicate that for the period 1979 to 1990, those in the bottom two-fifths of the income distribution continued to experience less-than-average income growth (see table 1.2). Growth occurred disproportionately in the higher-income categories (Ways and Means 1992).

What about those with substantial resources? This is the group that many policymakers would target for cuts in Medicare benefits. As table 1.2 indicates, the top 20 percent of elderly couples had incomes averaging $77,308 in 1990, and the highest one-fifth of singles averaged $34,149. The next highest quintile had an average income substantially below that of the highest quintile, dropping by more than half in each case. Should some elderly persons be asked to make substantially higher contributions toward their healthcare? This will be an important part of the debate and will hinge on how well-off we perceive older persons at the top of the income distribution to be. For

Table 1.2 FAMILY INCOME OF THE ELDERLY BY INCOME QUINTILES IN 1990
AND GROWTH SINCE 1979

Type of Family and Quintile	Income in 1990 ($)	Change in Income 1979–90 (%)
Elderly Childless Families		
Lowest	9,632	16.2
Second	17,358	19.0
Middle	25,209	21.1
Fourth	36,538	20.0
Highest	77,308	26.5
Total	33,205	22.8
Elderly Unrelated Individuals		
Lowest	4,256	8.6
Second	6,973	11.5
Middle	9,980	18.9
Fourth	15,103	20.6
Highest	34,149	15.8
Total	14,089	16.3

Source: U.S. Bureau of the Census (1991a and 1980).

example, compare the figures just cited to quintiles across all families, in which average income in 1990 in the top quintile was $94,404— substantially higher than for elderly couples, but also likely capturing larger family size (U.S. Bureau of the Census 1991a).[5]

In sum, the dichotomy between the wealthiest and the poorest older Americans continues, creating new challenges for public policy. We have opened the door for more debate regarding the treatment of older persons in programs like Medicare.

Prospects for the Future

If the trends of the last decade were taken as projections into the next, we would expect to see continued steady growth in average incomes of the elderly, continued improvement relative to the working population, and a general trend toward somewhat lower poverty rates. Evidence from the 1950–80 Censuses (Ross, Danziger, and Smolensky 1987) and from wealth surveys taken between 1962 and 1983 (Wolff 1987) indicates that the next generation of elderly—that is, those born between 1920 and 1935, and reaching age 65 between 1985 and 2000—will be considerably better off as they age than their older counterparts. This group had the good fortune to be in their prime working years during the period of maximum earnings growth of the halcyon 1960s, to find the value of their homes soaring during the inflation of the 1970s, and to be in the maximum liquid asset position to capture most fully the benefits of high real interest rates and the stock market boom of the early to mid-1980s.

But this suggests too rosy a scenario. There are several reasons for caution in assuming ever-rising increases in economic status for the elderly. The rate of growth of Social Security benefits has already slackened, and the slow growth in average wages for current workers will limit their benefits as retirees. Income from private pensions, which has shown rapid growth in recent years, now seems to be leveling off. The proportion of the population receiving pensions will not grow as rapidly in the future.

The changing age composition of the elderly will also retard the extent to which incomes grow over time. The very old will increase as a proportion of the elderly, and their lower average incomes are likely to help hold down overall rates of growth in income as compared to the growth of the 1970s. The younger old will be better off, but the over-85 age group will constitute an increasing share of the elderly population. In the near future, as the elderly population grows more as a result of longer life spans than because of new "entrants" to the 65 and over category, income growth will tend to be slower. In the 1990s, growth in the numbers of persons 65 and over will be concentrated in the over age-85 category, reflecting increased life expectancies. Individuals reaching retirement age will have been born in the 1930s, a period when birth rates were very low. Between 1990 and the year 2000, the population between the ages of 65 and 74 will grow by only 1.2 percent, while the group of those aged 85 and above will grow by 34 percent (Ways and Means 1992).

If these moderating influences on growth hold and the economy experiences relatively rapid real growth in the next decade, the status of the elderly relative to the young could again decline. More likely, however, the economic position of the elderly will stabilize relative to their younger counterparts. Growth in incomes for both the elderly and the young will likely average out to a moderate pace over the near term. This relative status of the elderly is likely to be important in any political debates over who should pay for Medicare, since many of the potential policy alternatives involve trade-offs between burdens on the old and the young.

Burdens from Health Spending

The percentage of income spent on healthcare by persons over age 65 is at an all-time high and will increase further. And as figure 1.4

Figure 1.4 HEALTHCARE SPENDING IN THE UNITED STATES AS SHARE OF
INCOME, PERSONS 65 AND OLDER, 1965–87

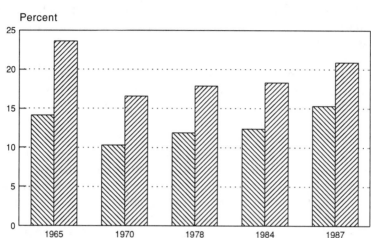

Sources: Waldo et al. (1989); U.S. Bureau of the Census (1990 and unpublished data).

indicates, whether compared to mean or median income, this spending now represents a critical burden for the elderly.[6] Incomes have
risen rapidly for this age group, but out-of-pocket health costs have
simply risen faster.[7]

Analyses of the acute-care portion of these expenses reveal considerable burdens on those with low or moderate incomes. The low rates
of private health insurance purchased by this group also leave them
vulnerable to very high potential healthcare liabilities. For example,
in 1986, elderly persons with a hospital stay and incomes of less than
$10,000 spent 18.3 percent of their own income for acute healthcare
services (Feder, Moon, and Scanlon 1987b). Since this is an average,
it understates the level of burden for a considerable minority of this
group.

The purchase of private supplemental coverage, often termed
"Medigap," is not a solution, since it tends to *raise* the average spending on healthcare. Since many older Americans pay fully for this
insurance, they are effectively still bearing the burden of healthcare
costs, plus paying an additional amount to cover the often substantial
administrative costs of the insurance (Feder et al. 1987a). Because so

many older persons have relatively high expenditures, this insurance does not spread the risks of health spending enough to result in lower costs for the average individual. It does help reduce the chances of high burdens in any one year, but Medigap does not address the basic problem of affordability.

Two major areas of protection are available for the elderly, one at each end of the income distribution. At the bottom, Medicaid fills in the gaps. In addition, about 30 percent of older persons have supplemental coverage from a former employer, which is at least partially subsidized (National Center for Health Services Research [henceforth, NCHSR] 1989). Although this employer coverage is usually only for acute care, it does offer important relief for those who have it. This relief is concentrated among persons with higher incomes.[8]

The costs of long-term care hold the potential for even more devastating reductions in economic status for older families. The burdens imposed by these costs are hard to evaluate in general, but on a case-by-case basis, an individual pays, on average, more than $30,000 for a year's stay in a nursing home. Medicare pays virtually nothing for long-term care, and Medicaid will only cover these costs once an individual has spent down nearly all of his or her assets. Even with the expanded Medicaid protection to lessen the impact of this "spend down" that was established by the Medicare Catastrophic Coverage Act, the spouse remaining in the community often faces a much-reduced standard of living. It is under these conditions that even middle-class elderly families find it impossible to meet their health-care needs.

The likelihood of incurring costs from both acute and long-term healthcare rise steadily with age—in reverse proportion to ability to pay. An elderly woman living alone is most at risk of needing long-term care services (Doty, Liu, and Wiener 1985). And the outlook for the future is not particularly reassuring. Rivlin and Wiener (1988) suggested that only a minority of older families will ever be able to afford long-term care expenditures. As yet, there are no indications that these burdens will diminish, raising the prospect of increasing burdens over time.

The burdens of healthcare will expand faster than the elderly's ability to pay for the foreseeable future. Over the same period that median incomes rose 34 percent, real out-of-pocket spending on healthcare rose by more than 80 percent (Moon 1991b). To conclude that we have solved the income problems of all older Americans is premature—now and for the foreseeable future.

THE ECONOMIC STATUS OF DISABLED PERSONS

Medicare is usually seen as a program for the over-65 population, but it covers younger disabled Americans as well. Relatively little is known about the economic status of the approximately 3 million disabled Medicare beneficiaries, who comprise about 10 percent of all Medicare beneficiaries. By definition, such individuals must be unable to work, so unless other family members are in the labor force, the family is likely to face severe economic constraints. Moreover, the onset of disability may occur in conjunction with high levels of spending on medical care and high rates of absenteeism from the workplace. Both of these factors may serve as a drain on the resources of the disabled worker and of his or her family. Moreover, disabled persons must then wait for over two years to become eligible for benefits.

One recent study found that disabled Social Security recipients were more likely to be poor in comparison to either the general population or persons receiving Social Security as retired workers (Grad 1989).[9] The rate of poverty was 19 percent for these disabled persons, and 30 percent were either poor or near poor. By comparison, only 17 percent of retired workers were poor or near poor. Moreover, disabled workers are even less likely to have assets upon which to draw than are their older counterparts, since the former have not had as many years or opportunities to accumulate wealth.

Thus, although details on the economic status of Medicare disabled beneficiaries are sketchy, this group appears to have much in common with older beneficiaries. Like the elderly, a disproportionate number are poor, and there is a considerable disparity between the rich and poor among them. Moreover, out-of-pocket healthcare costs are likely to represent a considerable burden on this group, since their average Medicare expenditures are higher than for the elderly.[10]

THE PROBLEM OF RISING HEALTHCARE COSTS

The problems driving Medicare costs upward are not unique to the public sector; rather, they are found throughout our nation's healthcare system. The crisis of rising healthcare costs affects payers: individuals, businesses, and governments. Although Medicare has been a leader in experimenting with options for curbing the costs of care, both in terms of increasing prices and use of services, costs continue to rise.

Prices

During the 1970s healthcare prices rose rapidly, but at about the same rate as all prices in the economy. In the 1980s, however, the general rise in consumer prices fell, whereas healthcare prices remained high. As figure 1.5 indicates, prices followed essentially the same track until 1975, when there was a slight divergence. After 1980, inflation in the

Figure 1.5 HEALTHCARE PRICE INFLATION IN THE UNITED STATES, 1965–90

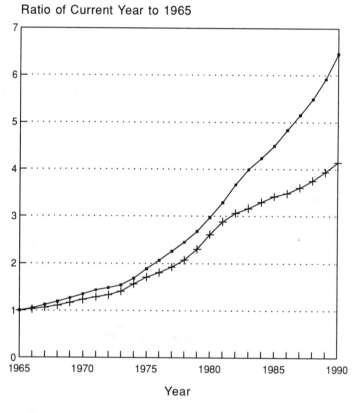

Ratio of Current Year to 1965

Year

— CPI Medical Care + CPI All Items

Source: Office of the President (1992b).

cost of healthcare occurred at rates substantially higher than that for the overall index. Since then, the medical care component of the consumer price index (CPI) has never been below the rate of growth of the remaining components.[11] Between 1980 and 1990, all consumer prices grew 58.6 percent, whereas the CPI for healthcare grew 117.4 percent (Office of the President 1992b).

What caused this inflation in healthcare prices during a decade when the rate of growth of other prices slowed substantially? Some economists point to the fact that healthcare is heavily service oriented, with rising wages in these areas translating directly into rising prices. It is difficult to find ways to cut costs per service. Productivity thus does not rise much in this sector of the economy. Yet, costs of manufactured goods like pharmaceuticals are also increasing faster than inflation in general.

Nor is it possible to blame the inflation in healthcare prices on strong demand for scarce services. The supply of physicians continued its rapid growth through both the 1970s and 1980s. For example, in 1970 the number of active physicians per 10,000 population stood at 15.6. By 1988, the number was 23.3 (National Center for Health Statistics [henceforth, NCHS] 1991). This greater supply of physicians has not, however, lowered their incomes, which rose an average of 8.6 percent per year from 1979 to 1988 (see figure 1.6). Further, hospitals

Figure 1.6 AVERAGE ANNUAL GROWTH RATES IN PHYSICIAN NET INCOME BY SPECIALTY IN THE UNITED STATES, 1979–88

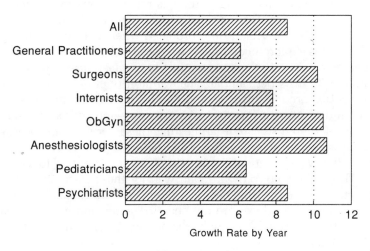

Source: American Medical Association, 1988.

operated at much less than capacity throughout the 1980s, with occupancy rates averaging about 66 percent in 1988 (American Hospital Association [henceforth, AHA] 1990).

Much of the explanation for rising prices undoubtedly rests with the fact that until very recently the price structure of the healthcare industry had not come under heavy scrutiny. Users of healthcare are typically not the payers; usually a "third party" such as an insurance company or the government pays for the care. Insured people do not choose who to see or what to use on the basis of the prices charged. Moreover, even when the patient is paying directly, people facing a medical crisis are unlikely to shop around for the least expensive care or to question the need for various services. In short, the market for healthcare goods and services does not foster price competition.

Use of Services

Despite these price rises, the use of services has also continued to increase over time. This occurs not so much in terms of overall numbers of visits but in the type and complexity of healthcare services (often referred to as "intensity"). To some extent, this is related to new technology that has given us new tools such as computerized tomography (CT) scans and magnetic resonance imagers (MRIs), or new procedures such as endoscopies and arthroscopies. These new sources of healthcare spending tend to operate as additions to goods and services consumed, rather than as replacements for old technologies or procedures. For example, people may now receive x-rays, CT scans, *and* MRIs to diagnose a problem, whereas before only x-rays (and perhaps exploratory surgery) were available. As another example, rather than subjecting a blood sample to one test, it is now simple to run 30 or 40 tests per sample. The availability of new tests and procedures that are less invasive and painful has surely improved diagnosis and treatment for many Americans—and increased the frequency of their use. Some argue that these services are overused, when less advanced tests or fewer alternative tests would be sufficient. But for the average patient, it may simply be too tempting to use these tools. Physicians not only are paid well for these extra tests, but the tests may reduce the time necessary to make a diagnosis.

These new procedures are not cheap. The median hospital charge for an MRI, for example, which was not available at all in 1980, was $850 in 1989 (Hospital Insurance Association of America [henceforth, HIAA] 1991). Similarly, the "scopes" also carry hefty price tags; for instance, the median physician fee for diagnostic knee arthroscopy was $708 in 1989 (HIAA 1991). New drugs to treat problems such as hypertension or blood clots after heart attacks also carry triple-digit price tags.

The number of physician contacts with specialists is also on the rise (NCHS 1991), and the supply of physicians reflects this trend. Between 1970 and 1987, the number of general and family practitioners increased only 7.8 percent, while the number of cardiovascular disease specialists grew by 155.7 percent, surgeons by 59.5 percent, and gastroenterologists by 328.4 percent (NCHS 1990). These figures also indicate that use is shifting to higher-cost services over time.

Surgery and other technical procedures continue to grow, albeit in different settings than in the past. The number of inpatient surgical operations fell by 4.6 percent between 1980 and 1989 (NCHS 1991), largely because of the enormous number of *outpatient* surgical procedures that now occur in a variety of settings. The American Hospital Association (AHA) has reported that 46.9 percent of total hospital-based surgeries are now performed in their outpatient departments, as compared to just 16.4 percent in 1980 (AHA 1990). And many procedures such as cataract surgery are now done in free-standing surgical centers or even physicians' offices.

The remaining inpatient surgeries are also becoming increasingly more complex and expensive. Across the 1980 to 1989 period, the rate of tonsillectomies dropped dramatically. In contrast, expensive procedures showed the opposite trend. For example, cardiac bypass surgery rates rose for men over the age of 65, from 2.6 per 1,000 in 1980 to 10.4 per 1,000 in 1989 (NCHS 1991).

The improved success of procedures such as hip replacements and cataract surgery means that outcomes have improved whereas the risks of surgeries have fallen.[12] In such cases, higher rates of use would certainly be expected and appropriate. The value of these procedures to individuals has increased over time. And lowered risks mean that older or disabled patients are particularly more likely to benefit now. It should not be surprising, then, that costs of care for these groups are rising rapidly. In fact, it is likely that some of the increase in use is a reflection of the greater value of such services, and of beneficiaries choosing to consume more of such services.

The problem, of course, is in determining what proportion of the overall increase is desirable and what proportion might indicate excessive use of services. Cataract surgery offers a good case study. We do not know what share of its explosive growth occurs because people with early cataracts are encouraged to obtain the operation before it is medically appropriate and what share reflects surgeries that truly improve the quality of life for patients.

These issues are not confined to Medicare; rather, they are pervasive in the U.S. healthcare system. In fact, Medicare has been relatively successful in holding the line on costs in the 1980s, as compared to health spending in general. As shown in figure 1.7, Medicare's share of total healthcare spending peaked in 1985 and since then has actually been falling.[13] This is particularly dramatic, given that the number of Medicare beneficiaries is growing faster than the popula-

Figure 1.7 MEDICARE BENEFITS AS SHARE OF TOTAL SPENDING ON HEALTH
SERVICES AND SUPPLIES, 1970–90

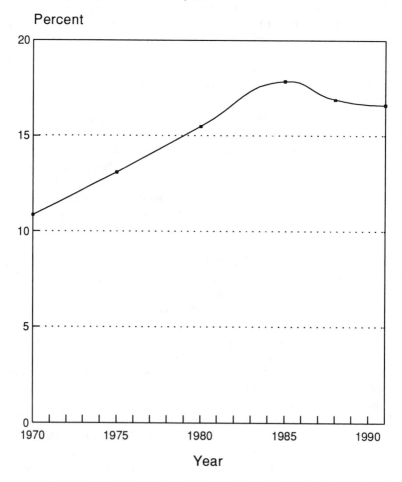

Sources: Ways and Means (1992); Office of National Cost Estimates (1990); U.S. Department of Commerce (1992).

tion as a whole—and is growing fastest among the very old, who are heavy users of healthcare services.[14] If measured on a per capita use basis, Medicare's costs look even more reasonable (figure 1.8).

But Medicare cannot be successful in holding down costs over the long run if healthcare spending in general is escalating. As stated, the pressures driving costs upward come from all parts of the healthcare system. Although Medicare commands a substantial share of the healthcare market, it cannot, by itself, fully control use or prices. When Medicare acts alone, the response by providers can be to "di-

Figure 1.8 RATIO OF PER CAPITA MEDICARE BENEFITS TO PER CAPITA SPENDING ON HEALTH, 1975–91

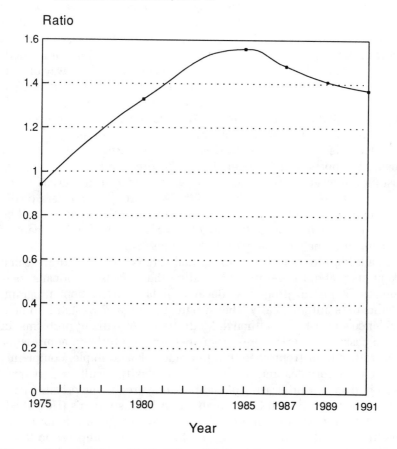

Sources: Ways and Means (1992); Office of National Cost Estimates (1990); U.S. Department of Commerce (1992).

vide and conquer," pitting one part of the system against the other. This constrains what Medicare can accomplish on its own. Any solution to the "cost problem" of Medicare should be tied ultimately to a broad-based solution involving the healthcare system as a whole.

MEDICARE AS PART OF FEDERAL BUDGET

Although, relative to total healthcare costs, Medicare has done rather well in the 1980s, it is still viewed as a runaway item in the federal budget. Its absolute size and rate of growth cause Medicare to stand out from most other domestic programs. Since Medicare is paid by tax dollars in an era of antitax sentiment, it gets more scrutiny than health expenditures paid for by individuals or businesses.[15] In the view of many policymakers, Medicare may be crowding out expenditures on other domestic programs and/or standing in the way of controlling the overall growth in federal expenditures. Such critics often argue that Americans will only accept a certain level of public spending, so if Medicare grows rapidly, it hurts other programs even if it has its own revenue source. This alone makes it a target.

Current law provides a fixed source of funding for the Hospital Insurance portion of Medicare—and the funding is not growing as fast as the level of spending, creating a possible future crisis when the trust funds become exhausted.[16] Even strong supporters of the Medicare program thus face the prospect that further changes will be needed, either increasing the payroll tax rate devoted to Medicare or reexamining the generosity of the program itself.

In addition to budget pressures, Medicare is viewed with the same skepticism about government spending that affects Americans' perception of public programs. Because it is a government program, Medicare is automatically labeled bureaucratic and wasteful. In fact, evidence suggests that although Medicare is not without problems, in some cases these arise more from spending too little on administration rather than from spending too much. For example, complaints about poor services and Medicare's complexity result in part from tight budgets for processing of claims. Compared to the private insurance sector, the Health Care Financing Administration's (HCFA) administrative costs for running the Medicare program are quite low, totaling only about 3 percent of benefit payments compared to larger proportional amounts—around 10 percent to 15 percent—for private insurers (Congressional Research Service [henceforth, CRS] 1989).

RETHINKING MEDICARE POLICY

This volume has two main goals: to describe and analyze the growth and development of the Medicare program and to assess future options for change. Medicare rapidly enrolled first persons over 65 and then disabled individuals, offering them access to mainstream medical care. But in so doing, it led to a demand for more services that helped to create rapid growth in federal outlays. Much of Medicare's recent history has involved efforts to hold the line on cost growth. And although its growth has continued, Medicare has been relatively successful at cost containment, compared to the rest of the healthcare system, with innovations in hospital and physician payment that have led the way for the private sector.

But despite its successes, Medicare leaves many of its critics unsatisfied. Further reductions in spending will be sought by those concerned with the "bloated" size of the program, and some of those cuts are bound to occur in areas where we have already seen considerable change: payments to healthcare providers. Additional pressures will be levied on beneficiaries to pay more. Even in the absence of changes to save costs, Medicare cost sharing is due for reexamination. It is too high in some areas and too low in others and was never carefully designed to influence consumption of healthcare services.

Some of the criticism calls for more substantive policy change. Incremental increases in premiums and cost sharing and in provider payments will not satisfy those who believe that the program should be severely scaled back. In that case, more dramatic realignments would be needed. Counterbalancing these proposals are suggestions for expanding Medicare—adding better catastrophic protection, covering prescription drugs, or, most dramatically, bringing long-term care under Medicare's umbrella.

These major restructuring proposals need to be viewed in the context of the broader debate over healthcare reform. To be consistent with many of the more generous reform options, Medicare would need to expand its coverage considerably, but it would also be consistent to ask those elderly and disabled persons who can pay more to help defray these costs. Long-term care expansions are sometimes part of reform options, but Medicare may or may not be the appropriate vehicle.

The first half of this book addresses the changes that Medicare has undergone and how well they have succeeded. Chapters 2, 3, and 4 divide Medicare's history into two general periods: first, an emphasis on access in the early years of the program, and then, beginning in the late 1970s, a shift to concern about cost containment. By the late 1980s, largely in response to cost-containment efforts, quality issues also became a secondary interest. Readers should note that the appendix at the end of this book will be of most interest to those unfamiliar with Medicare. The appendix defines basic components of the program (along with key terms) and can help put issues in context.

The second portion of this book begins with chapter 5's case study on a critical piece of legislation, the Medicare Catastrophic Coverage Act. The act's failure to elicit change in Medicare colors future policy for the program, strongly influencing how we get from here to "there." Chapter 6 considers possible marginal cost-containment measures as well as modest benefit expansions, whereas chapter 7 discusses broader options for reducing Medicare spending. Chapter 8 addresses the issues related to possible expansion of the system, particularly in the context of overall reform.

Finally, chapter 9 concludes with my personal view of how Medicare should change and its relationship to general health system reform. Some changes could be instituted in the system regardless of the direction of health policy for the rest of the population. But to make cost-containment strategies more effective, and/or to add benefits such as prescription drugs or expanded long-term care to Medicare, change must be coordinated carefully with policies that are adopted for the rest of our healthcare system.

Notes

1. Hospital Insurance (Part A) covers hospital care, skilled nursing care, and home health benefits. Supplementary Medical Insurance (Part B) covers physician and other ambulatory services. These two parts of the program are defined in more detail in the Appendix at the end of this book.

2. President Bush proposed a higher Part B premium for persons with incomes above $125,000 and has suggested caps on Medicare spending (Office of the President 1992a). Arkansas Governor Bill Clinton suggested that higher-income Medicare beneficiaries should contribute more to the costs of their care (*American Healthline* 1992). And Ross Perot proposed elimination of benefits for high-income persons.

3. The distinction between acute care and long-term care is never absolute, but acute care refers to services, particularly in short-stay hospitals and physician services, that are used to treat a particular medical condition. Long-term care usually refers to supportive services for persons with chronic disabling conditions.

4. For example, most of the "pay or play" proposals introduced in 1992 would do little to change Medicare, and President Bush's plan would also leave the program intact.

5. Cross-age comparisons when family sizes and other circumstances differ are subject to considerable controversy. There is little consensus about how to make adjustments to determine "equivalences."

6. Whereas the comparison here is with mean private health spending, mean income may not be appropriate since its distribution is so highly skewed. The comparison to median income, which more accurately represents a "typical" elderly person's income, is more appropriate (see Moon 1991b for a discussion).

7. Some have suggested that this situation simply reflects that healthcare is a "luxury" good and that as incomes rise, we should expect to see more healthcare consumed. Some of this phenomenon may indeed be occurring, but as is discussed later, much of the rise in spending goes beyond simple increases in use of services.

8. Moreover, the future of retiree coverage is somewhat uncertain as employers find the costs of covering existing employees burdensome.

9. Disabled workers in this study are those receiving Social Security disability benefits. Since there is a two-year waiting period before such individuals become eligible for Medicare, they do not represent exactly the same population. The characteristics of these two overlapping groups are likely to be very similar, however.

10. Disabled persons and the elderly are combined in this analysis, unless otherwise noted.

11. The medical care CPI captures "list" prices and thus may overstate actual price increases if consumers are receiving "discounts." Many insurance companies and health maintenance organizations have sought such price breaks from providers, especially hospitals in recent years. Nonetheless, healthcare price increases are so dramatic that the point remains valid even if the medical CPI is overstated.

12. As these various procedures have become more routine and less complicated to perform, it might be reasonable to expect facility and physician charges to fall—a phenomenon that largely does not occur. To some extent, this is related to the lack of a freely operating market for services.

13. The figures used here indicate the relationship between outlays on Medicare and personal health expenditures. The rise in the Medicare share in 1989 reflects the impact of the Medicare Catastrophic Coverage Act, which raised Medicare benefit payments in that year (see chapter 5).

14. That Medicare's share of total health spending has been falling since 1985 is an especially important point, since there is often a misconception that the aging of the population must be a major factor in Medicare's growth. The number of beneficiaries is rising, but only at about 1.1 percent per year.

15. Part A of Medicare is financed from earmarked payroll taxes—a mechanism that has largely protected Social Security from scrutiny. But interestingly, this has not insulated Medicare.

16. This represents a rollback of 3 years in the date of exhaustion of the trust fund since the previous year's report.

Chapter Two

ASSURING ACCESS

At its passage on July 28, 1965, the overriding goal of the Medicare program was to assure access to mainstream healthcare for persons over age 65. The elderly were underserved by the health system, largely because many older persons could not afford to obtain care. Insurance coverage as a part of retirement benefits was the exception and not the rule, and private insurance companies had shown a reluctance to offer coverage to older persons even when these individuals could afford it.

In the early 1960s, older Americans were also disproportionately poor compared to the rest of the population. The 1962 poverty rate for elderly families was 47 percent, as opposed to 13 percent for families headed by someone aged 25 to 54 (Council of Economic Advisors 1964). Moreover, many more older persons had incomes just above the official poverty level of income. Health insurance was not as expensive then as today, but these very low-income individuals could not afford even modest insurance.

Some public support for low-income older Americans was available, primarily in the form of Medical Assistance to the Aged (MAA). This legislation was originally part of the Kerr-Mills bill, passed in 1960.[1] MAA required a means test, but it was not restricted to persons receiving public assistance. Rather, it was a federal/state matching program and depended on the willingness of states to set eligibility limits.[2] Although MAA can be viewed as a precursor for Medicare and Medicaid, it remained a very small program. In 1963, only 148,000 elderly persons received MAA, compared to Medicare's enrollment of 19 million persons by 1967 (Newman 1972). In 1965, MAA provided $523 million in medical benefits to the elderly, compared to Medicare spending in 1968 of $4.4 billion. In its first two years of existence, Medicare spending on the elderly *poor* grew to $2.1 billion—a fourfold increase (Plotnick and Skidmore 1975).

For higher-income elderly persons, the story was mixed. About half of all seniors had health insurance (Davis and Schoen 1978). Generally, coverage could be obtained through former employers and from groups such as the American Association of Retired Persons. Indeed, health insurance was not merely an issue of affordability; it was also a question of whether it was available at any price. Private insurers had shown a reluctance to cover the elderly. Thus, although many of the elderly were needy with regard to healthcare, even in 1965 this was not a homogeneous group.

In contrast, coverage of workers through their employers was becoming increasingly common, underscoring the discrepancies between the elderly and nonelderly in access to care. Although health insurance was a relative oddity at the end of World War II, it quickly became an important benefit for many workers (Starr 1982). By 1960, the United States was separating into two camps: the healthcare haves and have nots, as defined by access to insurance protection. The elderly contained a disproportionate share of the have nots.

Thus, covering senior citizens was a logical starting point for government action. The 1965 Medicare legislation represented one of the major hopes of President Lyndon Johnson's Great Society. However, Medicare had its origins in the proposals first put forward by President Harry Truman in the late 1940s, when he called for a national program to pay for medical care for all Americans (Marmor 1970). It is there we should go to understand how Medicare—in the form we know it today—came to be.

THE GENESIS

Medicare was signed into law on July 30, 1965, by President Johnson in a ceremony in Independence, Missouri, honoring the important role that President Harry Truman had played in the national health insurance debate in the years since World War II. Truman never saw passage of a national healthcare program during his presidency, but his advocacy set the ball rolling. Over time, the debate shifted to ensuring coverage for the elderly as the most vulnerable—and deserving—subgroup of the population. The election of President Johnson in 1964 set the stage for Medicare's passage.

Evolution of the Legislation

Public provision of health insurance was not popular during the administration of Dwight Eisenhower; employer-provided insurance continued to expand, and healthcare costs remained low. Nonetheless, the long history of support for public health insurance contains many

Republican as well as Democratic supporters. For example, while governor of California, Republican Earl Warren proposed compulsory health insurance for the state in 1945 (Somers and Somers 1967). However, Republican opposition, coupled with the vociferous opposition of the American Medical Association (AMA), ended this and all other related national legislative initiatives through the 1950s.

The issue never died, however. A number of influential leaders in the field of social insurance, including Robert Ball and Wilbur Cohen, and two union leaders, Nelson Cruikshank (from the American Federation of Labor) and I. S. Falk (of the United Mine Workers), developed a bill that was introduced by Congressman Aime Forand of Rhode Island in 1957. Well-publicized hearings were held, and the bill, although failing to pass, represented the rallying point for the Democratic proposals in health (Campion 1984; Myers 1970). In 1959, President Eisenhower's secretary of Health, Education & Welfare, Arthur Flemming, released a report on options for providing hospital insurance to Social Security beneficiaries.

After supporting such legislation in the U.S. Senate, John F. Kennedy pledged in his presidential campaign to offer legislation for health insurance for the aged. Within a month of taking office, President Kennedy delivered to Congress a message calling for the legislation. Bills introduced by Congressman Cecil King of California and Senator Clinton Anderson of New Mexico became the focus of debate throughout the early 1960s (Marmor 1970).

But President Kennedy was unable to pass healthcare coverage for the elderly. Not until after his assassination did a more sympathetic environment for his proposals develop. The 1964 elections created a lopsided victory for the Democrats in Congress. In that period, President Johnson pushed Medicare and other Great Society legislation through Congress. With significant help from organized labor, which supported the legislation through its National Council of Senior Citizens, Medicare finally passed.

Even these efforts might not have prevailed without the "conversion" of Congressman Wilbur Mills. As the influential chairman of the House Ways and Means Committee, Mills was in a position to stop any legislation for health insurance. At first, Mills was not inclined to move; he had counted noses and did not have enough support in the House to pass the legislation. Mills was not a legislator who took on lost causes. But with President Johnson's landslide victory, some healthcare legislation seemed inevitable, so Mills took up the cause to control the outcome. Suspense then centered on what shape the plan would take.

Sensing that stonewalling was unlikely to work, opponents began to develop limited options. For example, the AMA, believing that the best it could achieve was to limit eligibility, lobbied relentlessly for restricting Medicare to the elderly poor. The AMA favored the Kerr-Mills Medical Assistance to the Aged approach (Derthick 1979), which would limit the size and influence of the public plan, effectively blocking it from becoming a mainstream healthcare program. The Republicans embraced this AMA alternative.

The supporters of Medicare viewed a means-tested approach as dangerous. One of the reasons for focusing first on the elderly had been to avoid creating a means-tested healthcare program.[3] Universal coverage offered the major political advantage of promising benefits for all, as had proven so popular with Social Security. Supporters felt this was crucial for Medicare as well.

The leaders stressed social insurance—that is, universal coverage paid for by broad-based taxes—and they went to considerable lengths to assert that all, or nearly all, the elderly had incomes too low to afford insurance (Marmor 1970). This was certainly an overstatement, but the claim was made to argue that it would not be worthwhile to means test the benefits.[4] Thus, the debate over means testing assumed a much broader significance, since both sides recognized that this issue would dramatically affect the public's perception of the plan and influence future policy moves in healthcare.

The breadth of services to be covered by this new health plan also became an issue. The King-Anderson bill, although making all the elderly eligible for benefits, was limited to hospital insurance. Proponents of social insurance saw the bill as a first step. Further benefits could be added later if the public accepted the concept of national insurance for hospital services for one portion of the population. However, supporters worried about the costs of the initial undertaking, so they proceeded cautiously.

Advocates of expanding coverage further came from both sides of the debate. Very liberal enthusiasts wanted fully comprehensive care. For example, the Forand bill, introduced in 1957, had been somewhat more inclusive, and some other advocates went even further with their proposals. Ironically, the major proponents of broader coverage were the conservatives. The AMA/Republican strategy was to argue that it was better to comprehensively cover the poor than to only partially serve everyone. Consequently, their alternative bill was much more inclusive than the Democratic proposal in terms of covered services.

Together these two issues of eligibility and coverage could have stalemated the entire process. For months the different parties wrangled with each other and threatened to divide the interest groups lining up for and against various approaches. The AMA and the unions expended enormous sums to influence both public opinion and Congress. In retrospect, the elderly interest groups often cited as key players today laid low during these debates. Only the newly created National Council of Senior Citizens, which was effectively a subsidiary of the AFL-CIO, was prominent. The American Association of Retired Persons (AARP), which already had a membership of more than 10 million in 1964, kept a conspicuously low profile. The AARP had testified in 1959 for a public-private partnership in which the Social Security system would serve only as a premium-collecting entity to help foster private insurance, such as its own Colonial Penn policies before the Senate Committee on Finance in May 1965. It is notable that none of the major histories of Medicare tout significant roles for the AARP (Davis and Schoen 1978; Marmor 1970; Myers 1970; Skidmore 1970; Somers and Somers 1967). The players important in the later policy changes in Medicare thus are quite different from those who led the charge in the beginning.

Medicare and Its Goals

No one anticipated the stunning outcome. The final package put together by Mills went beyond what either side had proposed. Mills' solution to the impasse over the competing approaches was to establish two programs: Medicare and Medicaid. Medicare would cover all those over 65 and would be divided into two parts: Part A, Hospital Insurance (plus skilled nursing care) and Part B, a voluntary, but subsidized, Supplementary Medical Insurance to cover primarily physician services. Medicaid would be targeted to low-income persons of all ages who were participating in other welfare programs.[5]

The basic structure of the Medicare program, with its large variety of benefits and patchwork of limitations and definitions, resulted from the negotiations between the House and the Senate. In particular, Senator Russell Long insisted on some changes to add further catastrophic protections (Myers 1970).[6] The outcome was a complicated structure of hospital benefits with coinsurance days and lifetime reserve days (defined in the appendix to this volume). The legislation as finally passed in July 1965 had a starting date of July 1, 1966 (then the beginning of the federal fiscal year). From that date on, Medicare and Medicaid fundamentally transformed the shape of American healthcare. Rather than sinking Medicare, the opposition of the AMA not only helped create Medicaid but fostered an expanded scope of Medicare benefits (Marmor 1970).

The rules that were established to govern Medicare did little to disrupt or change the way healthcare was practiced or financed in the United States. Claims processing was structured to resemble that in the private sector. And Medicare statutes specifically assured free choice of provider and no interference in the routine practice of medicine. Payment rates were designed to resemble those in the private sector, both in the mechanics and level of payment. Physicians' and other providers' groups that participated in the new program at least would not be put at a disadvantage. Thus, as previously stated, the emphasis in the early years of Medicare was on ensuring that individuals would be covered and included in mainstream medical care.

Nonetheless, no one was sure that the AMA would not get the last laugh. Their ominous warnings about those dangerous moves to socialized medicine carried the implicit threat that physicians might shun patients who were enrolled in either of these new programs. Indeed, in an article in the *New York Times* of August 12, 1965, the Association of American Physicians and Surgeons called for a boycott of Medicare.

These programs proved remarkably successful from the beginning. Large numbers of the elderly enrolled, and use of services expanded rapidly. There was no noticeable boycott by healthcare providers. By May 31, 1966, 17.6 million elderly persons had enrolled in the optional Part B plan—out of approximately 19 million who were eligible. And in the first three years of Medicare, about 100,000 eligible enrollees were admitted to hospitals each week (Myers 1970). Medicare led to a major increase in the elderly's use of medical care. For example, hospital discharges averaged 190 per 1,000 elderly persons in 1964 and 350 per 1,000 by 1973, with most of the change occurring in the early years (Davis and Schoen 1978).[7] Another study found that the proportion of the elderly using physician services jumped from 68 percent to 76 percent between 1963 and 1970 (Andersen et al. 1973).

Initially, *everyone* over the age of 65 was eligible. The legislation stressed access to care, without requiring a period of payroll tax contributions to achieve eligibility. This ensured a considerable windfall to persons aged 65 and older in 1966 and for many years thereafter. After the initial grandfathering in of all the elderly, Medicare eligibility was limited to persons both over the age of 65 and entitled to Social Security benefits, either as workers or dependents. But the payroll contributions that persons in their late 50s and early 60s made into the Medicare trust fund in those early years did not nearly compensate for the costs of healthcare they have received. Further, as costs of healthcare escalated into the 1970s, the "windfalls" to beneficiaries did not decline as anticipated; the rate of growth of costs of the program grew much faster than anticipated.

For example, Health Care Financing Administration actuaries estimated that an elderly individual with average covered earnings retiring in 1982 would have paid in $2,200 and would have had $31,500 in expected future lifetime benefits—a ratio of 14.3 to 1 (Congressional Budget Office 1983). A more recent study has found that the contribution for an average worker retiring in 1991 would total $15,416, but that expected lifetime benefits would be $44,368—a ratio of 2.9 to 1 (Christensen 1992). Throughout the history of Medicare, payments into the system by workers have been far less than the ultimate returns in benefit payments, although the ratio of benefits to contributions is declining.[8]

EXPANSION IN 1972

The second major push for access to care extended Medicare coverage to disabled persons and to persons with end-stage renal disease (ESRD). Like coverage of the elderly, there was a considerable history of calls for expansion to disabled individuals. Coverage for this group had been recommended by the 1963–64 Advisory Council on Social Security. And although disabled persons were left out of the 1965 legislation, the Johnson administration proposed including them in 1967. Instead, a new advisory commission was set up that, in 1968, again recommended coverage. This commission advocated coverage of all disabled beneficiaries and insured workers who had been disabled for three months, resulting in a shorter waiting period than that for cash benefits (Myers 1970).

Ultimately, inclusion of disabled persons under Medicare came in 1972 as part of the sweeping Social Security amendments that substantially increased the commitments of all aspects of the program.[9] The disability expansion was added by Congress, however, and was not part of President Richard Nixon's proposed amendments (Derthick 1979).

One concession to holding down costs for disabled persons was to limit Medicare eligibility to disabled persons who had been receiving Social Security for at least two years. This meant that workers not only had to qualify as permanently and totally disabled (a condition for Social Security benefits, including a five-month waiting period), but they had to have stayed on the rolls for 24 months. Generally, eligibility for Social Security disability requires the worker to have paid payroll taxes for 20 quarters (U.S. Social Security Administration 1991).[10]

The ESRD program was a last-minute addition to the Social Security amendments, but was not a new issue to Congress. Many bills had previously been offered to provide for treatment of end-stage renal disease, partly in response to publicity waged over the fact that this was a treatable disease for which treatment was largely unaffordable by average citizens (Rettig 1982). ESRD coverage was added by a floor amendment offered in the Senate at the end of the debate on the amendments, was then included in the conference report with less than 10 minutes of discussion, and hence became part of the final law (Rettig 1976).

Adding those with ESRD represented explicit coverage of a very visible group of persons with a specific, expensive ailment. Long-term kidney failure is fatal if the person does not receive dialysis (or a kidney transplant). Throughout the 1960s, growing attention was paid to the scarcity of kidney dialysis machines to treat patients. Waiting lists and rationing of this care highlighted a problem where patients were dying not because there was no effective treatment but because of budget constraints and the resulting limited supply of dialysis machines.

The creation of a category of patients eligible for Medicare based solely on a particular condition caused many to worry that there might be a "disease of the month," so that gradually more and more people would be made eligible for coverage. Indeed, the numbers of kidney dialysis patients expanded far more rapidly than many expected. Although ESRD was a highly visible and expensive problem area, it was by no means unique as an expensive, deadly disease. But other groups have not been added in this way to Medicare, perhaps in part because of how expensive the ESRD patients have been over the last 20 years.[11] By 1990, the number of ESRD patients had grown to 144,000, at an average cost of nearly $25,000 per beneficiary (Ways and Means 1991).

The two groups thus added to Medicare's rolls resulted in an instant expansion of 10 percent in the number of beneficiaries and an even larger boost to the costs of the program, since disabled persons tend to be more expensive to cover than the elderly, on average (Ways and Means 1992). The impact of these new beneficiaries can clearly be seen in figure 2.1 which tracks growth in the number of Medicare beneficiaries over time.

OTHER CHANGES IN ACCESS

Since 1972, Medicare has not been extended to any other broad group; indeed, changes that affect coverage have largely represented fine-tuning efforts at the margins, often to *restrict* access to the program. At least thus far, Medicare has not served as the first step toward national health insurance. Indeed, after serious debate in the 1970s, the issue was largely set aside until the late 1980s.

Figure 2.1 GROWTH IN MEDICARE ENROLLEES, 1966–90

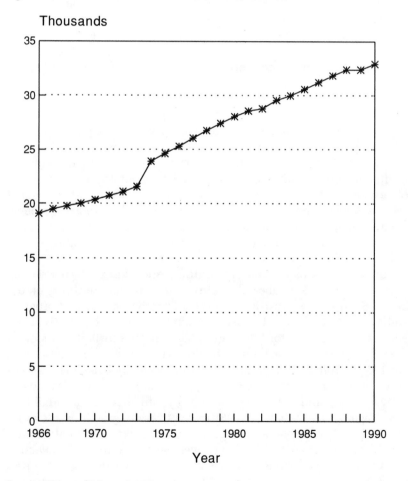

Source: Ways and Means (1991).

Changes after 1972 reflect the shift away from access toward cost containment. Take the case of "expansion" of Medicare to new federal workers, which was passed as part of the Tax Equity and Fiscal Responsibility Act (TEFRA) of 1982 (Ways and Means 1985). Initially, Medicare coverage was not offered to federal workers, since they had their own healthcare system. In practice, however, many federal workers became eligible for Medicare through other means. In some cases their spouses were eligible and they became entitled by virtue of being elderly dependents of covered workers. Moreover, many federal workers have shifted between the private and the public sector over the course of their working lives, resulting in eligibility for minimal Social Security benefits, and hence eligibility for full Medicare benefits. Consequently, they might have contributed very little but qualify for the full range of benefits. This "expansion" to new federal workers was thus actually a budget-reduction effort, requiring that all such workers pay the Medicare portion of the FICA tax for their full working lives.

Other TEFRA legislation limited eligibility for the working elderly (aged 65 to 69), also as a budget-reducing measure. This legislation dictated that Medicare be the "secondary payer" for employed persons who have access to employer-provided health insurance. Private insurance was made responsible for paying most of an individual's healthcare bills, with Medicare paying only for those services not otherwise covered. The intent of this change was to reduce federal Medicare spending while not lowering insurance coverage for beneficiaries. Instead, the costs are passed on to the employer. These workers are guaranteed at least all the benefits offered by Medicare; it is only a question of who pays for that coverage.

During the 1980s the Reagan administration moved to *restrict* access by enforcing tougher eligibility standards for disability under Social Security. Any restriction on access to the cash-benefit program spills over to Medicare by also reducing the number of individuals who become eligible for Medicare. These efforts substantially slowed the rate of growth in the number of new disability beneficiaries during the 1980s. From 1975 to 1981, growth in disability beneficiaries averaged 5.6 percent per year. However, growth came to a virtual standstill between 1981 and 1986, after which a small increase in eligibility began again. Over the entire 1981 to 1989 period, growth in the number of disability beneficiaries averaged just 0.7 percent annually (Ways and Means 1991). All of these changes were very limited, reflecting the retrenchment from expanding access at the beginning of the program. No major cuts have occurred in the two major groups covered by Medicare, although proposals in this area are now receiving more discussion.

The one important exception to these trends was the Qualified Medicare Beneficiary (QMB) program, which was instituted as part of the Medicare catastrophic legislation and survived the repeal of that legislation. This program covers Medicare cost sharing and Part B premiums for anyone with an income below the poverty level ($6,810 for an individual in 1992). The program also covers those between 100 percent and 110 percent of poverty, but only for the cost of the Part B premium. Thus far, however, participation rates have been low, since individuals must apply through the Medicaid program for the benefits, and states have not been anxious to publicize it (Families USA 1992).

WHO GETS WHAT?

Although the eligibility and scope of Medicare have remained basically the same and reflect uniform national benefits, the impact of Medicare still varies widely across individuals. In particular, the relatively high cost-sharing requirements of Medicare constrain the ability of vulnerable groups to utilize Medicare coverage. Karen Davis (1975) has long argued forcefully for improved protections from cost sharing, and has pointed out access problems for minority groups, for the low-income elderly, and for persons residing in certain regions of the country. If such persons do not use services, even though they are entitled to them, because of prohibitive out-of-pocket costs or supply problems, then Medicare is implicitly less universal than it appears on paper.

Thus, a discussion of access issues flows naturally into a concern about who gets what from Medicare. Such analysis could focus on a wide range of demographic indicators. For example, women tend to use more chronic care services, compared to men's heavier use of acute care. Since Medicare has done a poorer job of covering these chronic care services, women's coverage under Medicare in any given year is less generous than that for men—a difference that has persisted over time. On the other hand, Sandra Christensen (1992) has also pointed out that women's longer life expectancy raises their lifetime expected benefits enough to overshadow these annual differences. But for purposes of this discussion, the focus is on the two most important indicators of who gets what from Medicare: income and location.

Rising Burdens of Medicare Cost Sharing

Medicare cost sharing formally includes deductibles assessed under both Parts A and B of the program and coinsurance for many of the services provided. Coinsurance requires beneficiaries to pay a percentage of the costs of the service. The largest source of cost sharing is usually from the coinsurance on physician services. Extra billing by physicians for charges above what Medicare designates as reasonable also constitute a form of cost sharing. Finally, Part B premiums, although technically not cost sharing, constitute a substantial payment burden for those with moderate incomes. Table 2.1 contains an average per capita breakdown for these components.

The impact of increases in Medicare cost sharing over time has fallen disproportionately on those with low incomes who lack access to the Medicaid program. The RAND Corporation health insurance experiment of the 1970s indicated that cost sharing serves as a deterrent to use of services for persons with low or moderate incomes (Newhouse et al. 1982). Although that study contained no elderly persons, the striking results of a differential impact by family income would likely carry over to Medicare beneficiaries. A $20 coinsurance payment for a physician visit is simply more burdensome to someone whose income is $8,000 per year than to someone whose annual income is $20,000 or $40,000.

Many researchers have observed variations in the use of services by the elderly of varying income levels. For example, Christensen and Kasten (1988a) noted that Medicare benefits per enrollee generally rise with income, from $2,052 for the bottom 10 percent of the income distribution to a high of over $2,800 for those in the top half of the

Table 2.1 COMPONENTS OF MEDICARE COST SHARING, 1990

		Average per Capita ($)
Part A		183
Deductibles	132	
Coinsurance	51	
Part B		819
Deductibles	94	
Coinsurance	270	
Balance Billing	112	
Premiums	343	
Total		1,002

Sources: Data extrapolated from Ways and Means (1991) and Health Care Financing Administration, unpublished data.

distribution. These differences persist even after controlling for health status (Feder et al. 1987a).

Relief is available for persons eligible for Medicaid. Medicaid fills in where Medicare leaves off, paying the required cost sharing and adding other benefits. But less than half of the elderly poor receive Medicaid. States restrict eligibility to hold down costs by keeping income and assets limits very restrictive. Even the newly enacted Qualified Medicare Beneficiary program will only partly solve the problems of high cost sharing. This program will expand in 1995 to include those with incomes below 120 percent of poverty, but for anyone above the poverty level up to 120 percent, help will be limited to covering the Part B premium. Individuals will still have to pay for other cost sharing. (This protection is now available only for those between 100 and 110 percent of poverty.)

The affordability issue extends well beyond the poverty level. Medicare enrollees averaged about $1,000 in out-of-pocket liabilities just for Medicare-covered services in 1990 (Ways and Means 1991). Someone with an income of even 150 percent of the poverty level would have to contribute about 10 percent of his or her income to pay just for the average amount of required cost sharing under Medicare. And that individual would likely owe at least another 10 percent or more for noncovered services (Feder et al. 1987b). This person would be ineligible for help from Medicaid or the QMB program.

This calculation becomes bleaker each year as the costs of medical care—and hence the burdens on beneficiaries—rise. For example, as figure 2.2 shows, Medicare cost sharing is consuming an ever-increasing portion of the income of the elderly—and the story is likely to be the same for disabled persons as well. Thus, problems of access attributable to the burdens of cost sharing will almost surely continue for those of moderate means.

In practice, many of the elderly buy or receive as part of retirement benefits supplemental insurance to help pay for this cost sharing. Those who receive employer-subsidized coverage are at least partially protected from out-of-pocket costs; they have their cost sharing covered and do not have to pay the full premium costs for the protection. In 1987, this constituted about 30 percent of all the elderly (NCHSR 1989).

But purchasing "Medigap" insurance is not a solution for high average healthcare burdens. Such insurance can reduce the annual variation in the burden for moderate income Medicare beneficiaries, but it actually raises average costs. Medigap adds to the costs of care, since purchasers of this supplemental insurance pay for the marketing

Figure 2.2 MEDICARE COST-SHARING AS SHARE OF INCOME OF ELDERLY,
1975–90

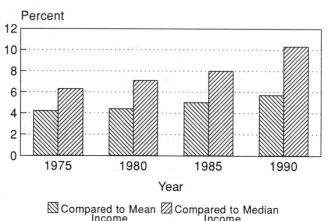

Sources: Ways and Means (1991); U.S. Bureau of the Census, unpublished data.

and administrative costs and profits for insurers, in addition to the
average costs of healthcare. In practice, this amounts to at least 20
percent to 30 percent above the expected benefits in premiums and
sometimes much more (Shikles 1990). If the problem of high cost
sharing were confined to a few high-cost patients, supplemental insurance would help. However, Medigap cannot solve the problem,
since even the median costs of Medicare-related liabilities are unaffordable for most moderate-income enrollees.

Geographic Variation

Variation in the supply of providers across areas of the United States
also restricts access of enrollees to Medicare benefits. Access problems may reflect where the enrollee lives, such as isolated rural areas
where the population is too small to support certain services. Or, these
problems may be related to enrollee incomes. If the enrollee lives in
a poor area, providers may not be located nearby. In some areas where
costs have risen rapidly and Medicare payments have not kept pace,
providers may be reluctant to see Medicare patients. These geographic
factors result in eligible persons who need Medicare services not
getting access to care.

Some of the large variations observed around the United States in
receipt of Medicare services likely reflect these supply problems. In

other cases, such variations in use of services reflect different medical practices that may or may not be indicators of major problems for patients. In 1988, for example, state-by-state breakdowns of the number of enrollees served by Medicare showed considerable variation, ranging from a low of 581.4 per 1,000 enrollees in Hawaii to a high of 848.2 per 1,000 in Maine. Reimbursement per person served ranged from $2,323 in South Dakota to $5,229 in the District of Columbia (Ways and Means 1991). If enrollees are divided into urban versus rural areas, Part B allowed charges indicate that urban enrollees had 31 percent higher expenditures than their rural counterparts in 1988 (Holahan unpublished data). Although some of the difference in dollars of expenditures reflects different payment levels around the country, use of services also differs substantially.

CONCLUSIONS

By most accounts, Medicare has improved access to healthcare by the nation's elderly and disabled populations. By 1970, it had enrolled nearly all of the elderly and, by 1974, a substantial number of America's disabled in a national healthcare program. Providing these population groups with access to mainstream medical care resulted in a dramatic rise in use of services.

But the other side of the story is that although Medicare offers universal coverage under a uniform federal program, use of services varies dramatically across beneficiaries. Access remains a problem for those with low incomes, for whom the costs of out-of-pocket expenses seem a substantial barrier to access. Variations in use extend beyond what would be expected by differences in health status, for example. A different set of problems besets those who reside in certain underserved areas—both rural and urban settings. Again use varies substantially—beyond what one might expect as a reasonable difference in attitudes toward care or need for services. Thus, the goal of ensuring access to mainstream care has not yet been fully achieved.

By 1990, the average Medicare beneficiary received $3,230 in services under the program. The "success" of the program contributed to the rapid growth in federal costs to maintain it. Thus was ushered in the second "phase" of Medicare—a concern for cost containment—the subject of the next two chapters.

Notes

1. In 1950 the Old Age Assistance program had also established a system of vendor payments to providers of healthcare for the elderly, but with even more limited federal dollars.

2. Some states continued their MAA programs after 1965, as allowed by law in lieu of Medicaid for the elderly. MAA was eliminated in 1969.

3. Ironically, accounts of this debate indicating concerns that means testing would undermine public support for Medicare sound very similar to the more recent controversy over the Medicare Catastrophic Coverage Act (see chapter 5).

4. However, health coverage was not, in turn, a major focus of those concerned about poverty per se during this period. To these groups, healthcare needs were an important, but not an extraordinary, concern. They emphasized income adequacy as the key to affordability of all basic goods and services. Healthcare's cost spiral had not yet become so great a concern.

5. Medicaid is, like MAA, a joint federal/state program in which the federal government sets some rules and provides matching monies to states. The states must provide benefits to those eligible for cash assistance and must offer certain benefits. Beyond that, the states may cover additional services and the medically needy as well as categorical eligibles. Medicaid is available to persons of all ages. Over time, its importance for the elderly has been primarily for long-term care services not covered by Medicare and as a supplemental program filling in Medicare's gaps for those with very low incomes.

6. Senator Long also argued for means-tested cost sharing. Although that provision was not included in the legislation, it is interesting that the issues raised by Long began to resurface in the late 1980s as a potential direction for change in Medicare.

7. Indeed, the system was so successful that critics both then and later pointed to the danger of increasing costs of healthcare—a criticism that proved well-founded. Perhaps the AMA got the last laugh after all. A *New York Times* article of August 19, 1966, indicated that physicians' prices for the elderly rose by 300 percent after the introduction of Medicare.

8. This ratio is likely to decline even faster now for those who pay at the maximum, since the cap on earnings subject to the tax increased in 1991.

9. The 1972 amendments also allowed individuals over the age of 65 to buy in to Part A if they were not otherwise eligible, and established a few minor expansions of services. These amendments also raised the Part B deductible from $50 to $60 and, in what would become an important change over time, tied premium increases in Part B to the newly added Social Security cost of living adjustment (COLA) (U.S. Social Security Administration 1991).

10. Younger workers have lesser requirements, and persons in other categories such as disabled adult children must meet other standards.

11. This issue has again been raised in the context of eligibility for the AIDS population. Many AIDS victims will die before becoming eligible for Medicare through the traditional disability program. Advocates for AIDS patients thus urge that, as is now the case for ESRD, there should be no waiting period.

Chapter Three

CONTAINING COSTS:
IMPACTS ON PROVIDERS

It was not long before the Medicare system began to be viewed with alarm, not because of its failure, but because of its success. The rapid initial growth in the cost of the program testifies to how quickly the system began to fulfill its original goal of offering mainstream medical care to older persons. The addition of disabled and end-stage renal disease patients in 1972 further enlarged program costs.

It is not surprising, then, that the second major "phase" of Medicare involved a fixation on controlling program costs. Indeed, immediately after passage, many observers expressed concern at Medicare's growth. Healthcare costs received attention from President Richard Nixon during the period of wage and price controls. Predictions of Medicare's "bankruptcy" also began to surface. In 1970, Chief Actuary Robert Myers predicted an enormous deficit in Medicare for 1995 (Feder 1977). The 1981 report on the Federal Hospital Insurance Trust Fund indicated that the fund would be in deficit by 1991 (HI Trustees 1981). These projections of future spending indicated that something had to give, that higher taxes or lower spending would be necessary to keep the Medicare trust fund solvent.

Worry over costs in the 1970s spurred a number of cost-containment efforts. However, it was the prospect of enormous federal deficits and efforts to reduce them that provided the executive and legislative branches with additional impetus for major cost-containment measures in the decade following. By 1980, Medicare was the second largest federal domestic program and the fastest growing one, making it a target for those concerned about the size of government in general. Decisions about Medicare in the 1980s thus reflected general concern not only about rising healthcare costs but also about the size of the federal budget deficit.

Under each budget submission by the Reagan administration, Medicare was accorded a central place in proposals to reduce the size of the federal budget deficit. These proposals focused almost exclusively on reducing spending. Policy was as much budget-driven as centered on devising innovative new approaches to provider payments. Nonetheless, many of the cost-containment strategies chosen have revolutionized the way we pay providers in the United States, and Medicare often has been used as a model for other payers seeking to hold down costs.

Enthusiasm for cost cutting within Medicare extended to all aspects of the program. Most of the emphasis centered on reducing payments to providers of Medicare services, but beneficiaries also faced reductions in benefits and increased requirements for cost sharing. A study by the Congressional Budget Office (1991) concluded that in 1990, Medicare spending was 20 percent below what it otherwise would have been without the changes of the 1980s. Nonetheless, throughout the 1980s, Medicare maintained its distinction as the fastest growing domestic federal program. Future serious attempts to bring down costs will certainly occur, but the easiest cuts have already been made.

This chapter examines these increasing costs and assesses major cost-containment efforts that have been directed at the provider level, especially with regard to hospitals and physician services. Chapter 4 addresses the impacts of cost-containment efforts on beneficiaries.

SOURCES OF GROWTH IN MEDICARE SPENDING

Expenditures in all parts of Medicare have risen dramatically. Like the growth in aggregate healthcare spending, Medicare expenditures reflect both price inflation and increases in the use of services. Hospital expenditures led the way in the 1970s, and physician spending took off in the 1980s. Although use of services contributed to this growth, the bottom line is that prices were responsible for much of the growth in the late 1970s, making price controls a natural place to start any cost-containment strategy.

Table 3.1 provides breakdowns for some of the components of expenditure growth for the two parts of Medicare over three periods: 1968–75, 1975–84, and 1984–91. The first period coincided with the highest growth in the number of enrollees in the program. Reimbursements grew rapidly as well, particularly for hospital care, but picked up considerably in the late 1970s. From 1975 to 1984, per enrollee expenditures, which is the combination of persons served and reimbursement per person served, were above 17 percent per year, on average (Ways and Means 1991). Consequently, it is not surprising that

Table 3.1 AVERAGE ANNUAL PERCENTAGE CHANGES IN MEDICARE, 1968–91

Period	Hospital Insurance			Supplementary Medical Insurance		
	Growth in Number of Enrollees	Growth in Persons Served per 1,000 Enrollees	Growth in Reimbursements per Person Served	Growth in Number of Enrollees	Growth in Persons Served per 1,000 Enrollees	Growth in Reimbursements per Person Served
1968–75	3.2%	1.1%	10.3%	3.5%	4.5%	5.5%
1975–84	2.4	1.5	15.8	2.5	3.6	13.0
1984–91	1.6	− 3.1	8.8	1.7	1.6	9.2

Sources: Ways and Means (1985, 1992).

this period provided the impetus for the cost-containment efforts of the 1980s, and that the initial focus was on the hospital. And although there were considerable legislative cost-containment efforts from 1981 through 1983, the impacts did not begin to have much effect until 1984 or 1985. At least on the surface, some of these efforts would appear to have been successful after 1984, when growth in both the proportion of beneficiaries using services and their average expenditures declined. However, overall rates of inflation in the economy were also lower from 1984 to 1991 compared to the late 1970s and early 1980s.

The figures in table 3.1 also help to identify the sources of the problem of rapidly rising Medicare costs. Growth in numbers of enrollees has been only a minor factor since 1975. For Part A, consisting mainly of hospital services, growth in the proportion of enrollees using services was also a limited contributor to the problem. Indeed after 1984, the rate of enrollees using services fell substantially, particularly for hospital and skilled nursing facility (SNF) care.[1] But Part A reimbursements per beneficiary using services grew rapidly—at a rate of nearly 16 percent from 1975 to 1984. These changes reflect both rising prices and increasing intensity of services offered in the hospital. Each year, more tests and services were performed, but more important, the prices were higher.

Figure 3.1 illustrates the growth of Hospital Insurance (HI) costs per enrollee in nominal dollars and growth after adjusting for inflation, using two alternative indices. The overall consumer price index (CPI) offers an adjustment that indicates what happened to Part A spending relative to constant purchasing power. That adjustment indicates that the general rate of inflation, which was extremely high in the late 1970s and early 1980s, accounted for a substantial share of the higher Part A spending per enrollee.

Figure 3.1 PER ENROLLEE HI BENEFIT PAYMENTS ADJUSTED BY ALTERNATIVE
PRICE DEFLATORS, 1975–90

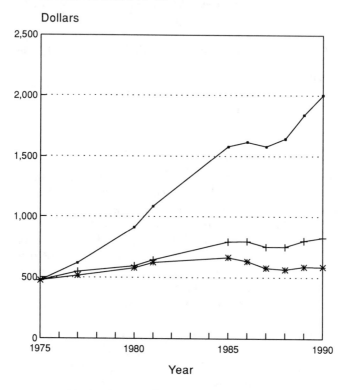

Sources: Office of the President (1992b); Ways and Means (1991).

If the spending figure is adjusted, instead, for the rate of price
increases just in healthcare goods and services, the growth line is
flatter still. This means that much of the growth in per capita spending on Medicare Part A can be attributed to healthcare inflation. This
comparison is most relevant for the 1975–82 period, before Medicare
prices began to be controlled. After that point, Medicare was subjected
to stricter rates of growth in payments than occurred in the economy
as a whole.[2]

Thus, not unexpectedly, much of the emphasis in cost control for
hospital care centered on controlling the price of care. The blank-
check approach of the original legislation was always of concern to
those who worried about costs of the program. Hospitals were essen-

tially paid on the basis of what they spent on Medicare beneficiaries. Long lengths of stay and redundant services were rewarded with higher levels of reimbursement to hospitals.

The picture is somewhat different for Part B (Supplementary Medical Insurance [SMI]); costs of the program continued to grow, passing the rate of growth in Part A after 1984. This part of the program shows a much more substantial growth in the number of persons receiving benefits each year. The low level of the SMI deductible, raised only once between 1973 and 1991, meant that price inflation increased substantially the number of enrollees exceeding the deductible limit and hence receiving benefits each year. By 1991, over 80 percent of all Medicare enrollees exceeded the deductible amount, compared to 52 percent in 1975 (Ways and Means 1992). Reimbursements per person grew at a slower rate after 1984, but were still above 9 percent annually (table 3.1).

Prices also played a major role in SMI growth, as indicated in figure 3.2. Again three growth lines are shown: the top line uses dollars uncorrected for inflation, the middle line corrects for general inflation in the economy, and the bottom indicates growth after accounting for price increases in physician services. Again, the bottom line is most relevant before Medicare policy began to restrict price growth. Before 1984, price growth in Medicare largely mirrored that for physicians as a whole.

Since 1984, Congress has set the maximum annual rate of increase in physician payments by law and has used that as a policy lever to control costs of Part B services. The mechanism was the Medicare Economic Index (MEI), which sets limits on the rate of growth of Medicare's prevailing charges for physicians.[3] For example, beginning on July 1, 1984, the MEI was frozen for 16 months. Thus the MEI in the last half of the 1980s was considerably lower than the overall rate of inflation for such services. Nonetheless, this line in figure 3.2 is not as flat as that for the hospital side of Medicare, shown in figure 3.1, indicating more real growth in the intensity of services in this part of Medicare.

CHANGING MEDICARE'S RELATIONSHIP WITH PROVIDERS

When Medicare was enacted in 1965, much of the debate on implementation centered on achieving the confidence of hospitals and physicians. Mainstream medical care would be offered to older persons

Figure 3.2 PER ENROLLEE SMI BENEFIT PAYMENTS ADJUSTED BY
ALTERNATIVE PRICE DEFLATORS, 1975–90

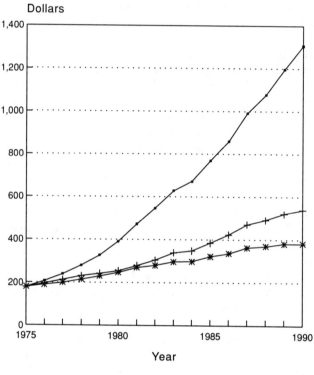

Sources: Office of the President (1992b); Ways and Means (1991).

only if the program could overcome the stigma of "socialized medicine" and the rancorous debate over passage. Because of these concerns, Medicare was set up to operate as much like private insurance as possible. Private insurance companies were selected to process the claims (and were referred to as "carriers" for Part B and "intermediaries" for Part A). Generally, a different company served each state, ensuring that physicians and hospitals would deal with familiar faces. The rules for processing claims were decentralized, creating considerable area variation. Carriers and intermediaries enjoyed (and still have) great latitude in their relationships with healthcare providers concerning claims processing.

In the early years of Medicare, physicians, in particular, were subject to almost no controls on the care they provided, nor on billing practices. This was done in large part to reassure physicians and to guarantee their acceptance of Medicare. Doctors used whatever forms they had used before Medicare's passage. At their option, they could either bill Medicare directly for each service or bill the patient. Although Medicare established limits on what the government would pay (called allowed charges), physicians were free to bill the patient the full amount of their actual charge, collecting any difference between actual and allowed charges from the patient. Moreover, because Medicare's allowed charges were computed in much the same way that Blue Cross/Blue Shield calculated reasonable charges, they were not much of a restraining force.

Over time, Medicare's allowed charges strongly reflected the historical rates in various areas and began to be viewed as anachronistic. The levels did not respond well to changes in the general market for physicians' services or to changes in technology that made procedures simpler or more complex over time. A number of interim steps were taken to modify the payment structure, but until physician payment reform passed in late 1989, Medicare physician payment schedules were largely based on historical patterns established in 1966.

Hospitals were also treated generously in the beginning of the Medicare program. They were allowed to bill on a cost basis with no oversight about the appropriateness of the services rendered. But hospitals were the first to be subjected to stringent cost controls—in part because of the rapid growth in costs in this sector, but also because the sector is the largest and most formally organized part of the healthcare system. Policymakers felt they had a handle on hospitals' behavior and could thus seek to mold it over time.

HOSPITALS TAKE THE FIRST HIT

From 1965 to 1974, Medicare paid hospitals on the principle of "reasonable and necessary costs." Hospitals had to fill out detailed cost reports and face auditing of their expenses, but essentially they billed Medicare for whatever services were provided. These were not the published charges that hospitals generally apply to patients, but were costs for each hospital as calculated by Medicare's intermediaries. Hospitals could not charge whatever they liked, but once costs were established, there were no constraints on the amount of care provided.

Although this was the initial bargain struck to help secure Medicare's passage, debate began almost immediately on how to control hospital costs. But although the concern was there, consensus on major reform was lacking (Feder 1977). Robert Myers (1970) noted, however, that even in the first several years of Medicare there was interest in a per capita payment system for hospitals.

A number of more limited constraints were introduced over this period. In 1972, Professional Standards Review Organizations (PSROs) were established to review and control beneficiaries' use of services (Feder et al. 1982). Beginning in 1974, a reimbursement cap was added to prevent any hospital from charging more than 120 percent of the mean of routine costs found in similar facilities. Thus, this first constraint on hospitals required them to hold their costs in line with those of other hospitals in the area. Over time, this limit (called a "223" limit after its Social Security statute) was ratcheted downward to 112 percent (Office of Technology Assessment 1985). But this approach did not force major efficiencies on hospitals, since they were still being paid on the basis of what they spent, and the limits applied only to basic services.

In 1974 and 1975, Hospital Insurance payments grew at rates in excess of 20 percent, prompting the administration of Jimmy Carter to propose national hospital rate setting (Feder et al. 1982). This dramatic proposal was defeated when hospitals pledged voluntarily to hold down costs. During consideration of that legislation, hospital cost growth did slow substantially, even though the period was generally marked by very high rates of overall inflation. But the impact proved only temporary. In 1980 and 1981, growth rates in HI once more approached 20 percent, even though inflation was abating elsewhere (see figure 3.3). No longer could the industry credibly argue that it could police itself.

The confluence of efforts to cut Medicare spending as part of general budget reductions and concerns about rampant growth in the hospital sector made hospitals an obvious target for budget cuts in the 1980s. Since over two-thirds of Medicare payments went to hospitals, they were the place "where the money was." Cost cutting on hospitals in the 1980s did not start with the Prospective Payment System, (PPS), as many believe; rather, its origins were earlier. The Omnibus Budget Reconciliation Act of 1981 tightened the "223" limits on what hospitals could receive as reimbursement for routine operating costs to 108 percent of mean costs (Office of Technology Assessment 1985). That is, a hospital could receive no more than 108 percent of costs averaged across all similar hospitals. But this was only the beginning.

Figure 3.3 ANNUAL RATES OF GROWTH IN MEDICARE HOSPITAL PAYMENTS,
1975–90

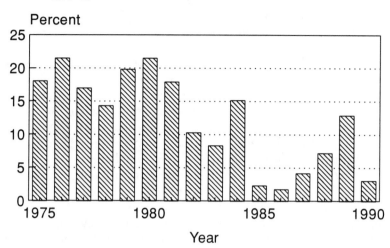

Source: Ways and Means (1992).

Substantially more stringent restrictions were added by the Tax Equity and Fiscal Responsibility Act of 1982 (TEFRA). TEFRA expanded the 223 limits, and added a new hospital-specific target rate on costs per case.[4] The initial 120 percent limit was scheduled to be reduced over three years to 110 percent. But the most important change was that these limits would no longer be based on spending each year, but rather on costs up to a ceiling trended forward through time. This meant that each year the restrictions would be more severe and more binding (Office of Technology Assessment 1985).

TEFRA also introduced several new concepts into hospital reimbursement. First, the per case limits moved away from retrospective payments to a payment schedule set in advance. TEFRA replaced the old per diem approach to hospital payment with a per case approach and permitted hospitals to benefit, at least partially, from any cost savings they generated.[5] For the first time, hospitals had incentives to seek efficiencies in the provision of care.

But the stringent TEFRA limits left hospitals with little room to maneuver, that is, without enough flexibility to benefit from the efficiencies they introduced. The climate set by the TEFRA limits led many hospitals to conclude that almost any other plan would be preferable, thereby smoothing the way for introduction of radical payment reform. Indeed, TEFRA called for the U.S. Department of Health and

Human Services (DHHS) to devise a new plan for reimbursing hospitals, indicating that TEFRA changes were meant as interim rules.

This new hospital payment reform was implemented quickly. The DHHS presented its proposal to Congress in December 1982, with many unresolved details left open for negotiation. Some pundits predicted that prolonged debate and lobbying would delay passage. The Reagan administration and Congress worked feverishly in the spring of 1983 to hash out the compromise that led to the legislation. Although the DHHS and the Congressional Budget Office undertook considerable analysis of the impacts on hospitals, the deadlines for enactment dictated that many of the adjustments were ad hoc and that many of the potential specific impacts remained unclear.

The new legislation, called the Prospective Payment System (PPS), came into being in April 1983. Because PPS was tied to critical legislation to protect the solvency of the Social Security system, the PPS amendments likely received less attention than if they had been proposed as standalone legislation. The final details were not debated or subjected to the scrutiny of interest groups, which might have slowed the process.

PPS began as a great experiment in systemwide reform, with no one certain of the outcome. In fact, Congress also established a Prospective Payment Assessment Commission (ProPAC) to oversee the implementation of this complicated new system and advise on the inevitable changes that would be necessary to fine-tune it over time. Despite the many issues and concerns still outstanding (detailed in the discussion following), PPS counts as a major coup for Congress and the administration; it radically changed payment policy to hospitals with a minimum of disruption to the healthcare system.

How PPS Works

The basic justification for the new Prospective Payment System was a desire to stop paying hospitals on a retrospective cost basis; such a system was widely recognized as contributing to health inflation, since hospitals had no incentive to seek more efficient ways to provide care. To reward efficiency, PPS needed not only to move away from a cost-plus system but to establish a payment mechanism that hospitals could understand and that was sensitive to legitimate differences in costs of care. The presumption was that a system was needed that would pay a fixed amount set in advance for services and avoid some of the pitfalls of merely reimbursing hospitals for whatever costs they incurred (Russell 1989). Further, such a system would be based on national or regional rates and not the costs of the individual hospitals. Very efficient hospitals would be rewarded, whereas those with higher costs would be forced to economize. The payment levels needed to reflect differences in patients, in types of services offered, and in variations in input prices over which hospitals had no control. Since hospital services vary dramatically—from simple procedures performed on relatively healthy individuals to highly complex treatments or surgery on individuals with multiple, complicated health problems—the system had to be flexible enough to change over time as medical practice and patient needs also changed. And it must not encourage hospitals to respond merely by admitting only lower-cost patients.

PPS established payment schedules for hospitals by setting prices for diagnoses. Patients are classified into a diagnosis-related group (DRG), and total payments to a hospital reflect the mix of patients as indicated by the DRGs.[6] In addition to separating patients into groups depending upon the problem for which they are admitted and the procedures performed, some attempt is made to identify patients requiring heavier care.[7] There is also special provision for cases that are outliers from the norm—requiring additional payments to cover unusually expensive cases.[8]

The DRG is assigned a weight indicating the level of hospital costs for persons in that group relative to a standard case. The weights, which help establish the prospective payment for the patient, are set nationally and reflect the costs of care for Medicare patients. For example, the weight for a simple appendectomy without complications was .7745 in 1991, compared to 12.9086 for a heart transplant or .4822 for an allergic reaction by a patient over the age of 17 (Ways and Means 1991). Table 3.2 includes additional examples of DRG groups and their weights.[9]

The actual payment level for a hospital reflects a multistep process; DRGs are only one component. First, the hospital is assigned a basic fee for a standardized case, calculated on the basis of the average cost of a hospital stay for that type of hospital (i.e., whether it is located in an urban, large urban, or rural area). The basic rate is then adjusted by the weight for the particular DRG into which the patient is classified. Adjustments to that rate are then also made—for example, for differences in local wages or for cases in which the hospital serves a disproportionate share of low-income patients, is the sole community hospital, or is a teaching hospital. Thus, whereas the rates are set nationally, considerable variation occurs as a result of the location or other characteristics of the hospital.[10]

Table 3.2 MOST COMMON DRGs AND THEIR WEIGHTS

DRG[a] Number and Description	1989 Discharges (in thousands)	1991 Weight
Total DRGs	9,879.5	
127 Heart failure and shock	539.5	1.0040
140 Angina pectoris	359.0	.6296
089 Simple pneumonia and pleurisy[b]	348.3	1.1878
014 Specific cerebrovascular disorders except transient ischemic attack	325.2	1.2212
182 Esophagitis, gastroenteritis, and miscellaneous digestive disorders[b]	243.6	.7497
096 Bronchitis and asthma	215.0	.9568
209 Major joint and limb reattachment procedures	218.7	2.3689
296 Nutritional and miscellaneous metabolic disorders[b]	196.6	.9387
138 Cardiac arrhythmia and conduction disorders with cardiovascular complications	171.2	.8331
015 Transient ischemic attack and precerebral occlusions	139.2	.6420
320 Kidney and urinary tract infections[b]	145.0	1.0055
121 Circulatory disorders with acute myocardial infarction and cardiovascular complications, discharged alive	146.1	1.5772
410 Chemotherapy	140.5	.5123
174 Gastrointestinal hemorrhage with cardiovascular complications	140.2	.9537
243 Medical back problems	120.2	.6580

Source: Ways and Means (1991).
a. DRG, diagnosis-related group.
b. Age greater than 17, with complications.

The goal of PPS is to encourage hospitals to find efficient ways to deliver care. The payment calculated for a hospital for a particular DRG is made regardless of the actual costs of treating the patient. If hospitals are able to deliver care at less than the amount of the prospective payment, they may keep the difference. Furthermore, although hospitals may lose on particular patients or in particular DRG categories, the assumption is that *on average* the hospital should be able to cover its costs—or even make a profit. The system was never designed to fully cover the costs of all patients in each DRG; rather, the gains and losses for individual cases are expected to even out over the year. Implicitly, the system also assumes that there are a sufficient number of cases for the averaging to occur.

No longer is there an incentive to keep patients for long periods or to perform many procedures that will be reimbursed at cost. Rather, hospitals find it in their financial interest to limit lengths of stay and tests or procedures performed. The downside of such a system is the possibility that patients will be discharged too early (referred to as the "quicker and sicker" issue) and that necessary tests will not be performed. Thus, some of the simplest responses that hospitals can make may put patients at risk. Further, hospitals may find it beneficial to discourage admission of high-cost patients within particular DRGs or patients with certain DRGs that are costly to that hospital.[11]

The other major problem anticipated by the legislation was the likelihood of "DRG creep." This could arise if hospitals were to "game" the system by assigning patients to DRGs with the highest possible weights, by careful attention to the diagnosis codes used. But such gaming is also difficult to separate from the natural response of physicians to take more seriously the reporting of diagnoses when that report is tied to payment. Early studies of the potential impact of PPS were based on data in which diagnoses were not related to payment and hence were not well reported. Thus, some "coding creep" was expected as a legitimate part of the adjustment to the new system.

Since 1984, a number of ad hoc adjustments to PPS have been enacted by Congress, particularly with regard to geographic location or hospital characteristics. Usually these changes have shifted the categories to which certain hospitals are assigned or have added new dimensions to the payment system to compensate for what, at least politically, have been the perceived failings of the system in dealing with particular hospitals. Hospitals often argue that special circumstances apply that cause them to be subject to higher costs.

Spirited lobbying and negotiation over these adjustments have kept Congress busy nearly every year since the passage of PPS. For example, hospitals that serve a disproportionate share of Medicare patients were granted additional payments beginning in 1986. In many cases, special treatment for some hospitals then lowers the payments made to others to keep budget neutrality in Medicare payments. This approach has effectively kept the hospital industry divided over the appropriate strategy for dealing with these changes.

The PPS system was phased in over several years to allow hospitals time to adjust their behavior. Payments during this transition were a blend of the hospitals' 1982 costs (updated) and regional and national DRG rates. The actual phase-in took longer than the initially planned four-year period, finally shifting to full national rates in November 1987 (Russell 1989).

Since passage of PPS, a consistent theme of federal budget reduction efforts has been to fund lower increases in payment rates to hospitals than that established in the original legislation. The PPS legislation called for an annual increase in payment levels, based on the prospective payment input price index (a "market basket" of hospital goods and services), adjustments for technological change, and an adjustment for changes in the mix of DRGs (a "case mix index") as a result of changes in coding and reporting accuracy (Ways and Means 1991).

The full update as calculated by the legislated formula has seldom been applied, however. Since 1985, the usual pattern has been for the administration to propose a very low update, which in turn is raised by Congress in its budget deliberations, reinstating some but not all of the increase that would have occurred if the original formula had been applied. These limits on the update modify the process established for the PPS system. They represent efforts to generate budget savings, but are also supported on the grounds that PPS began as a more generous system than was originally envisioned. As described next, hospitals, on average, did well financially during the early years of PPS. Nonetheless, hospitals often complain that although they are willing to abide by PPS, the reductions in the update penalize them for finding ways to cut costs. Together with PPS, the reduced updates resulted in a substantially lower rate of growth in hospital payments in the last half of the 1980s (figure 3.3).

The Immediate Response in Delivery of Care

The world did not stand still while PPS was being implemented. The healthcare environment for hospitals and other providers changed dramatically: developments in the practice of medicine affect what procedures are done in the hospital; other payers of healthcare have instituted their own strategies for holding down healthcare costs; states have revised their Medicaid payment methods; and many employers and insurers have sought discounts from hospitals as part of cost-containment efforts. Consequently, any analysis of trends in hospital care over the period captures what was happening in general and not just the specific impact of PPS.[12]

Nonetheless, some rather large jumps in key variables at the time PPS was implemented suggest that it had an important influence on healthcare. For patients, providers, and taxpayers, PPS has led to crucial changes in healthcare delivery and costs. Two major changes in the way care is delivered occurred almost immediately: lengths of stay per admission and number of admissions fell after the implementation of PPS.

Hospitals moved swiftly to discharge their Medicare patients earlier. From 1983 to 1985, hospital stays for Medicare patients fell from

9.7 to 8.7 days, a decline of over 10 percent (NCHS 1991), accelerating an existing trend (see figure 3.4). Moreover, these reduced lengths of stay occurred for Medicare patients of all ages and across most DRG categories.

Admissions also dropped off sharply, as shown in table 3.3. Although shorter lengths of stay were anticipated as a response to the new incentives, the decline in admissions was surprising. In fact, to help avoid the problem of unnecessary hospitalization and to oversee the quality of care being delivered, a system of local Peer Review Organizations (PROs) was established simultaneously with PPS. It

Figure 3.4 AVERAGE LENGTH OF STAY IN NONFEDERAL SHORT-STAY
HOSPITALS, 1980–90

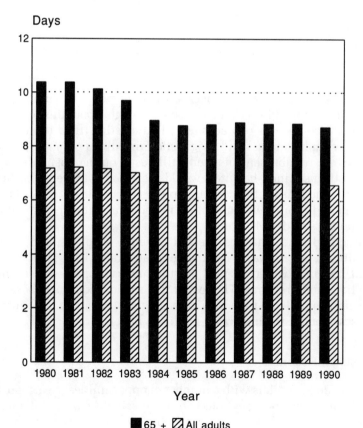

Source: ProPAC (1991).

Table 3.3 RATE OF CHANGE IN HOSPITAL ADMISSIONS FOR MEDICARE
ENROLLEES, 1980–89

| Year | Community Hospitals | | |
	All (%)	Urban (%)	Rural (%)
1980	3.0	2.9	3.1
1981	0.8	3.5	− 7.4
1982	− 0.2	0.1	− 0.9
1983	− 0.6	0.7	− 5.2
1984	− 2.8	− 2.0	− 5.2
1985	− 4.9	− 3.9	− 8.4
1986	− 3.2	− 2.3	− 6.8
1987	− 2.4	− 1.6	− 5.7
1988	− 0.5	− 0.1	− 2.0
1989	− 1.1	− 0.7	− 2.7
Cumulative Change:			
1979–83	3.0	7.4	− 10.3
1983–89	− 13.9	− 10.2	− 27.3
1979–89	− 11.3	− 3.6	− 34.7

Source: ProPAC (1991).

has been suggested that the uncertainty of the new legislation and/or
the scrutiny of the PROs over admissions brought about this response.
PPS may also have merely accelerated an existing trend toward performing simple surgical and diagnostic procedures on an outpatient
basis. Since reimbursements were still based on the hospitals' costs
in outpatient settings, hospitals would prefer to shift care to that area.
Whatever the reason, the combination of shorter stays and fewer admissions led to a dramatic decline in the total number of inpatient
hospital days under Medicare.

These and other changes affected patients, hospitals, and federal
spending in major ways. By changing so dramatically the way in
which hospitals would be paid, all the interested parties faced new
incentives and problems. The rest of this section examines those impacts on hospitals and the Medicare program, deferring to chapter 4
an assessment of the impact on Medicare beneficiaries.

Impacts on Hospitals

PPS provided hospitals with a number of opportunities to earn profits
by reducing costs. But they could do so either at the expense of quality
or by improving efficiency. Certainly the most dramatic response to
PPS was the sharp increase in the trend toward shorter lengths of stay
for Medicare patients. But limiting lengths of stay and reducing the

numbers of nurses on staff represent straightforward responses; hospitals have been less likely to radically restructure their organization or administration to achieve further efficiencies.

From the hospital's perspective, shorter periods of hospitalization *may* be associated with lower costs of care, but the savings may be considerably less than proportional. That is, if the number of tests and procedures remain the same, but are consolidated in fewer days of care, costs per case will not fall proportionately with shorter stays. When shorter lengths of stay simply translate into more empty beds on average over the year, the fixed costs of the hospital will increase on a per case basis. Since the shorter length of stay occurred at the same time as a downturn in admissions, hospitals were faced with problems of excess capacity. Indeed, the American Hospital Association has reported that in 1990, across all hospitals, one-third of beds were empty, up sharply over 1980 (AHA 1991). For hospitals to truly achieve savings, they must either do less for each patient or provide the same services more efficiently (i.e., at less cost).

Hospitals sought to reduce staff per patient—in particular, nursing staff (ProPAC 1991). But if the average patient is sicker than before and more procedures are packed into fewer days, reducing the nursing staff may, at some point, achieve cost reductions at the expense of quality. The fact that other types of hospital personnel have not been cut has fueled arguments about deteriorating quality of care. For example, among the fastest growing departments in hospitals over this period were administrative services (ProPAC 1991). Some of this growth no doubt reflects heavier burdens of dealing with the new environment created by PPS, but it may also reflect reluctance to make more sweeping changes. Hospitals have indeed been slow to institute more fundamental reforms that alter the type of care delivered. For example, one hope was that PPS would promote more emphasis on cost-saving, as opposed to cost-increasing, technologies (Lave 1990). This lack of innovative change has been a disappointment to some early supporters of PPS.

The result of all of these changes has been a steady decline in hospitals' Medicare operating margins. These operating margins—defined as the difference between Medicare payments and Medicare-allowed inpatient operating costs—indicate how well Medicare covers the costs that hospitals incur in providing Medicare services. When PPS was introduced in 1983 and 1984, the level of payment to hospitals was quite generous, and hospitals' immediate response of reducing lengths of stay allowed many of them to do very well. Operating margins for Medicare averaged more than 14 percent in the first two years of the payment system but declined thereafter, actually reaching a deficit in the sixth year of PPS (figure 3.5)[13] (ProPAC 1990). Although the initial generosity of Medicare payments was to some extent intended to gain the acceptance of hospitals, the margins were higher than many had anticipated.

Since then, the update factors have consistently lagged behind the market-basket adjustment that was supposed to protect hospitals from inflation and technological change. On the other hand, because of large changes in the mix of DRGs over time toward higher weighted

Figure 3.5 AGGREGATE PPS OPERATING MARGINS: FIRST SEVEN YEARS

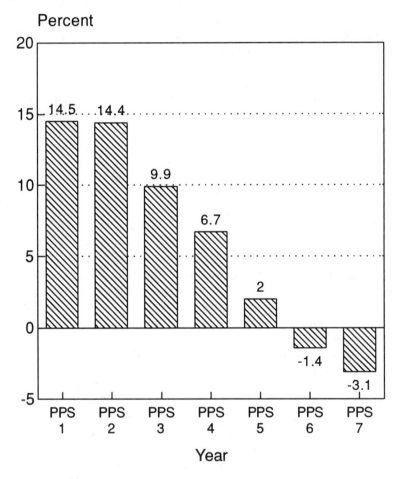

Source: ProPAC (1991).

cases, actual payments per discharge grew more rapidly than indicated by the update factor.[14] Over this period payments actually rose 69 percent. Nevertheless, many hospitals are finding it more difficult to cover the costs of providing care to beneficiaries. Frequently hospitals have not acted aggressively to hold down the costs of care. Consequently, they must either face losses or find ways to shift costs onto other groups paying for hospital care (such as patients covered by private insurance). Projections indicate that this trend in negative operating margins will continue and even worsen over the next few years (ProPAC 1991).

Averages do not tell the whole story. Even in the early years of PPS when payments were more generous, individual hospitals varied substantially in their gains or losses in Medicare operating margins. Systematic variations also occur, causing certain types of hospitals to do better than others. As shown in table 3.4, major teaching hospitals and large urban disproportionate-share hospitals consistently have done much better, on average, than other hospitals (ProPAC 1991). Since these types of facilities receive additional payments for each case, the findings are not surprising. Rural hospitals with less than

Table 3.4 DISTRIBUTION OF PPS OPERATING MARGINS, BY HOSPITAL GROUP, PPS 6

Hospital Group	Operating Margin by Percentile		
	10th (%)	Median (%)	90th (%)
All hospitals	− 29.3	− 3.2	15.6
Urban	− 25.8	− 2.7	15.5
Rural	− 33.3	− 3.9	15.7
Large urban	− 27.1	− 3.5	15.7
Other urban	− 24.1	− 2.0	15.1
Rural referral	− 20.5	− 3.0	13.6
Sole community	− 42.3	− 7.9	11.3
Other rural	− 33.5	− 3.0	16.5
Major teaching	− 13.5	7.4	23.7
Other teaching	− 20.5	− 1.2	14.8
Nonteaching	− 31.9	− 4.2	15.2
Disproportionate Share:			
Large urban	− 24.6	0.8	18.5
Other urban	− 21.1	0.5	16.8
Rural	− 27.9	0.9	20.6
Nondisproportionate share	− 31.3	− 4.5	14.4

Source: ProPAC (1991).

Note: Excludes hospitals in Maryland. PPS 6 refers to the sixth year since the Prospective Payment System went into effect for hospitals.

50 beds have always had lower average Medicare operating margins than large urban hospitals.

Within each type of hospital there are also major gainers and losers. Some major teaching hospitals have consistently low operating margins, whereas some small rural hospitals display consistently high operating margins. Indeed, a common complaint about Medicare PPS is this mismatch. Hospitals receiving the same payment levels may have varying costs that are not recognized by the system (ProPAC 1990). PPS is not able to fully capture differences in costs across hospitals, a failing of the payment system.

How serious are the declines in Medicare operating margins? To a large extent, many hospitals have avoided tough choices in changing the way they operate. Medicare margins have not fallen far enough to place most hospitals in overall financial distress. Rather, hospitals have cross-subsidized their operations from other more lucrative payers (i.e., private insurers). This safety valve of cost shifting effectively postpones the day of reckoning for hospitals, but it does not eliminate it. Could hospitals become more efficient? When their Medicare margins turn very negative and/or other payers do not provide enough revenue to maintain business as usual, hospitals will be forced to make major adjustments. This will come sooner for financially distressed hospitals. Indeed, Sheingold (1986) argued that most of the cost-saving efforts to date under PPS have been associated with hospitals in poor financial condition.

But this creates a dilemma. If hospitals respond only when they have to, more cuts may be necessary to induce those who are now shifting costs or who have positive margins to seek meaningful reforms in their operations. But further cuts may create enormous pressures on those hospitals that have responded well to PPS but nonetheless have higher-than-average costs.

Impact on Medicare Administration

From the federal government's perspective, PPS has been very successful. It has achieved substantial reductions in benefit payments over time, not in absolute dollars, but in terms of what Medicare would otherwise have had to pay for care. This impact can be seen in the decline in the rate of growth of payments for inpatient services (figure 3.3). After the introduction of PPS, the rate of growth in hospital payments declined substantially.

One consequence of these changes has been the steady outward progression of the date of projected exhaustion of the HI trust funds (see figure 3.6). In 1981, exhaustion was predicted by 1991. As indicated in previous chapters, policy changes have helped to steadily push off the date, so that by the 1991 trustees report, the date was 2005 (HI Trustees 1991). (The passage of PPS helped to protect the trust funds, and some of the low increases in hospital payments in later years—especially the updates for 1986 and 1990—were influential in postponing the date of exhaustion.)[15] However, between 1991 and 1992, a year when no legislative changes occurred, the date of exhaustion of the trust funds again slipped back to 2002—less than a decade away (HI Trustees 1992).

Figure 3.6 ESTIMATED BALANCE IN FEDERAL HOSPITAL INSURANCE TRUST FUND, SELECTED YEARS, 1982–2003

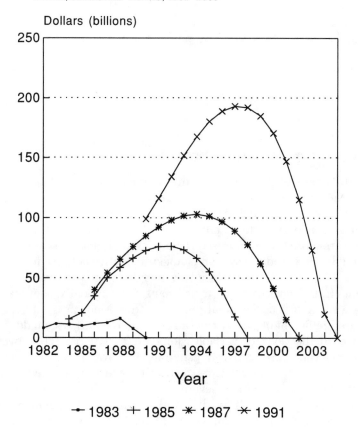

Source: Board of Trustees, Federal Hospital Insurance Trust Fund, annual reports, selected years.

From a wider perspective, PPS may have shifted some of the costs to settings totally beyond the hospitals' doors. PPS is often cited as one reason for the accelerated shift of treatment to standalone outpatient centers or physicians' offices. If so, some of the reduced spending on inpatient services will show up elsewhere, effectively offsetting the apparent cost-containment achievements of PPS. Shifts to skilled nursing facilities (SNFs) and to home health for postacute care would be captured by the trust fund projections in figure 3.6, but greater reliance on hospital outpatient services or physicians' offices is not captured by that indicator; these are Part B services. It is possible to look at the combined growth in hospital outpatient services, inpatient services, SNFs, and home health in contrast to inpatient services alone. Between 1980 and 1988, hospital inpatient services grew 3 percent per year in real terms—that is, above the overall rate of inflation in the economy. When all four service categories are examined, the total growth rate is 4 percent per year—an amount fully one-third higher. Not all of the additional growth in these services is attributable to PPS, nor would these offsets eliminate PPS savings; but PPS savings may be less than would be indicated by focusing only on changes in hospital inpatient services. Decreases in cost in one part of the system have a nasty habit of popping up elsewhere.

Changes to Improve Hospital Payment

Overall, hospital payment reform has been successful in holding down Medicare's costs, although there have been some concerns about quality (discussed in chapter 4). But as the financial pressures on Medicare continue to dictate tight budgets, weaknesses in the PPS system are more likely to cause problems. Not all hospitals are equally affected by PPS, and the system is not sufficiently sensitive to capture all the variations in costs faced by hospitals or differences across patients in the severity of their problems. Consequently, some hospitals are likely to face financial pressures from Medicare, not because they are inefficient or poorly run but because the PPS system does not capture all the relevant variables for their situations. When overall payment levels were relatively generous, this was less of a concern. As these budgets become more restrictive, the problems with such hospitals will become more severe.

Few serious critics call for dismantling prospective payment; it is now an ingrained part of Medicare. Instead, there has been considerable interest in modifications to the PPS system that may strengthen it over time. One approach would be to reintroduce some hospital-specific costs into the formulas, recognizing that the payment factors in the current formula do not capture all the relevant variation (Hadley, Zuckerman, and Feder 1989; Lave 1990). This could provide protection for hospitals that have higher costs not accounted for by other adjustment factors and relieve one of the major criticisms leveled against PPS.[16]

Another proposal often discussed is to improve measures of severity to protect hospitals that treat sicker-than-average patients within each DRG. This solution focuses on one of the specific problems of PPS—the relative insensitivity of the system to differences across patients within a given DRG. If a hospital has an unusually high share of severely ill patients, they may effectively be penalized by PPS. Averaging across patients may not help if there is a persistent differential. Although the outlier policy was designed to ease this problem, it does not help if many patients are *moderately* sicker than average, as opposed to a few extreme cases.[17]

Others advocate further within-DRG adjustments or even alternatives to DRGs. Among the alternatives suggested are classifications systems that use objective, clinical data to generate more sensitive indicators (Office of Technology Assessment 1985; ProPAC 1986). But much of the attention directed to these types of adjustments to DRGs came in the mid-1980s, and interest since then seems to have waned. Lave (1990) has also proposed "rebasing" the PPS system to capture the effects of changing costs of treatment across DRGs and increasing the number of adjustment factors. This would require reestimating the DRGs to better capture differences across hospitals in the costs of care provided to patients.

All of these issues will likely increase, rather than decrease, as greater efforts by the government to hold down costs put further pressures on hospitals. Unless new techniques refining DRGs that more effectively explain differences in costs can be developed soon, it makes sense to reintroduce some hospital-specific costs to the formula. Pressure needs to be applied to all hospitals to hold down costs, rather than just to those currently under financial stress. If we develop more confidence in the fairness of the payment mechanism, more stringent controls can be justified.

PHYSICIAN PAYMENT REFORM

From the outset, Medicare sought to encourage physicians to participate. Initial payment levels were relatively generous, and doctors were promised no restrictions as to the care they could provide. For the first 20 years of Medicare, physician reimbursement went largely unchanged. But physician payment growth became a major issue in the 1980s. Not only was growth high absolutely, but it was growing relative to hospital payments, which were moderating. Physicians also represent a target for cost-cutting efforts because of their high income levels and control over the rest of the healthcare system as well.

Starting in 1984, payments were reduced through several mechanisms, including a freeze on how fast charges were allowed to grow. This fee freeze, first instituted on July 1, 1984, was viewed by many as a first step toward broader reform. This legislation permitted no increase in the "prevailing charge" for physicians—which acts as the absolute cap on Medicare allowed charges.[18] Since this represented a situation analogous to the TEFRA changes that helped push PPS for hospitals, many felt that reform could be hammered out before the freeze was lifted. But consensus remained elusive, and Congress failed to enact broader reform. After one further extension, the freeze was finally lifted in May 1986.[19] Whereas the passage of fee reform stalled, recognition of the problem increased. As figure 3.7 shows, despite the fee freeze, costs of the physician services portion of Part B continued to grow at an alarming pace.

Figure 3.7 ANNUAL RATES OF GROWTH IN MEDICARE PHYSICIAN PAYMENTS, 1975–90

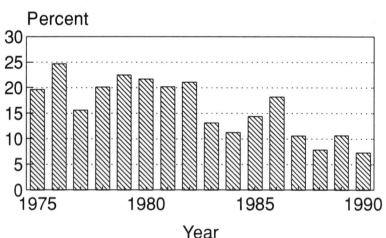

Source: Ways and Means (1992).

Many policymakers had long expressed doubts about Medicare's Part B payment structure, on the basis that it locked in historical inequities. These imbalances sent the wrong signals to physicians by paying relatively more for expensive, high-technology services while offering few incentives for careful geriatric assessments or other basic care. Further, payments in some rural areas of the country were viewed as too low, discouraging physicians from practicing in such areas. Finally, physician payments varied enormously around the country and even within the same area for the same services—creating an extremely complex system that was not only difficult to manage but was also unable to provide appropriate incentives to physicians through the payment structure. Consequently, the old payment mechanism did not allow Congress or the Health Care Financing Administration (HCFA) to change incentives for physicians; a new mechanism was needed.

The desire to adopt reforms so as to control costs and eliminate payment inequities led to debate in the early 1980s about what approach to take. Some policymakers wanted the government to be able to set fees and streamline the payment process; others sought more dramatic schemes to pay physicians, not on a fee-for-service basis but, rather, on a flat amount per patient (referred to as "capitation" approaches). Often, this latter approach focused on using formal groups such as health maintenance organizations (HMOs) to oversee the volume of all service use (and not just physician services) The goal of simplifying the system so that it could be better controlled was also an important factor in the debate.

In an attempt to speed the development of consensus on reform, Congress established a Physician Payment Review Commission (PPRC) in 1986 and charged it with hammering out the details of a reform package to propose to Congress and the Reagan administration. In March 1987, PPRC recommended a resource-based relative value scale approach (PPRC 1987).[20] PPRC noted that this would not rule out further reforms to move away from a fee-based system; rather, the fee schedule was emphasized as a necessary first step. The administration remained skeptical of relying only on a fee schedule, preferring more radical change to move away from a fee-for-service approach. Nonetheless, HCFA funded the major study that would later serve as the basis for the fee schedule used in the payment reform. The groundwork was being laid for reform.

Debate continued to be waged until 1989 when Congress, at the eleventh hour, passed the Medicare Fee Schedule as part of the Omnibus Budget Reconciliation Act of 1989 (OBRA89). Like PPS, it was

added to other more comprehensive legislation. The payment reform
began on January 1, 1992, and, after a five-year transition, is scheduled
to be fully in place by 1996. The fee schedule does not reduce the
overall level of payments to physicians, but it does substantially reduce payments for surgeries and procedures (which were deemed
"overvalued") while increasing payments for basic office visits.

The implementation of the fee schedule has not been smooth, however. First, doctors were alarmed by a preemptive strike on reform
with a budget agreement in 1990 that essentially instituted some of
the cuts in the "overvalued" procedures without offsetting increases
in "undervalued" ones. But the most controversial move prior to the
January 1, 1992, starting date was the release of proposed regulations
for the fee schedule on June 5, 1991, in the *Federal Register*. Physicians'
groups exploded. Led by the AMA, doctors cried foul, not over the fee
schedule but over the initial starting value (the "conversion factor"),
which they felt violated the promise that the fee schedule be budget
neutral. Two major sets of adjustments would effectively have resulted
in a 16.5 percent cut in the conversion factor used to set fee levels.[21]
The result would be lower fees after the transition than physicians
had expected to face. For example, HCFA calculated that an intermediate office visit for an established patient would rise only from $26
in 1991 before the fee schedule to $27 in 1992—not much of an in-
crease for one of the fees that the schedule presumably sought to favor.
There was thus little good news in fees to offset the bad news of larger
cuts in other fees.

After much acrimony and threatened congressional intervention,
HCFA produced its final regulations on November 11, 1991. The
agency softened the cut in the conversion factor. As a consequence,
that same intermediate office visit would now rise to $30 in 1992,
rather than $27. The cuts were also reduced. For example, coronary
artery bypass surgery would have fallen from $3,178 in 1991 to $2,726
in 1992 under the initial rules, but only to $2,892 under the November
rules.

Details of the Medicare Fee Schedule

Versions of a relative value scale had often been floated as a policy
option in the debates over physician payment reform.[22] Policymakers
are very attracted to the concept of directly establishing payment
levels for various services, both absolutely and relative to each other.
A relative value approach sets maximum levels of fees with the con-
scious goal of establishing justifiable differences across type of serv-

ice. These relative values can then be translated into dollar fees at any absolute level desired.

The first sets of relative value scales in the United States were established using interviews with physicians to determine appropriate relationships among services. They represented standardization efforts more than attempts to rethink how fees are set. Early work by William Hsaio and William Stason (1979) moved the relative value scale in another direction, emphasizing a method for establishing values that was not dependent on existing fees or physicians' general perceptions regarding fees. They proposed a resource-based relative value scale (RBRVS), which would set the relative value units (RVUs) according to time and complexity of the service performed. The results of this study indicated RVUs at odds with earlier fee schedules and average reimbursement levels by various payers. For example, office visits were weighted more heavily relative to surgical procedures in the Hsaio-Stason approach.

The Hsaio-Stason findings appealed intuitively to many policymakers. First, they reflected a "scientific approach" that sought to establish RVUs objectively, rather than on the basis of historical precedent or individual physician judgment. Equally important, the approach suggested that high-technology procedures, which were growing rapidly and seemed well compensated, should fall relative to more basic services. If the findings of Hsaio and Stason had been in the opposite direction, it is likely that they would not have been nearly so well received. But this initial work was not undertaken in a vacuum. The "goals" of any new fee schedule were to raise fees for management and evaluation services and reduce those for surgery and other "overvalued" procedures. The Hsaio-Stason approach was assured of leading in that direction.

The RBRVS approach also has many critics, who point out that prices in competitive markets reflect the value of services to consumers and not the costs of the inputs to produce the services (Hadley et al. 1986). Thus, the RBRVS may not produce relative values that reflect what individuals are actually willing to pay, and may lead to undesirable distortions in prices. These critics often favor instead a negotiated approach where the goals of the fee schedule and the market pressures can be reconciled directly.

The Medicare Fee Schedule (MFS), passed by Congress on December 19, 1989, uses a resource-based relative value scale. In anticipation of a payment system using RVUs, Hsaio and others at Harvard University were commissioned by HCFA to create a new resource-based relative value scale, building on the earlier work. Published in 1988

(Hsaio et al. 1988), this work served as the basis for establishing the relative value units adopted by HCFA in 1991 (*Federal Register* 1991a).

The Harvard analysis used several techniques to devise RVUs. First, national surveys of 3,200 physicians and technical consulting groups representing 18 specialties were used to rate 23 key services in each specialty. These efforts resulted in within-specialty RVUs that then had to be compared across specialty. The next step was thus to "calibrate" these specialty-specific scales relative to each other, taking two specialties at a time. For a particular pair of specialties, several key services in each specialty were compared by expert panels to provide rankings that could link the specialty-specific scales.[23] Then the whole package was combined. This yielded a set of key RVUs that then served as the basis for establishing rankings for other services. Within a specialty existing charges for groups of services were used to set the final RVUs.[24]

The process was expensive and time-consuming, and represented a careful effort to establish an objective measure of "value." However, it is certainly not perfect science, nor did it satisfy everyone. The cross-specialty linkages were subject to considerable debate, and many physicians believed their services were ranked too low. In general, however, there was considerable acceptance of the study's methodology, and the findings again had intuitive appeal. Physicians' groups, who viewed some type of reform as inevitable, generally agreed to this type of approach.

The RBRVS constitutes only one part of the Medicare Fee Schedule. Essentially, the fee schedule establishes "national uniform relative values for all physicians' services" that are the sum of the RVUs that reflect physician work, practice expenses (net of physician liability insurance), and the cost of professional liability insurance. These national relative values are modified by a geographic adjustment factor. A conversion factor is then applied to the adjusted RVUs to achieve dollar values for the fees. Unlike the earlier RBRVS by Hsaio and Stason, the Medicare Fee Schedule has no adjustments for specialty. Consequently, specialists who concentrate on surgeries or procedures that were substantially cut will face large reductions in Medicare services.

HCFA turned to studies by Stephen Zuckerman, W. Pete Welch, and Gregory Pope (1990) in developing a geographic adjustment factor for the Medicare Fee Schedule. The geographic practice cost index (GPCI) proposed by these authors represents an effort to measure the relative costs of inputs used in practices across the United States. In many cases, data on the relevant price variation do not routinely exist, and proxy data needed to be used to derive the index. For example, it is very difficult to obtain information on office rents in some areas of the country, necessitating that apartment rent differences be included as a proxy. Although the original data on the GPCI included professional liability expenses (for malpractice), these were specifically established as a separate factor in the legislation, recognizing that these adjustments were likely to be subject to further change in the future.

Another element of physician payment reform consists of volume performance standards (VPS), which were designed to create incentives to moderate the rate of growth in expenditures for physicians' services. These standards are then used by Congress in setting the rate of growth of physician payments each year. If Congress fails to act on a specific rate, a default formula dictates the level of payment. Essentially the formula creates a penalty that varies in inverse relation to the rate of growth in the volume of services over the previous five years not attributable to enrollee growth, regulation, or legislation. At present, there are two VPS calculations: one for surgery and one for nonsurgery. Each is applied on a national level. Critics contend that this scale is too broad to have the desired effect on physician behavior and that the standards may end up penalizing physicians who are not gaming the system. Further study is being conducted on how to disaggregate these adjustments, perhaps at the specialty or area levels.

Finally, the reform legislation limited the ability of physicians to bill their patients above Medicare's fees. This was a compromise between consumer groups who wanted to require Medicare fees to represent payment in full and physicians who opposed all such limits. Limits on such extra billing protect the financial resources of the elderly and those with disabilities, but also may result in restrictions on access to care if physicians consequently decline to take on Medicare patients. Physicians argued that without such opportunities for additional billing, fees would be undesirably restrictive, preventing differences across physicians on the basis of the quality of care, for example. In the end, the limits adopted were quite stringent. When fully implemented, physicians who decline to "accept assignment" (see note 19) will be able to bill only about 10 percent above the fee levels.[25]

The Likely Impact

The Medicare Fee Schedule will have an impact on physician behavior, patients' access to care, and the overall costs of Part B. How much of an impact is the question. Implicitly, HCFA has weighed in with its assessment that volume will increase substantially, since it proposed to reduce the conversion factor even before the fee schedule takes effect. Moreover, a number of physician groups hostile to the new fee system have suggested that the payment level changes will result in reduced willingness by doctors to treat Medicare patients. As yet, however, there has been little evidence of any actual decline.

One objective *not* achieved by the fee schedule is simplicity. With over 7,000 codes and 233 geographic areas, the MFS consists of thousands of separate fees, although it does represent an improvement over the current system. It will be a challenge for physicians to keep track of their own fees, although at least now they can be known in advance. Moreover, the regulations of this complicated system took up 317 pages in the *Federal Register* (1991a), and it is likely that each year will bring additional nuances and regulations as various groups jockey for preferential treatment.

The HCFA has calculated the impact of the Medicare Fee Schedule by physician specialty, based on the composition of services now attributable to each specialty area. As shown in table 3.5, the biggest gainers are general and family practice physicians. They rely most heavily on office visits—an area where fees will rise—and much less on surgical procedures. Since the fee schedule will not distinguish among specialties, optometrists, chiropodists, and podiatrists will also gain, since their fees are now considerably lower than those for

Table 3.5   1996 IMPACT OF MEDICARE FEE SCHEDULE BY PHYSICIAN SPECIALTY

Specialty	Changes in Payments per Service (%)
Family practice	28
General practice	27
Cardiology	− 17
Internal medicine	5
Gastroenterology	− 18
Neurology	− 4
Psychiatry	3
Urology	− 8
Radiology	− 22
Anesthesiology	− 27
Pathology	− 20
General surgery	− 13
Ophthalmology	− 21
Orthopedic surgery	− 11
Thoracic surgery	− 27
All specialties	− 6

Source: Health Care Financing Administration (1991a).

physicians. In contrast, the biggest losers are thoracic surgeons, anesthesiologists, and radiologists.[26]

The regional adjustments are furthermore intended to reflect differences in the costs of practicing medicine across the United States. As indicated earlier, there are 233 separate geographic areas where the practice cost index will be applied. This system also creates winners and losers across physicians as compared to the previous system. As might be expected, Manhattan has very high practice cost weights—for example, the malpractice weight there is set at 1.647, compared to .504 in Texas. Practice expense weights also show considerable variation. San Francisco is at the upper end with a weight of 1.303, compared to .763 for Puerto Rico or 1.001 for large Pennsylvania cities (Federal Register 1991a).

Finally, impacts within various specialty groups in a particular area will also vary, depending upon the relative level of physicians' fees under the current system. A major impact of the new fee schedule will be to even out existing variations. Earlier research simulating a fee schedule illustrated how dramatic the adjustments can be (Moon 1986). In that simple simulation, a fee schedule using average charges as the fee resulted in over 38 percent of general surgeons experiencing gains or losses in reimbursements in excess of 10 percent, for example. The impact of the MFS will likely be less than indicated by that study, for several reasons. Since the early 1980s, physician payment differentials have likely been reduced—for example, the reductions in overpriced procedures will have had an impact. Moreover, allowances are made for reduced payments to those in their first few years of practice.

The impact on Medicare expenditures in the first few years of the MFS should be minimal. Indeed, the fee schedule is billed as a budget-neutral change and as reform rather than cost containment per se. Furthermore, if the volume response of physicians is higher than anticipated, the program could fail to be budget neutral, and could actually raise costs.

The volume performance standards were designed to address exactly this issue, but it is not clear how well they will work. If physician payment reform can develop strong volume controls, it may help to hold down costs. It is also possible that cuts in surgical fees and fees for other procedures might discourage use at the same time that other changes such as effectiveness and outcomes studies and practice guidelines demonstrate the desirability of doing less in some areas. If so, the MFS may prove quite successful. Finally, there is a strong likelihood that the conversion factor will be used to hold down cost growth in Part B over time, just as growth in the PPS update factor has been constrained. Pressures for further cost containment make this a very likely scenario.

OTHER PROVIDER CHANGES

Although most of the cost-containment attention has been directed at inpatient hospital and physician services, which represent the biggest shares of Medicare, other areas have also been subject to the budget ax. Indeed, the effort has been so extensive that micromanagement of budget cutting reached new heights in the 1990 budget deal. To achieve the $43 billion in five-year savings, almost no part of Medicare remained unscathed. For example, payments for prosthetic devices were frozen, further restrictions were added to the coverage of seat-lift chairs and power scooters, and a further reduction was made in laboratory fees. These changes produced only a tiny portion of the $43 billion, but spread the pain across many providers.

During the 1980s, additional areas were subject to rather substantial cost-saving efforts. For example, home health and skilled nursing care benefits were constrained by interpretation of regulations rather than from legislative changes—as discussed in the subsections following. Savings in other areas have been a bit more illusive. Outpatient hospital services, which have grown enormously, received considerable attention and some cost cutting, but major policy change in that area has proven illusive. Payment policy for outpatient services remains a hodgepodge of ad hoc adjustments (Sulvetta 1992). Scheduled payment reform has been delayed several times in this area. Congress first mandated recommendations from HCFA by April 1989 (Ways and Means 1989). In 1992, HCFA was still working on its final recommendations. When those changes come they are likely to result in a PPS-type system. Finally, some limited efforts have also focused on fraud and abuse—such as attention to physician referrals to laboratories or testing facilities in which they have a financial stake.

Home Health Services

Home healthcare under Medicare has always been limited to "skilled" care, thereby restricting its size. Nonetheless, the benefit has undergone a number of "phases." In the early years of the program, growth was relatively restricted, in large part by limits on the number of services and the existence of cost sharing. Those restrictions were fully lifted by 1980, resulting in a rapid rate of growth in the benefit. A period of extremely tight regulatory control then followed in the mid 1980s, with a subsequent easing of restrictions after an important court case (discussed later here) at the end of the decade. These policies are reflected in the unusual pattern of growth of reimbursements shown in figure 3.8.

Home health services represent a medical benefit to which enrollees are eligible if they are under the care of a physician, confined to home, and need skilled nursing services on an intermittent basis. Coverage is also available for those who need physical or speech therapy (and at least earlier have met the other criteria). The coinsurance requirement for home health was removed in 1972, and further liberalization in 1980 eliminated the deductible, the 100-day limit, and the prior hospitalization requirement. This means that nearly all home health services effectively were shifted to Part A.[27] In addition, in 1980, proprietary agencies were permitted to operate without licensing requirements, leading to a rapid expansion in the supply of home health services—and likely having the greatest impact on use of services (Kenney 1990).

Concern about rates of growth in reimbursement for home health in excess of 25 percent a year between 1980 and 1983 led HCFA to closely scrutinize intermediaries' adherence to the eligibility requirements and types of services received. HCFA clamped down on activities and instructed its intermediaries to closely examine claims. Denial rates increased (Leader 1988) and the rate of growth of reimbursements slowed noticeably, at a time when the introduction of PPS would have been expected to accelerate the growth in the program. By 1986, the rate of growth in reimbursements slowed to 1.1 percent, and actually declined in 1987 (Ways and Means 1991).

The regulatory strategy to hold down costs proved very effective. In 1984, HCFA issued new guidelines to the fiscal intermediaries regarding the interpretation of the part-time and intermittent requirements. The 1984 guidelines required that an otherwise eligible individual would qualify for the benefit only if the care were both part-time (less than eight hours per day) and intermittent (four or fewer days per week). Eligibility also required that the individual be homebound. This meant a virtual Catch 22, where the individual had to be so incapacitated as to be unable to operate outside the home, but well enough to need only part-time care.

Figure 3.8 BENEFIT PAYMENTS FOR SKILLED NURSING FACILITY, HOME
HEALTH, AND HOSPICE CARE, 1975–90

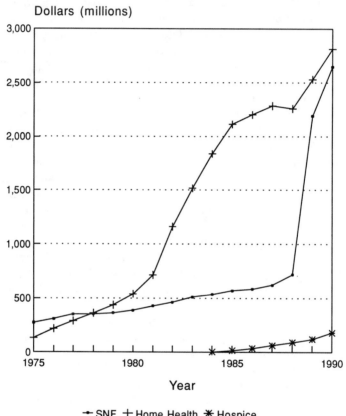

Dollars (millions)

Year

⚊ SNF ➕ Home Health ✳ Hospice

Source: Ways and Means (1991).

Since that time, an important lawsuit, *Duggan v. Bowen,* has helped
to ease these requirements substantially.[28] Beginning in July 1989, the
definitions of medical necessity changed, the definition of intermittency was relaxed, and the guidelines to intermediaries were rewritten
to establish more consistent treatment. The impact seems to have been
an important opening to further expansion of services beginning in
1989, as indicated by figure 3.8. Thus, the period of strong cost containment in home healthcare seems to be over, at least for the time
being.

Skilled Nursing Facility Care

Like home healthcare, skilled nursing facility (SNF) services have always been constrained by their definition as skilled care. SNF benefits are restricted to enrollees who have had a three-day prior hospital stay and who need skilled nursing or rehabilitation services. In 1969, they were limited to those on a course of recovery. These limitations restrict the number of persons eligible and have ensured that Medicare has never become a substantial provider of long-term care services (Smits, Feder, and Scanlon 1982). In addition, intermediaries had regulatory discretion over what conditions qualified for the SNF reimbursement and the duration of benefits. These interpretations tended to vary widely across the United States (Liu and Kenney 1991). The actual regulations have been in place since the beginning of the program and were not modified in the 1980s. Indeed, earlier studies criticized the arbitrary and after-the-fact rulings about coverage that discouraged nursing home participation (Smits et al. 1982). Nonetheless, they represent an important cost constraint on SNF care that seems to have become more important during the mid-1980s, when PPS was leading to earlier hospital discharges than ever before. Perhaps most crucial, however, have been the relatively low reimbursement rates under Medicare.

In the 1980s, cost-sharing requirements became more severe. The level of SNF cost sharing (assessed against days 21 through 100) is tied to the hospital deductible, which rose rapidly in the 1980s and outpaced the growth in the costs of SNF care. In fact, at one-eighth of the hospital deductible, the SNF cost sharing turns out to be higher than the daily payment to some providers of SNF care. Consequently, for many beneficiaries, the SNF benefit essentially became only a 20-day benefit (Liu and Kenney 1991); it may prove cheaper to make other private arrangements after that. Again, with no formal policy interventions, growth in SNF care was limited substantially until 1988 (see figure 3.8).

The situation for SNF changed substantially beginning in April 1988, when a legal ruling established more uniform coverage guidelines, taking away one of the barriers to receiving care. Much of the discretion employed by intermediaries in interpreting what services were covered was eliminated. Consequently, patients such as those requiring tube feeding became eligible for the first time (Liu and Kenney 1991). SNF reimbursements took a sharp upward jump in 1988. That movement continued in 1989 with the addition of the benefits from the Medicare Catastrophic Coverage Act (described in chapter 5).

CONCLUSIONS

Overall, Medicare's achievements in cost containment have been remarkable. At a time when many payers of healthcare—insurers and employers—have complained about costs but shown little inclination to experiment with dramatic solutions, Medicare forged ahead. Prodded by Congress, the Health Care Financing Administration undertook sweeping changes affecting payments for hospitals and physicians. These revolutionary new payment mechanisms cost millions to develop and implement. And, although there have certainly been problems, the innovations offered by the government have both held down costs and served as a model for others to emulate or build upon. Indeed, many of the healthcare reform proposals of the early 1990s have drawn upon Medicare payment policy as a model for broader systems of cost containment.

The hospital Prospective Payment System helped to bring down the growth in costs of healthcare for the Medicare program and, at least for innovative hospitals, provides incentives for improved efficiency. Perhaps the greatest failing of PPS is its inability to account for some legitimate differences in costs that lead to overly generous payments for some hospitals and insufficient levels for others. Further tinkering and adjustment of the system will undoubtedly continue. But it is also equally unlikely that Medicare will reject the PPS system and either return to the old ways or seek some radically different approach. Some concerns about quality (discussed in chapter 4) also warrant continued monitoring of the system.

Physician payment reform has represented a considerable improvement over the previous payment scheme. The tools are at hand to discipline both price and volume growth, although this will likely lead to major confrontations with the physician community. As with PPS, many physicians and groups of physicians will likely believe they are being treated unfairly by the system and will seek legislative redress. But the RBRVS, volume performance standards, and some type of balance billing limits are also likely to be part of the payment landscape for some time to come.

Cost containment did not just affect the providers of healthcare, however. Directly and indirectly, beneficiaries have also faced many changes in Medicare. These impacts are addressed in the next chapter.

Notes

1. The picture would likely vary considerably if hospital *outpatient* services were included, since much of the drop in hospital use reflected a move to outpatient services.

2. Once Medicare payment rates differ from the general rate of price increases in the economy, the medical price index does not neatly separate price and volume differences. Care should thus be taken in assuming that use of services grew little after 1982, as implied by figure 3.1.

3. The MEI establishes the limit on the yearly increase in physicians' prevailing charges under Medicare. Prevailing charges reflect the 75th percentile of all physician charges for that particular service in a given area. Since not all physicians' bills are as high as the prevailing charges in an area, this is not an absolute cap, however.

4. The limits now applied to ancillary departments and special care units, and for each case, the hospital would get its target or 120 percent of the average cost for similar hospitals, whichever was lower.

5. Hospitals with costs below both sets of limits could keep one-half of the difference between their costs and the TEFRA limits.

6. A unique DRG is assigned to a patient depending upon diagnosis at admission and the type of treatment received (i.e., whether surgery was performed). Diagnoses and procedures are identified by codes defined in the International Classification of Diseases (referred to as ICD-9 codes). This system had been developed at Yale University and was used in the state of New Jersey. However, no one had studied applications of DRGs specifically for aged and disabled persons.

7. In the early years of PPS, "age 70 or over" was used as a proxy to capture more expensive cases; that has now been replaced by "complicating condition" (Lave 1990).

8. Outliers are those patients whose length of stay in the hospital or whose costs of care are well above the average for other patients in the same DRG. Outlier limits are established for each DRG and generally apply to only a small fraction of patients (about 5 percent).

9. These weights are updated annually to reflect changing relative costs. New procedures are added occasionally; there are now 475 DRGs in use. Moreover, as patterns of care or treatments change, the weights for the DRGs also change. This "recalibration" attempts to keep DRGs current with technology and other factors that affect the costs of hospital care.

10. When PPS was passed, capital costs—those associated with building or modifying facilities and purchasing equipment—were excluded from the calculation of other costs. Such costs vary substantially from year to year and offer major challenges for payment design. Rather than trying to design that part of PPS at the time of passage, capital payments were retained as a "pass through" in the formula. Payments used the pre-PPS methodology and were simply added to a hospital's PPS payment each year. Congress instructed the U.S. Department of Health and Human Services to devise a

prospective payment scheme for capital costs. The Health Care Financing Administration has adopted regulations for capital payments that are essentially comparable to the methodology used for establishing PPS payments. The rates will be fully prospective and not related to actual spending levels by hospitals. And like PPS, there will be special provisions and exceptions for certain types of hospitals. A longer, 10-year transition to this new system has been proposed, recognizing that hospitals make decisions regarding capital investments well in advance.

11. These issues are discussed in chapter 4.

12. Some studies were able to examine the staggered transition to PPS to analyze its impact on hospital care. These have suggested that PPS was indeed important (Coulam and Gaumer 1991). In addition, a few states received waivers that allowed them to avoid using the PPS system. Some studies have used these states' experiences as controls for examining PPS impact, although these waivered states certainly do not constitute a random control group.

13. The Prospective Payment Assessment Commission (ProPAC) estimates operating margins according to time elapsed since the beginning of the PPS for each hospital. Since hospitals vary in their fiscal years, they entered the system at differing dates in 1983 and 1984. PPS year six would be approximately 1990.

14. Some of this discrepancy is likely accounted for by real increases in the severity of cases and some is an artifact of DRG "code creep."

15. A study by the Congressional Budget Office (1991) also illustrates the relative success from the federal perspective of the cost-containment efforts in the 1980s in the hospital area. Between 1975 and 1980, hospital inpatient services per enrollee grew 7 percent annually after adjusting for general inflation. That growth rate declined to 3.4 percent for the 1980 to 1990 period. Actual spending in 1990 was only 71 percent of what it would have been if the 1975 to 1980 trend of spending had continued in the 1980s. However, although PPS and the scrutiny of the PROs may account for some of that trend, admission rates for persons of all ages also fell over this period, likely reflecting changes in the ways we use hospitals in the United States, more reliance on outpatient services, and perhaps even changes in the overall health of our citizens.

16. To guard against returning payment to a cost-plus environment, however, the costs could use a base year trended forward using an index independent of behavior. This would be similar to the methodology employed under TEFRA.

17. Implicitly, adjustments for disproportionate-share and teaching hospitals have also sought to offer such protections, but these are proxy measures targeting hospitals likely to have such patients. Disproportionate-share hospitals refer to those with an unusually high proportion of Medicare and Medicaid patients. Teaching hospitals are those institutions that train a substantial share of medical interns and residents. In both cases, these types of hospitals, it is argued, are likely to have sicker patients or patients with other complicating conditions that make them more expensive to treat. But these approaches do not address problems of higher costs for hospitals that do not fit into a protected category, however.

18. Physicians whose charges were below the prevailing rate could receive higher payments over this period until they hit the prevailing cap.

19. Actually, the freeze was only lifted for those physicians who agreed to "accept assignment" for all their Medicare patients (i.e., "participating" physicians who agreed to bill Medicare directly rather than demanding that their patients pay in full at the time of service). Physicians who did not agree to accept assignment for all patients remained under the freeze until January 1, 1987.

20. This approach, defined in more detail in the text upcoming, would set fees for physicians on the basis of physician time and practice costs necessary to perform the service.

21. The more controversial of the reasons for these adjustments was HCFA's decision to anticipate the likely response of physicians, resulting in an increase in the volume of services. Consequently, HCFA allowed for a "behavioral offset" by reducing the conversion factor by 10.5 percent. This adjustment was disputed on several grounds, especially the assumption that physicians would game the system. It thus condemned them before the fact. The second reason for the adjustment was a technical issue related to the transition rules established by Congress.

22. Using a fee schedule to set payments was also debated, however. One camp argued for negotiated fees, to be decided after tough bargaining between the government and groups representing physicians; others advocated relative value scales that would establish new fees based on time spent and/or intensity of effort. A lack of consensus on appropriate strategies for change also slowed efforts to reform Medicare payment policy (Hadley et al. 1986).

23. These panels consisted of but a small number of physicians, an aspect of the Harvard study (Hsaio et al. 1988) that has been criticized.

24. Since then, further analysis has been undertaken by the Harvard researchers to analyze more procedures and more specialties. Moreover, the legislation adopting the Medical Fee Schedule also drew on modifications in the methodology provided by the PPRC (1989).

25. The actual limit is 15 percent, but nonparticipating physicians will be paid only 95 percent of the fee level.

26. Actually, anesthesiologists have their own fee schedule that they negotiated with HCFA. They are affected by the conversion factor that HCFA uses, however.

27. Originally, the benefit was covered under Part A for patients who had either been hospitalized or admitted to a skilled nursing facility for at least three days, or under Part B for patients without prior hospital or SNF admissions. Once benefits were exhausted under Part A (after 100 days per spell of illness), they were available under Part B, but were subject to the Part B deductible and coinsurance.

28. Duggan v. Bowen was a lawsuit designed to clarify home health eligibility criteria. It was settled out of court when HCFA agreed to make certain changes (Dubay, Kenney, Liu, and Moon 1991).

"YOUR BLOOD PRESSURE AND TEMPERATURE ARE WAY UP, BUT YOUR MEDICARE COVERAGE IS WAY DOWN. LOOKS AS IF YOU CAN GO HOME TODAY, MRS. FITCH!"

Chapter Four

CONTAINING COSTS:
IMPACTS ON BENEFICIARIES

Cost-containment efforts affect beneficiaries directly by raising what they are required to pay (cost sharing) and indirectly through requirements on hospitals, doctors, and other healthcare providers. In turn, these activities influence the quantity and quality of care delivered. Most of the policy changes in Medicare during the 1980s focused on restrictions in reimbursements to providers, but direct and indirect burdens on beneficiaries also increased over the period.

The Medicare program offered nearly $2,887 in benefits for the average enrollee in 1990. However, the Congressional Budget Office has estimated that patients' liability averaged $1,002 in 1990—or about 26 percent of the costs of Medicare-covered services (Ways and Means 1991). These expenses stem directly from Medicare's Part B premium and cost-sharing provisions. Noncovered services raise beneficiaries' share of healthcare costs even further, to about 30 percent of all acute-care services.

Growth in the burdens on beneficiaries for these Medicare-covered services reflects the rapid growth in overall spending on Medicare, as well as policy changes that shift the burdens as a means to save federal dollars. Moreover, limitations on coverage and other reimbursement changes have indirect effects not captured by standard out-of-pocket spending measures, so the burdens may be even higher. For example, beneficiaries facing shorter stays in hospitals have likely substituted with noncovered services, such as homemaker aides. Those costs do not show up in traditional measures of Medicare enrollee liability, so it is not apparent how much patients' liability may have grown. Also, if less care that could extend life or improve its quality is delivered over time, beneficiaries also clearly suffer. Declines in the quality of care represent less tangible, but no less important, potential impacts of cost containment.

DIRECT CHANGES IN BENEFICIARY COST SHARING

Legislative changes in the 1980s altered the degree to which beneficiaries are required to pay additional shares of the costs of their Medicare-covered acute care. Although none of these increases individually proved very significant, when added together they generated
substantial savings to the Medicare program and added noticeably to
enrollees' average liabilities. In every budget submission by Presidents
Reagan and Bush, proposed cuts in Medicare affecting beneficiaries
have constituted a substantial share of the domestic budget reduction
agenda. In turn, Congress has included beneficiaries in each of the
major budget reduction reconciliation acts, although generally to a
lesser degree than the administration has advocated. Thus, the elderly
and disabled populations were not immune to the budget cutting of
the 1980s.

Sources of Higher Beneficiary Burdens

The largest Medicare cuts in the first budget that was passed during
the Reagan administration (1981) occurred in beneficiary cost sharing.
That budget reconciliation act raised the deductible amounts for both
parts of Medicare. The deductible under Part B rose from $60 to $75—
a 25 percent one-time rise. The 1990 budget summit further increased
the deductible to $100 per year, although this level is still below the
deductible amounts often associated with private insurance for the
under-65 population. The impacts of this and other legislated changes
are shown in table 4.1.[1]

For Part A, Hospital Insurance, the deductible rose by about 12
percent beginning in 1982 through a technical change in the formula.
Although the hospital deductible increase was proportionally smaller
than that for Part B, the dollar amounts were greater, and more im-
portantly, this increase was permanently incorporated into the calculation of the deductible, so that its impact rises each year as hospital
costs rise. That adjustment thus effectively increased the Part A deductible by $31 in 1982, but by about $78 in 1992 over what it otherwise would have been. The Part A deductible is $676 in 1993, higher
than that found in most private insurance policies. In addition, coinsurance for Part A for both hospital and skilled nursing facility (SNF)
care is tied to the deductible, so these charges also displayed similar
proportional increases.

The hospital prospective payment system (PPS) also increased the
Part A deductible. Until 1986, the average daily cost of a hospital stay

Table 4.1 SOURCES OF INCREASED ENROLLEE LIABILITY FOR MEDICARE
BENEFITS, 1991

	Per Capita Amounts ($)
Total enrollee liability[a]	1,110
Direct increase in liability from changes in:	
Part B premiums	156
Part A deductibles and coinsurance[b]	48
Part B deductible	31
Miscellaneous[c]	−25
Total increase	210
Medicare's net contribution[d]	3,598

Source: Author's estimates extrapolated from Congressional Budget Office and Health
Care Financing Administration data.

a. Includes cost sharing, Part B premiums, and excess physician charges.
b. Includes impact of the Prospective Payment System on deductibles, as well as direct
increase.
c. Includes radiology/pathology changes, balance billing changes, and others.
d. Net of Part B premium contributions.

served as the basis for calculating the deductible and coinsurance
amounts. But since PPS helped induce shorter lengths of stay, the
average cost per hospital day rose faster than before, as more tests and
procedures are delivered in a shorter period of time, particularly in
the early years of the program. Consequently, the average daily cost
rose faster than the overall costs of the program. The deductible
amount increased from $400 to $492 between 1985 and 1986—a 23
percent rise in just one year. If, instead, the deductible had risen at
the same rate as per capita costs of hospital care over the period, the
1986 deductible would have been only $430.[2] All the coinsurance
amounts tied to the Part A deductible would have been smaller as
well.

The Omnibus Budget Reconciliation Act of 1986 recognized this
problem and changed the deductible formula to reflect increases in
costs per case rather than per diem. That change returned the growth
in the deductible to a calculation more in tune with the overall cost
growth in hospital services. The formula now uses the hospital update
factor and case mix index to raise the amount each year. After 1986,
rates of growth in the deductible returned to an average annual rate
of 5 percent. Nonetheless, the high rates of increase in 1985 and 1986
remain in the base, so that the 1991 deductible of $628 was about $80

above the level it would have been if the 1986 formula had taken effect simultaneously with the advent of PPS.

Together, the two sets of changes affecting the Part A deductible raised the amount paid by beneficiaries by approximately $146 in 1991. Without these two changes, the deductible would have been about $482.

These increases in cost sharing are likely to be covered by the "Medigap" policies that many individuals carry. But that does not mean the burdens are not real to Medicare enrollees, since these higher charges translate directly into premium increases for supplemental policies.[3] Thus, directly or indirectly, most enrollees who use health services were affected by these legislated changes, and their healthcare burdens rose accordingly.

The largest beneficiary cost increase in the 1980s resulted from changes in the formula for calculating the premium for Part B services. When enacted in 1965, beneficiaries were required to pay one-half the costs of Part B insurance coverage. But the rapid increase in the costs of the program outstripped the growth in Social Security benefits. The 1972 Social Security Amendments limited the rate of increase in premiums to the rate of growth in the consumer price index used each year to calculate Social Security cost-of-living increases. Since the cost of Part B services continued to rise at double-digit rates through the end of the 1970s, Part B premiums came to represent a smaller and smaller share of the total costs of the program.

Legislation in 1982 reversed this trend and set the premium at one-fourth of the costs of the program (for elderly beneficiaries) for three years. That requirement has been extended several times; in 1990, the requirement was once again renewed, this time through 1995. The costs of this change have long-term consequences for enrollees, since program costs have been rising rapidly in recent years. By 1991, the premium would have risen to only about $16.90 per month under the 1972 calculations, so the 1991 monthly premium of $29.90 cost beneficiaries about $156 more for the year. That figure will continue to rise each year, and at a faster rate than the incomes of elderly and disabled individuals.

Offsetting Reductions in Beneficiary Burdens

Other changes in Medicare reduced out-of-pocket burdens on the elderly, but not nearly enough to offset the increases.[4] Enrollees benefited particularly from federal activities to limit spending for physician services. Both the level of the premiums and the amount of the Part B cost sharing are tied to Medicare spending and hence to allowed charges. So if such charges rise more slowly because of policy, cost sharing will also be limited. For example, the freeze on physician payments for fiscal year 1985 (and extended through May 1986) meant that beneficiaries' cost sharing per visit was also frozen. During 1985, however, per capita expenditures on physician services grew at a rate in excess of 10 percent, suggesting that some physicians may have billed for more complex procedures or may have seen patients more frequently in response to the freeze (Ways and Means 1991). Savings to beneficiaries from this source thus were limited.

Of greater impact were policies designed to restrain beneficiaries' liabilities beyond Medicare's allowed charges. These extra bills accounted for about 16 percent of beneficiary cost sharing in 1985 (Ways and Means 1991). In the mid 1970s, the proportion of bills being accepted on assignment dipped from over 60 percent to about 50 percent and showed little change through the early 1980s. When extra billing did occur, charges usually averaged between 20 percent and 30 percent above Medicare's allowed amounts.[5]

The legislation that established the freeze on physicians' prevailing charges also offered preferential treatment for physicians who agreed to accept Medicare's reasonable-charge determination as the full payment for services. As indicated in the previous chapter, such physicians are termed "participating" physicians if they *always* accept Medicare's allowed charges as payment in full. Although this legislation did not offer full protection from "balance billing," it did help to turn around the trend toward low assignment rates. The result has been a steady increase in the number of physicians who do not charge patients additional fees for their services. HCFA estimated that between 1984 and 1985, excess (or balance) billing for physician claims fell by $16 for the average enrollee—a decline of 16 percent in just one year. By 1991, participating physicians accounted for 73 percent of total Medicare spending, and by January 1, 1992, 52.2 percent of all physicians had signed participation agreements (Physician Payment Review Commission 1992).

Over the next few years, rates of assignment continued to rise, providing an important source of relief to beneficiaries (see figure 4.1). This was one of the few important examples of better protection for the impact of higher costs on Medicare beneficiaries. But participation rates by physicians still vary widely across both specialties and location, meaning that some beneficiaries have little opportunity to seek

Figure 4.1 ASSIGNMENT RATES FOR PART B CLAIMS FOR MEDICARE, 1969–90

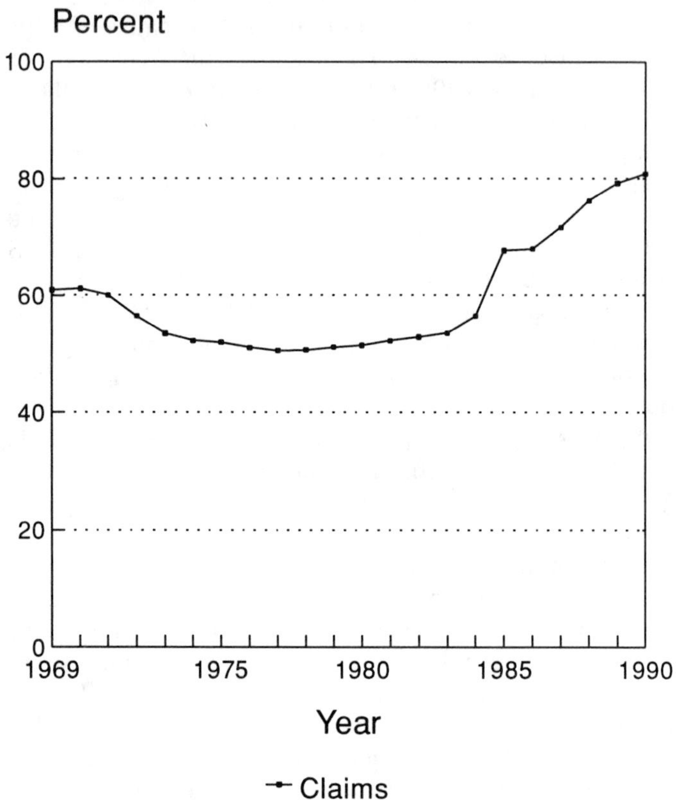

Percent

Year

— Claims

Source: Ways and Means (1991).

out such participating physicians and instead must pay additional amounts for physician services above their 20 percent coinsurance amounts.[6]

Legislation enacted when the fee freeze was lifted also limited what physicians who chose to continue to "balance bill" patients could charge. Termed the maximum allowable actual charge (MAAC), the formula was extremely complicated, and its actual impact is thus difficult to assess. But the goal was to place a cap on the amount that physicians could balance bill (Ways and Means 1988). Few physicians and perhaps few carriers understood how the MAAC worked, so it may not have operated as a binding constraint. It has now been replaced by much simpler, and likely more effective, limits—as part of

Medicare's physician payment reform. Ultimately, nonparticipating physicians will only be allowed to charge patients 15 percent above their allowed amount—an amount set at 95 percent of that paid to participating physicians.

Overall, balance billing declined as a share of total Medicare costs between 1980 and 1985, and again in 1990 (Ways and Means 1991). The average balance billing amount per beneficiary was estimated by the Congressional Budget Office as $112 per enrollee in 1990, representing almost no real growth since 1985 (during a period of rapid growth in physician spending) (Ways and Means 1991). If the relationship between Part B copayments and balance billing had stayed the same in 1990 as in 1980, the billing limits would have been $148—$36 higher than what occurred. Thus, substantial progress was made in holding down this source of out-of-pocket spending.

Physician payment reform may also result in savings to some beneficiaries. Legislative changes in 1987 and 1989 previewed the reforms with cuts in "overvalued procedures." These changes brought about some of the reductions at the high end, but without raising the "undervalued" procedures. Research by Zuckerman and Holahan (1992) indicates that these changes led to substantial reductions in the fees for affected procedures. For example, although most prices for physician services increase each year, sonography and ambulatory eye procedures each declined by over 3 percent between 1987 and 1988, when substantial shares of those procedures were subject to the policy changes.

The Medicare physician payment reform legislation, on the other hand, is set to be "budget neutral" in terms of physician reimbursement, so that the increases in fees established for some physicians will be offset by decreases for others. Consequently, the impact across all beneficiaries will also be budget neutral for the basic fee schedule, although there will be individual gainers and losers. Those gaining the most will be beneficiaries undergoing surgical and other procedures where payments are being substantially cut. On the other hand, individuals with chronic illnesses who are heavy users of physician office visits may experience noticeable increases in cost-sharing burdens, since each dollar of increase in physician charges for an office visit translates into a 20-cent increase in required cost sharing. In simulating the impact of these changes, Mitchell and Menke (1990) found little variation across definable population groups. About the only noticeable change would be for rural residents who would, on average, "lose" under the fee schedule. On the other hand, the balance billing limits that were also part of the legislation will result in savings for beneficiaries.[7] And the savings are enough to offset most losses from higher fees. The biggest gainers according to Mitchell and Menke's simulations were beneficiaries who were hospitalized during the year, largely because balance billing tends to be higher than average among specialists and surgeons.

DISTRIBUTION OF THE IMPACT

On balance, direct changes in Medicare cost sharing increased what beneficiaries paid for care. The combined impact of these benefit and cost-sharing changes led to a reduction in Medicare benefits of about 5 percent in 1991—compared to what would have occurred if no changes had been made in Medicare policy in the 1980s—and a 19 percent increase in enrollee liability for Medicare-covered services.[8] The shift in liability from Medicare to its enrollees as a result of policy changes in the 1980s averaged about $210 in 1991 (see table 4.1).

But not all Medicare enrollees suffered equally. Needs and use of care vary dramatically across individuals; so, too, do the resulting financial burdens. For example, a Medicare beneficiary with an extended hospital stay would pay nearly $400 more in a given year as a result of these changes.

One way to systematically look at some of this variation is to consider age differences. That is, the heaviest users of healthcare services are the oldest beneficiaries—the group that is also rising the fastest within the Medicare population (see table 4.2). Skilled nursing care

Table 4.2 PERSONS SERVED PER 1,000 MEDICARE ENROLLEES, BY AGE

| | Ratio of Users Compared to Age 65–69 Group | | | | |
Age of Enrollee	Hospital Inpatient	Hospital Outpatient	Skilled Nursing Services	Home Health	Physician and Other
65–69	1.00	1.00	1.00	1.00	1.00
70–74	1.26	1.11	2.06	1.13	1.08
75–79	1.52	1.20	4.03	1.54	1.15
80–84	1.81	1.26	7.24	1.82	1.21
85 and above	2.11	1.33	12.42	1.63	1.28
Disabled	1.47	1.26	1.27	.78	1.04

Notes: Data for hospital and physician services are from 1986; data from home healthcare and skilled nursing facilities are from 1988.
Sources: Health Care Financing Administration (1990), and Ways and Means (1991).

leads the list of Medicare services dominated by older beneficiaries. Persons aged 85 and above are over 12 times more likely to use Medicare skilled nursing facility (SNF) benefits. Next in importance for the "oldest old" is inpatient hospital care. Indeed, all Part A services are particularly heavily used by the oldest beneficiaries.

Use of physician and outpatient services is considerably less correlated with age, however. Persons over age 85 are only 28 percent more likely to see a physician than is a beneficiary between the ages of 65 and 69 (see table 4.2). This is an especially dramatic statistic, given the higher use of hospital care by older beneficiaries, suggesting that ambulatory visits are less important for older beneficiaries than for younger beneficiaries. Indeed, the average rate of use of these services peaks for persons aged 75 to 79.

Dollars of expenditures on each of these service areas display a similar pattern. The oldest beneficiaries always have higher expenditures than younger ones, but the differences are greatest for Part A services. Skilled nursing and home health benefits are most often used by those who have complications—including frailty associated with age—that lengthens periods of recovery from acute illnesses.

Except for inpatient and outpatient hospital care, disabled beneficiaries are less likely to use services overall than are elderly beneficiaries. But in every case, reimbursements per person served are higher. Thus, although a smaller proportion of disabled persons generally use services at any given time, their use of care is more intensive. For example, in 1986, 68.5 percent of disabled enrollees used physician and other medical services as compared to the elderly, but per person served, the disabled enrollee had $992 in reimbursed services compared to $835 per elderly person served (Office of National Cost Estimates 1990). As with the elderly, the probability of a disabled person using services tends to increase with age.

These age differences are borne out in the cost-sharing liability that individuals (or their insurance companies) must pay for covered Medicare services (see table 4.3).[9] Again, the greatest differences appear for Part A cost sharing. In 1987, enrollees over the age of 85 had liabilities over 20 percent higher than enrollees aged 65 to 69 under Part A, but only an 11 percent differential under Part B (Waldo et al. 1989). But Part A liabilities are smaller on average than those for Part B services, so that when looking at total burdens, differences by age diminish. Part B premiums also reduce the overall differential in burdens.

The oldest old are disproportionately represented among those with very high cost-sharing burdens. In 1984, although persons over age 80

Table 4.3 VARIATIONS IN MEDICARE OUT-OF-POCKET LIABILITIES, BY AGE, 1987

Age of Enrollee	Hospital Care		Physicians' Services	
	Average Liability ($)	Ratio to Age 65 to 69	Average Liability ($)	Ratio to Age 65 to 69
65–69	312	1.00	380	1.00
70–74	327	1.05	389	1.02
75–79	341	1.09	398	1.05
80–84	355	1.14	407	1.07
85 and above	376	1.21	420	1.11
All elderly	333		393	

Source: Waldo et al. (1989).

constituted less than 23 percent of enrollees over age 65, they accounted for 31 percent of all the beneficiaries with reimbursed expenses of $5,000 or more (Congressional Budget Office 1983). Again, this is likely to reflect differences in Part A liabilities. A more recent study, Mitchell and Menke's (1990), found that those aged 65 to 69 were less likely to have high Part B liabilities, but that the oldest old were not disproportionately represented in that high-cost group.

Thus, any change in cost-sharing or reimbursement policy that affects beneficiaries in one part of the program and not another will have differential effects by age. Only premium changes will be age neutral, that is, affecting all beneficiaries equally. Changes in physician cost sharing will be more evenly distributed by age and will vary less within each age group, since most Medicare beneficiaries (about 80 percent) have reimbursable Medicare physician expenses. This is particularly true for changes in the Part B deductible, as opposed to the coinsurance, which will fall more heavily on those with heavy use. (And since heavy users of physician services are also very likely to have a hospital stay, they will suffer the double burden of having cost-sharing liability from both parts of the program.)

What about the specific burdens of the direct changes in beneficiary cost sharing implemented during the 1980s? About three-quarters of the direct changes described in table 4.1 would be spread evenly across most enrollees. These include the changes in the Part B premium and the Part B deductible. The Part A deductible and coinsurance increases and the change in radiology and pathology services (which would be largely felt by those who are hospitalized) would fall disproportionately on older beneficiaries, who are also those least able to afford the higher burdens of cost sharing.

PPS AND INDIRECT BURDENS ON BENEFICIARIES

Reimbursement changes dominated the cost-cutting efforts under Medicare in the 1980s. Overall, savings to the federal budget from changes directed at providers have been about twice the level of changes that have fallen directly on beneficiaries. For instance, in the changes from the 1990 budget summit, the balance was 3-to-1, provider-to-beneficiary changes (Ways and Means 1990). Nonetheless, the implicit consequences of some of the changes targeted to providers are to increase costs to beneficiaries as well. And, although it is not a financial burden per se, the effects of policy changes on the quality of care are also of great importance to beneficiaries.

The most significant single provider change implemented in the 1980s was the introduction of the hospital Prospective Payment System (PPS). This serves as a compelling case study for the relevance of examining beneficiary impacts. In many respects, the introduction of PPS has likely brought about more efficient delivery of care with no adverse consequences on beneficiaries. For example, prior to PPS, the old cost-based reimbursement system was widely criticized as promoting lengthy hospital stays for Medicare patients. Stays would sometimes be extended for patients' convenience rather than for sound medical reasons. Eliminating these extra days would improve efficiency and lower costs, and might furthermore prove beneficial to patients if earlier discharge reduced their risk of developing hospital-based infections. On the other hand, some PPS-induced changes may have merely shifted the costs of care onto the beneficiaries or reduced the quality of service as hospitals changed their behavior in response to PPS.

To develop specific estimates of the impacts of such changes on beneficiaries constitutes a formidable task. Causation is difficult to establish, and some of the "costs" are intangible and thus hard to measure. Yet such efforts are needed to fully evaluate the impact of provider changes. The true efficiency effects of the reduced costs of providing healthcare should be distinguished from those that sacrifice quality or merely shift burdens.

Consider three sources of potential burdens to beneficiaries from PPS: shorter hospital stays; shifting the site of service; and less care while in the hospital. Each of these is discussed here in turn.

Effects of Shorter Hospital Stays

Perhaps most important of all these changes has been the movement toward shorter hospital stays by Medicare patients. Hospitals are paid the same amount for a particular type of admission (by diagnosis-related group [DRG]), whether the patient stays 5 days or 10 days, for example. And the length of the hospital stay is one of the simplest elements for a hospital to control. Further, the trend in length of stay (LOS) had been downward for some time, both for Medicare beneficiaries as well as the population in general. The response to PPS was a substantial acceleration of that trend, as shown in figure 4.2. From 1983 to 1985, average hospital stays for Medicare patients fell from 9.7 to 8.7 days, a decline of over 10 percent (NCHS 1991).

The quality issue raised by these shorter lengths of stay is whether they represent desirable or undesirable changes in medical practice. Changes in medical practice and in procedures themselves led to at least some of the historical decline in LOS. New techniques often speed recovery and reduce the need for long hospital stays. Moreover, hospitals are dangerous places where risks of postoperative infection may be high; in general, patients recover better at home. And historically, some hospital days were more for the convenience of Medicare patients or their families than for medical necessity.

On the other hand, when patients are told that their DRGs "have run out," the discharges may reflect hospitals' budgetary concerns more than patient needs. Although hospitals are supposed to keep patients as long as medically necessary, and there is technically no such thing as DRGs "running out" for patients, hospitals make such claims to hold the line on costs. If patients are discharged too early, they face higher risks of dying, of being readmitted to the hospital, or of taking longer to recover at home—this has been called the "quicker and sicker" issue. In addition, those who must return home without someone to care for them may need follow-up services to substitute for hospital care—services not covered as part of this policy change.

Thus far, only a few studies have examined the impact of PPS, and then only for the early years of the program. What is more, most studies have looked at only the crudest indicators of quality—mortality rates and rates of readmission. A worsening of these statistics would suggest severe problems from PPS. To date, the evidence overall

Figure 4.2 AVERAGE LENGTH OF STAY IN NONFEDERAL SHORT-STAY
HOSPITALS, BY AGE, 1980–89

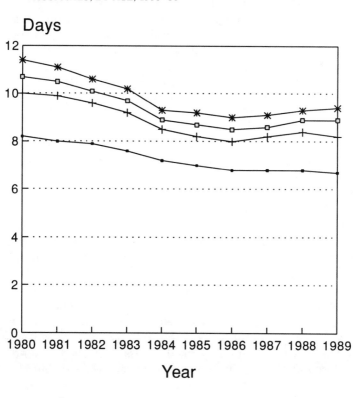

Days

Year

Age

― 45-65 **+** 65-74 **✳** 75 + **▫** 65 +

Source: U.S. Public Health Service (1990).

does not support claims that PPS had such impacts. Generally, studies
of mortality, the grossest outcome measure, have failed to detect any
significant changes (Coulam and Gaumer 1991). Another potential
concern addressed in the studies is the previously mentioned risk of
patients' readmission to the hospital if discharged prematurely.

The most dramatic findings on PPS's impact come from a study by
the RAND Corporation released in 1990 (Kahn et al. 1990).[10] Despite
a relatively positive overall assessment of PPS, the results were actually mixed. The RAND study found that for four of the health conditions studied, readmissions fell post-PPS, while increasing for my-

ocardial infarction (Kahn et al. 1990). The study did find, however, that patients were discharged earlier and sicker after the introduction of PPS. There was a 22 percent increase in the proportion of beneficiaries discharged in an unstable condition after PPS, compared to a similar pre-PPS group (Kosekoff et al. 1990).[11] And for those discharged home as opposed to an institutional setting, there was a 43 percent increase in instability. These findings portend undesirable health outcomes as well, since the study also found that instability at discharge was associated with a higher probability of dying within 30 days.[12]

Earlier discharges may result in greater reliance on other less-intensive care. Patients may need home health or skilled nursing care more frequently following a hospital stay. Shifting the type of service is not necessarily an undesirable outcome, if such services are available. But no specific provisions were made to enhance the availability of care after the introduction of PPS, so beneficiaries had to rely on services that were already in place. Since both SNF and home healthcare under Medicare were tightly controlled in the mid-1980s by conservative interpretations of regulations, beneficiaries could not rely on these for follow-up care. The tightened requirements for reimbursement made some nursing homes and home health agencies reluctant to take on some patients, for fear of being denied reimbursement. To the extent that this represented a major constraint, PPS may have caused early discharges in which patients lacked access to needed "step-down" care. Alternatively, some patients may have received care but crowded out other traditional recipients of nursing home or community-based services (Wood and Estes 1990).

In 1985, there were 22.8 million fewer hospital days as compared to 1983. On average, about one-third of those days were for Medicare beneficiaries with long-term care needs who were likely to require further assistance in recuperating from a hospital stay.[13] But the number of Medicare-funded SNF visits actually decreased from 1984 to 1988 in response to restrictive Medicare coverage provisions implemented in 1984 (Feinglass and Holloway 1991). In fact, in 1987 covered days of care for SNFs were only 81 percent of the 1983 level, despite growth in the number of Medicare beneficiaries. Converting this figure to days per 1,000 elderly beneficiaries, coverage declined from 338 to 248 over the period, meaning that, per enrollee, benefits were only 73.4 percent of the 1983 level in 1987 (Silverman 1991).

And although home health visits increased over this period, the *rate* of growth in these visits declined after PPS as well (Kenney 1991). Kenney found that PPS stimulated use of home healthcare over what it would have been otherwise, but from a declining base. Home health-care visits per 1,000 enrollees also declined by 7.4 percent between 1983 and 1988. Although SNF and home healthcare currently comprise only a small piece of Part A, the demands generated by PPS for follow-up care should have increased use of SNF and home health services after 1983. But increases in spending for these two services were at or below their pre-PPS average rates of change between 1983 and 1985.

Together, Medicare SNF and home health benefits did not rise enough to replace the number of hospital days lost under PPS. Instead, individuals may have sought less formal arrangements. They may have obtained noncovered services such as homemaker services that they financed out of pocket. In these cases, the individual would incur additional costs for care (or do without), but these burdens generally would not be captured by traditional measures of out-of-pocket spending. The "quicker and sicker" claim thus was one of the negative side effects of PPS. Studies do not find dramatic impacts on mortality, but there are indications that early discharge may create problems, particularly related to quality of life.

Shifting the Site of Service

After PPS, many inpatient services moved to settings outside the hospital. For example, more surgery and tests are now performed in hospital outpatient departments or even physicians' offices; tests are routinely "unbundled" and are now performed on an outpatient basis before or after a hospital stay.

Inpatient admission rates for Medicare enrollees fell dramatically and continued to fall throughout the 1980s. Some procedures that used to be performed on an inpatient basis, such as cataract surgery, are now done almost exclusively in outpatient settings, a change that would likely have occurred without PPS, albeit perhaps more slowly. Between 1980 and 1989, the number of inpatient surgeries for extraction of a lens decreased from 335,000 to 60,000 (NCHS 1991). But on the outpatient side, that same procedure increased even more. Expenditures on ambulatory eye procedures, dominated by cataract surgery, grew at an annual rate of 13.3 percent from 1985 to 1989, much of that accounted for by volume and intensity (Zuckerman and Holahan 1992).

Shifting surgery and other major procedures to the outpatient setting reflects, to some degree, changes in these procedures that make them safer and easier. For example, laser surgery of the eye has led to remarkable improvements in cataract surgery, and thus it is not surprising that these are now almost universally outpatient procedures. But very frail patients or those with poor home circumstances that may impede recovery may be placed at a disadvantage when operations are performed only in outpatient settings. The shift outside of the hospital seems to have occurred with equal frequency for beneficiaries of all ages, suggesting that accounting for other factors has not played a major role in the decision making (Leader and Moon 1989).

Effects of Less Inpatient Care

Enrollees will not receive needed care if, in response to PPS, hospitals become reluctant to accept some types of patients and physicians do not press for these admissions. In some cases, people who were previously hospitalized for tests or treatment are now getting less care or care of a different sort. Although there has been an increase in the severity of the condition of patients treated in the hospital setting since the introduction of PPS, use of technology has remained largely unchanged (Sloan, Morrisey, and Valvona 1988).[14] Chesney (1990) found that the composition of patients using intensive care units (ICUs) did not change after the introduction of PPS, but that the severity of patients *not* admitted to ICUs did increase. What is not clear is whether less care received during the stay has resulted in adverse outcomes. These reductions may reflect more efficient care—a desired result of PPS. More study is needed on this issue.

The analyses to date suggest that PPS did shift incentives to a preference for less, rather than more, care. After controlling for patient severity, fewer resources are now directed to patients in terms of length of stay, technologies used, and even decisions to admit to the hospital. Interestingly, many of these trends have carried over to non-Medicare patients as well. Often these reductions may actually be desirable. And even when they are not, the problems may be related more to a lack of step-down care rather than to PPS itself. In the past, errors were made on the side of delivering too much care; however, now the incentive is to provide too little. Such changes are inevitable in an environment of concern about controlling costs, but they also raise the need for heightened oversight of quality.

QUALITY OF CARE

In the early days of Medicare, little emphasis was placed on quality of care. If access to mainstream care were assured, it was reasoned,

Medicare enrollees would enjoy the best in healthcare that the nation could offer, and quality would be a "nonissue." Spurred in part by a changing climate for healthcare in general and Medicare in particular, interest in quality issues has been on the increase. Part of the concern arose with introduction of PPS—it was felt that more vigilance was required when there were incentives to use less care. Beyond the effect of PPS, there has been some scrutiny of the impact of the new Medicare Fee Schedule on physician payment and enrollees' participation in health maintenance organizations (HMOs). Another source of concern for quality has arisen from questions about cost-effectiveness in general. Is some care not only unnecessary but harmful? At least in this instance, quality improvements and cost containment would be compatible. Finally, some health researchers have raised alarms about the lack of self-enforcement of standards by providers, allowing problems to go undetected and/or uncorrected.

Medicare Physician Payment Reform and Quality

A major issue for the quality of future care will be the impact of physician payment reform on beneficiaries' access to care. How will physicians respond to this new system? Much of the attention thus far has focused on the financial consequences of this change. But doctors who face lower fees may also respond by having patients return more frequently for visits and procedures, by spending less time with patients on any given visit, or by refusing to take Medicare patients. The assumptions that led the Health Care Financing Administration (HCFA) to project a "behavioral response" implies that physicians would increase the volume of their businesses, charging for more visits and procedures. That would likely mean less time on each activity and perhaps subjecting patients to unnecessary and sometimes risky procedures. Regarding the possibility that lowered fees may cause doctors to substitute other patients and refuse to take on new Medicare patients—or perhaps even turn away existing Medicare patients—the American Medical Association has reported some increase in physicians declining to treat Medicare patients, although there is little hard evidence on this yet (Freudenheim 1992). This is a particular concern in underserved areas where patients have little choice of what doctor to see. Further reduction of access to care in such areas could exacerbate some of the regional variations in use of services.

Actually, it is possible that both of these scenarios could occur, with some physicians eschewing Medicare patients and others becoming "Medicare mills," treating many patients but spending little time with each; this would be a worst-case scenario. Discrimination against Medicare patients is less likely if other payers follow Medicare's lead and move to a similar fee schedule—a change that becomes more plausible as employers and other payers seek further ways to rein in rising healthcare costs. So long as the differential in payments between other payers and Medicare does not increase, it is unlikely that physicians will discriminate against their Medicare payers. In addition, in cases where physicians will be paid more than they are currently for management and evaluation services, some beneficiaries may actually receive better care than at present.

HMOs and Quality

In the 1980s, the Medicare program embraced the prospect of achieving cost savings through enrollee participation in health maintenance organizations, first as an experiment and then as a permanent part of the program. Qualified HMOs that choose to participate must take any Medicare enrollee who applies. They must cover at least the same benefits as Medicare, and in return they receive a flat payment based on the enrollee's characteristics. The HMO is then at risk.

There are many potential advantages to enrollment in HMOs. As inducements, beneficiaries often receive broader coverage than Medicare offers. Filing of claims is eliminated, and cost sharing is usually reduced and simplified. Moreover, a high-quality HMO can provide good coordination of care and help to patients in wending their way through the healthcare system.

On the other hand, just as PPS raised issues of quality in a system that offers incentives to reduce the level of care offered, HMOs and other capitated systems pose similar concerns. Since Medicare essentially turns over all responsibility to the HMO, it does not receive any information of the quantity of care received and thus cannot track whether appropriate services are being delivered. In addition, although the Peer Review Organizations (PROs) are formally charged with oversight of the quality of care received in HMOs, the process of developing standards for these groups has been painfully slow.

Moreover, there have been some notable failures in the Medicare HMO program, suggesting that beneficiaries may have been placed at risk. These problems were particularly notable in the early years of the program when, to encourage HMOs to participate, exceptions were granted to established standards. In fact, although HMO coverage started as a demonstration, the program was expanded in 1985 before the results of that demonstration were available (Congressional Budget Office 1990). Consequently, several HMOs that rapidly enrolled many beneficiaries overestimated their ability to integrate these new types of patients. Several dramatic failures in the late 1980s, such as that of IMC in Florida, cast doubt on HCFA's oversight (U.S. General Accounting Office 1992).

The track record for the industry has since improved, however, and well-established HMOs have been able to effectively serve beneficiaries. Still, the proportion of beneficiaries enrolled in HMOs—only about 5 percent—remains small.

Peer Review Organizations

Medicare established Peer Review Organizations (PROs) for two reasons: to oversee use of services for purposes of cost containment and to monitor the quality of care received by Medicare beneficiaries.[15] By most accounts, PROs have concentrated on this first mission, often to the detriment of the quality-control portion. PRO contracts with HCFA have generally specified that much of their time be spent on activities such as hospital preadmission screening, sampling of inpatient records, and DRG validation. Although these activities may have quality components, the emphasis certainly has been more on controlling the use of services. In addition, PRO activities have focused primarily on hospitals; there is almost no oversight of ambulatory services (Lohr 1990).

With respect to quality oversight by PROs, use of generic screens, which tend to result in review of many cases, can bog down the process in paperwork. Moreover, at the end of the process, PROs have little flexibility in the types of sanctions they can use against offending physicians or institutions; the choice is between severe sanctions or none at all. Moreover, all of the PROs' monitoring activities focus on care received. To the extent that problems also arise from lack of care, Medicare has no tracking mechanisms or ability to oversee problems. Thus, much of the quality effort is directly tied to what is done for Medicare enrollees, and hence is linked to some notion of effectiveness. PROs look for errors of commission, but not errors of omission. No broader assessments are made regarding what the level of overall care should be. For example, in evaluating the PPS, there is no mechanism for assessing whether too little care is being delivered or whether some who should be admitted to hospitals have been excluded.

The PRO program could be substantially improved to better serve the Medicare enrollee population. A 1990 report by the Institute of Medicine detailed recommendations to shift the focus of quality assessment and assurance by Medicare away from the current punitive, adversarial approach that focuses on outliers rather than the overall standard of care (Lohr 1990). The report advocated a new system that would enlarge the role of Medicare in quality, in part by expanding the definition of quality of care, by redirecting the activities of the PROs, by emphasizing improved research and measurement of quality issues, and by preparing professionals to address such issues. A gradual process was stressed, using the existing PRO structure. In many cases, the recommendations were not specific, since many of the ideas for improving quality were as yet untested. Furthermore, considerable federal investment of funds would be required.

No formal efforts have yet been undertaken to institute these changes or to otherwise expand the PRO system. Implementation of HCFA's goal to expand PRO activities to assess quality in ambulatory settings or in HMOs has also been slow in coming. On the other hand, some areas of improvement that were stressed by the Institute of Medicine's report are now under way. In particular, analysis of the effectiveness of medical care is being given priority by the government health research community, and the fourth scope of work for the PROs emphasizes quality to a greater extent than in the past.

Using Effectiveness Studies to Improve Quality

In the late 1980s the promise of achieving cost savings while also enhancing quality came to be associated with research on the effectiveness or appropriateness of healthcare. For example, an early study by the RAND Corporation on carotid endarterectomies suggested that this procedure was often inappropriately performed, not only raising Medicare costs but also potentially harming patients who were exposed to unnecessary risks from this major surgical procedure (Merrick et al. 1986). Later studies of coronary artery bypass (Winslow et al. 1988) and coronary angiography (Chassin et al. 1987) also came to similar conclusions. The suggestion that there is not only a considerable amount of unnecessary surgery, but that it could be identified and its prevalence reduced, was welcome news to many seeking "magic bullets" to achieve healthcare savings. Indeed, some researchers have argued that healthcare costs could be reduced by as much as 20 percent or 30 percent if such unnecessary procedures could be eliminated.

One tangible indicator of the enthusiasm of the policy world for such solutions is the dramatic increase in funding for effectiveness research by the federal government. Millions of dollars of new monies have been targeted for these studies, and the National Center for Health Services Research changed its name to the Agency for Health Care Policy and Research and reoriented its research agenda to focus support on this effort. Research on effectiveness and on practice guidelines that seeks to establish recommended approaches to given medical problems is now in progress.

Will such efforts prove to be the magic bullet that makes cost containment palatable? And will these dollars improve the quality of care received by enrollees? The jury is still out on these questions, particularly the impact on the cost of healthcare. In a recent article on the consequences of these research efforts, a pioneer in this research, Robert Brook, has argued that although overuse of services is a problem in some areas, further study will also identify areas of underuse that suggest we should spend more and not less to achieve high-quality care (Brook et al. 1989). Thus, these research efforts are best evaluated in a discussion of quality improvement rather than cost containment.

There will likely be a long lag before findings on research effectiveness are available and disseminated widely enough to have a notable impact on behavior. That is not to say that there will not be impacts, however. Take, for example, the case of Cesarean sections for childbirth. Dissemination of information about the excessive reliance on that procedure seems to have had an impact on the proportion of births delivered by Cesarean section in recent years, although it took a combination of empirical evidence and efforts to publicize the results to change behavior (Myers and Gleicher 1988).

Program Satisfaction

The quality of care under Medicare can be broadly defined to encompass many concerns. One concern yet to be discussed relates to beneficiary satisfaction with the program. How well does Medicare meet perceived needs? Can "user-friendly" improvements help boost the perceived quality of the program? And what about broader concerns relating to coverage of services under Medicare?

Medicare fares relatively well in measures of consumer satisfaction. Polls generally indicate that the program is popular with beneficiaries and that they are happy with their doctors and the care they receive. Their major complaints often center on the program's complex paperwork they have to fill out and the communication problems they have with HCFA regarding billing. These are certainly less critical issues than standard quality concerns, but they ought to be addressed by the program. Cost sharing makes such paperwork almost inevitable, but simplification and clarification of forms could aid beneficiaries. For budgetary reasons, funding for administration under Medicare has also been constrained in this period of cost containment; such constraints seem likely to continue. Nevertheless, minimal expenditures in this area could pay considerable dividends in patient satisfaction. For example, more rapid response to queries or complaints and improved forms might reduce the time burdens on individuals in dealing with the system.

The other major source of dissatisfaction with Medicare—its lack of coverage for specific kinds of care—would be much more expensive to resolve. By excluding certain key types of healthcare services, enrollees may not get a well-rounded course of treatment or may misuse the system to make up for its shortcomings. For example, exclusion of prescription drug coverage under Medicare may result in patients who have access to physicians but are unable to comply with a course of treatment if they cannot afford the increasingly expensive drugs that the doctor prescribes. Although drugs may often be an extremely cost-effective way to treat certain conditions, this is one area where patients with limited means skimp on care. The result may be unnecessarily more intensive care later when the problem is left untreated. Is this a Medicare quality problem? For many beneficiaries, the answer is yes.

Lack of coverage of long-term and chronic care is particularly likely to lead to poor quality outcomes. Lack of coverage for supportive services may result in more hospitalization and treatment in the acute-care setting than would occur if coverage were not an issue. Before PPS, long hospital stays may have been, in part, a reflection of lack of options for follow-up care by Medicare enrollees. Inappropriate use of services can be harmful—for example, patients may be exposed to greater risk of infection as inpatients, while still not getting care that is most relevant to their needs. On the other hand, the fact that such patients are now discharged earlier may simply mean that they return home with inadequate support, an equally undesirable outcome.

These problems have largely been viewed as beyond the scope of Medicare. However, individuals are unlikely to focus on fine distinctions about what is covered when they are receiving inadequate care. Moreover, when such problems exist, broad indicators such as outcomes are more difficult to use as a gauge of quality. Many experts in quality assessment stress the need to look not just at inputs but at the consequences of care—such as mortality rates or quality-of-life measures. But if beneficiaries have increasing rates of mortality over time, can these be attributed to quality of care of the services *received*, or are they more likely to reflect other factors such as lack of access to needed drugs?

CONCLUSIONS

Although, ironically, Medicare is one of the most popular of all government programs, it has also been subject to large and continuing budget cuts. How can we reconcile these two facts? Most argue that since cuts in the program have largely been directed at providers, beneficiaries have not been affected. However, this overstates the degree to which beneficiaries have been insulated from change.

Medicare cost-sharing liability for enrollees has risen substantially compared to its level in 1980. Some of this has resulted from direct increases in premiums, deductibles, and coinsurance, the cumulative and continuing effects of which reduce Medicare payments significantly.

As Medicare clamps down on providers and experiments with new ways to hold down costs, it is likely to influence the quality of care received as well. For example, earlier hospital discharges may place the frail and vulnerable elderly at greater risk of death or complications, suggesting that enrollees have an important stake in the broad range of cost-containment strategies pursued by the government. The new physician payment fee schedule may also result in changes in access to certain services—changes that could have a positive or negative impact on quality.

Fortunately, Medicare in the early 1980s started from a base of high-quality care, with generous payments to providers and a substantial subsidy provided to enrollees. Thus, erosions in financial support or in the quality of care need to be assessed against this initial base. Nonetheless, it is incorrect to argue that Medicare cuts have been painless for enrollees. Nor are beneficiaries likely to be satisfied simply with the knowledge that erosion in quality has been relatively small.

Most of these changes have failed to ignite the passions of elderly and disabled persons. One change did—the Medicare Catastrophic

Coverage Act (MCCA) of 1988, which was designed to expand Medicare's reach.[16] A new era in Medicare policy began with the passage and nearly instant revocation of the MCCA. The controversy over the MCCA—and its pivotal implications for future Medicare policy—are the subject of the next chapter.

Notes

1. Assessing the cumulative effects of these many changes is a difficult task. Savings in each year reflect assumptions about the growth in benefits over time that are not constant. Thus, it is difficult, for example, to compare 1982 changes with those made in 1989 and group them all in a table for 1991.
  A number of other smaller changes also boosted the proportion of Medicare expenditures that beneficiaries must pay. For instance, hospital-based radiologists' and pathologists' charges used to be fully covered by Medicare. Now, these physicians' fees are subject to the normal 20 percent coinsurance that beneficiaries must pay. In another example, before 1981 some costs of physicians' services from the previous year could be carried over and applied to the current year's deductible. This is no longer allowed.

2. If the increase had been to only $430 in 1986, the effect of the legislation increasing the deductible by 12 percent would have meant a $46 impact. Thus, the indirect impact of PPS on the deductible in 1986 was 35 percent greater than the impact of a change specifically designed to raise the Part A deductible.

3. Some Medicare enrollees have either Medicaid or employer-provided insurance that may render them largely immune to these changes. However, unless the employer fully absorbs the premium costs of the insurance, beneficiaries will bear some of the burden. Most employer-provided coverage requires at least some contribution from the retiree.

4. Minor changes include the extension of Medicare coverage to include hospice benefits for the terminally ill. Although this broadened the range of choices open to beneficiaries, it represented a very limited expansion. Similarly, as part of a move to establish a fee schedule for independent laboratory services, patient cost sharing was eliminated on July 1, 1984.

5. These additional charges may not always be assessed against the beneficiary. They are the amounts reported to the Health Care Financing Administration; patients may or may not pay all these charges.

6. In addition, balance bills are often not covered by private supplemental insurance, so that even beneficiaries who have Medigap coverage may have to pay out of pocket for physician services.

7. Mitchell and Menke's (1990) simulations were based on 1986 data, however, when balance billing was relatively more important than it was in 1991, the year before the fee schedule was set to begin. Thus, these results are likely to be more dramatic than what Medicare beneficiaries will experience over the next few years.

8. Although beneficiaries' overall share of Medicare costs actually stayed about the same through the 1980s, that share would otherwise have declined over time if no legislative changes had occurred. This is because the Part B premium was tied to the rate of increase in the Social Security cost-of-living adjustment from 1973 to 1981, which grew more slowly than the costs of Medicare.

9. These estimates include cost-sharing liability for excess billing by physicians who do not accept assignment or for services not covered by Medicare. Earlier estimates of such age-related cost-sharing liabilities showed greater discrepancies (Moon 1988).

10. This effort assessed health outcomes from PPS by contrasting data on 16,758 Medicare patients hospitalized prior to and subsequent to the introduction of PPS in five states. The first set of results focused on five disease categories: congestive heart failure, acute myocardial infarction, pneumonia, cerebrovascular accident, and hip fracture during the first several years of PPS (Kahn et al. 1990).

11. That is, after PPS, 18 percent were discharged in unstable condition, as compared to 15 percent before PPS.

12. Most other studies of such outcomes have been done on a smaller scale and offer a mixed picture. See, for example, Fitzgerald et al. 1987, Palmer et al. 1989, and Gerety, Doderholm-Difatte, and Winograd (1989).

13. This reflects the numbers of Medicare beneficiaries who have chronic health limitations that might normally require special assistance. Early discharges for such individuals would likely require extraordinary help. And, of course, others who have no additional complications might also need assistance if the discharge is truly premature.

14. That is, as easier cases are being treated outside the hospital, the more severe cases are left to the inpatient setting.

15. Effectively, PROs replaced the Professional Standards Review Organizations (PSROs), which were instituted by the 1972 Social Security Amendments. These organizations did some early work on quality-of-care issues, such as auditing medical records to analyze quality problems.

16. Moreover, strong objections to the first package of Medicare cuts in the 1990 budget summit helped send the negotiators back to the drawing board. The final package of Medicare cuts was much less stringent on beneficiaries.

Chapter Five

THE MEDICARE CATASTROPHIC COVERAGE ACT

The Medicare Catastrophic Coverage Act (MCCA) represents one of the shortest-lived pieces of social legislation in the United States. But even more, the act marked a turning point in Medicare policy. Unlike earlier additions to the Medicare legislation, such as the 1972 amendments that added disabled and end-stage renal patients, the Catastrophic Coverage Act was intended to be budget neutral, requiring beneficiaries themselves to fund the additions to benefits. It also constituted a marked departure from earlier proposed legislation of the Reagan years that sought to restrict Medicare coverage and reduce costs at the expense of both providers and beneficiaries. After years of cost-cutting efforts, the MCCA sought to expand Medicare benefits. It also embodied many of the constraints faced by legislation in the 1980s that sought to expand the role of government despite the high federal deficit and the Gramm-Rudman-Hollings budget restrictions. Thus, it must be viewed in a broader political context as well.[1]

The MCCA offers important political and economic lessons. In political terms, the act launched an unprecedented debate about the future of Medicare—as well as of other domestic policy initiatives—that will likely shape policy choices to come. Economically, it became clear that even minor changes in Medicare come with large price tags, price tags that may be undervalued by beneficiaries if they are asked to pay for them directly. Further, the use of a flat limit on spending is too constraining, since if it is kept affordable in terms of financing, it is unlikely to be sufficiently generous to aid those most in need. This has become more of an issue as the diversity in the well-being of the Medicare population has grown over time.

RECOGNIZING THE NEED FOR CATASTROPHIC PROTECTION

Rapidly rising healthcare costs both generated interest in cost-containment efforts under Medicare and exerted further pressure on elderly and disabled beneficiaries to share more of the costs of their own care. By 1987, elderly beneficiaries were spending about the same share of their incomes on healthcare as they did before Medicare was introduced. A considerable portion of that burden came from the rising deductible and coinsurance requirements of Medicare, as well as the increasing fees for critical services that Medicare did not cover. In 1987, when the MCCA was first being debated, persons aged 65 and over had average per capita expenditures of $5,360 on healthcare, only $3,356 of which came from public sources (i.e., Medicare and Medicaid) (Waldo et al. 1989). The elderly were even liable for nearly a quarter of the costs of hospital and physician services ($726 in 1987), which are relatively well covered by Medicare. They also lacked coverage for nursing home care—the largest source of uncovered services for older persons—and for other crucial healthcare expenditures such as prescription drugs, dental and vision care, and homemaker services. After excluding Medicare out-of-pocket liabilities, older persons faced an average liability of $1,278 for these other expenditures.

As averages, these figures do not give a clear sense of how high the liabilities can be for persons with even relatively modest health problems. For example, individuals who trigger hospital coinsurance had average out-of-pocket spending for Medicare-covered cost sharing of $7,852 in 1988 (Congressional Budget Office 1987). Beneficiaries who did not trigger the coinsurance but had at least two hospital stays averaged $2,387 in cost-sharing liabilities. And those dollar figures do not capture spending on other services such as drugs that Medicare does not cover.

Many Medicare beneficiaries rely on private supplemental insurance ("Medigap") to fill in at least some of these gaps. Insurance companies such as Blue Cross/Blue Shield or organizations such as the American Association of Retired Persons offer Medigap policies. Standard plans usually cover the deductibles and coinsurance that Medicare requires, and sometimes small amounts of additional benefits, but the comprehensiveness of the benefit package varies substantially across policies. For example, at considerably higher premiums, drug coverage is sometimes available to individuals. The costs of such additions are high not only because the benefits are costly, but also because individuals who choose higher coverage are more likely to use the services.

Some fortunate beneficiaries receive coverage as part of retirement benefits. These policies are often either free to the retiree or at least partially subsidized. Benefits are usually more generous under these plans, which are intended to raise coverage to the level held by these individuals when they were active employees. For example, many employer-based plans include prescription drugs. In 1987, about 31 percent of the elderly had such employer-based coverage (NCHSR 1989).

Those most in need of protection—low-income elderly and disabled persons—are the ones least likely to have private supplemental protection. Such individuals tend not to have employer-based coverage and often cannot afford Medigap policies. Given the costs of Medigap, it is surprising that low-income individuals actually purchase such policies. Moreover, although Medigap has helped smooth out the variations in acute-care liability for those who have it, individuals with coverage spend an even higher share of their incomes on health than if they had no Medigap protection, since they pay high administrative costs for relatively modest protection (Feder et al. 1987a). And for the low-income beneficiaries, comprehensive protection is simply unaffordable. Over half of the elderly (56.2 percent) with incomes of $10,000 or less had out-of-pocket spending totaling more than 15 percent of their incomes in 1986 (Feder et al. 1987b) (see table 5.1). Thus, the needs for these low-income groups are particularly high. It was felt that only a universal public program that offered special protections to these individuals could solve the problem.

Setting the Stage for the Legislation

The Medicare Catastrophic Coverage Act owed its initial political impetus to the Bowen Commission—a group headed by former Secretary of Health and Human Services Otis Bowen. The Commission was charged by President Reagan with studying problems associated with catastrophic health expenses, including both acute- and long-

Table 5.1 PROPORTION OF ELDERLY IN THE UNITED STATES WITH OUT-OF-POCKET SPENDING MORE THAN 15 PERCENT OF INCOME, BY INCOME AND HOSPITAL USE, 1986

| Income | All Elderly (%) | Proportion of Elderly Spending More than 15 Percent of Income | |
		Elderly with a Hospital Stay (%)	Elderly with No Hospital Stay (%)
All Incomes	23.9	39.9	19.5
$10,000 or Less	37.0	56.2	31.6
More than $10,000	5.6	16.2	2.8

Source: Feder et al. (1987b).

term care for persons of all ages. Testimony to the commission stressed the critical need for long-term care protection for the elderly, in particular. But the Bowen report, released in fall 1986, only proposed legislation to deal with the problem of gaps in acute care for Medicare beneficiaries (U.S. Department of Health and Human Services 1987). This issue was viewed as the "easiest" to solve of the major healthcare access problems, because it was likely to be least expensive, requiring only marginal changes to address the problem.[2]

The original Bowen proposal called for a simple expansion of benefits financed with a flat $59 annual premium assessed on all Medicare enrollees. This was to be added to the existing Part B premium, fully covering the costs of the program. The benefit improvement would consist of an annual $2,000 limit on each beneficiary's out-of-pocket expenses arising from hospital and physician deductibles and coinsurance. Once the beneficiary paid $2,000, the Medicare program would forgive all further Medicare cost-sharing under both Parts A and B in that calendar year. In addition, hospital cost-sharing would be limited to no more than two deductibles per year. Otherwise, Medicare would remain the same. This simple proposal added so-called stop-loss protection to Medicare similar to that found in many employer-covered policies. It made no distinction across beneficiaries; the $2,000 cap would be the same for everyone.

EVOLUTION OF THE LEGISLATION

The willingness of the Reagan administration to support a $2 billion expansion in Medicare benefits took many by surprise. This legislation was proposed in 1986 at a time when previous annual budget submissions by the administration had routinely sought reductions in Medicare spending of at least that amount (e.g., Office of the President 1986). Not surprisingly, when the White House agreed to support the Bowen proposal, it did so with a number of stringent constraints attached—namely, that new benefits must be self-financed by the beneficiaries and that the financing must come from premiums paid by beneficiaries rather than from general taxes. The flat premium of about $5 per month that was part of the proposal was to be a straightforward increase in insurance coverage. Thus, although the bill would expand the scope of government benefits, it would not expand subsidies to elderly and disabled persons. In this sense, it was consistent with administration goals not to raise taxes—although it would still have expanded the scope of the federal government.

Despite some initial concerns, Capitol Hill staff and lobbyists generally accepted the framework established by the Reagan administration as a starting point. Any hope that long-term care would be added by Congress was fleeting. Further, even the idea of a flat cap on spending as a desirable means for offering catastrophic protection went largely unchallenged, even though many in the research community had questioned the effectiveness of caps, given differences in income (Berki 1986; Congressional Budget Office 1983; Feder et al. 1987b; Varner 1987; Wyszewianski 1986). Capitol Hill staffers and interest groups such as the American Association of Retired Persons (AARP) began to develop their own versions of legislation, but worked within the broad outlines of the Bowen proposal.

Within this framework, the contents of the benefit package were soon transformed. The Democrats in Congress, vowing not to be outdone by the Republicans in offering new legislation to expand Medicare, were handed a tough challenge: to enhance the benefits while keeping to the constraint of self-financing through premiums insisted upon by President Reagan. How much could be added without risking a presidential veto?

Defining the Benefits

During the spring of 1987, a number of modest additions to Bowen's package began to surface. For example, an early draft from the House Committee on Ways and Means added a limit on Part B out-of-pocket liabilities, simplified the hospital benefit, and improved coverage for home healthcare and skilled nursing facility (SNF) care. (As described in chapter 3, stringent regulations had restrained growth in the latter two benefits. Moreover, the requirement of three days' hospitalization before entering an SNF, as well as an unduly high coinsurance beginning on day 21 of a stay, also discouraged beneficiaries from claiming further benefits.)

Changes in home health and SNF care were viewed as minor improvements in the long-term care area. Even many supporters of publicly provided long-term care thought that a major move to include it in this legislation was too radical an addition, largely because of its cost. When Congressman Claude Pepper tried to interest members in adding his home care bill to the package, there was strong opposition from all quarters.[3]

But as the spring progressed, two other broad additions were made by the House of Representatives. First, major Medicaid expansions were added to provide relief from Medicare coinsurance and deductibles for the low-income elderly, as well as to improve the financial protection of spouses of nursing home residents. The first of these changes required that the program pay Medicare coinsurance, deductibles, and premiums for all Medicare beneficiaries with incomes below poverty. (Less than half of poor Medicare recipients had Medicaid coverage in 1987, since states' eligibility standards for Medicaid were generally stringent.) This was a way to add further protections for low-income beneficiaries without differentiating coverage within the Medicare program itself. The approach recognized that a $2,000 cap on spending was not sufficient to protect the poor, and since the change was to be added through Medicaid, it would not seem to be "means testing" the benefits.

The spousal impoverishment provisions raised the amount of income and assets a spouse remaining in the community could keep when the husband or wife received Medicaid support for nursing home expenses. The liberalization of these protected amounts would expand the number of people eligible for benefits and help to financially protect their spouses. Although modest, this addition recognized the need of many of the elderly for long-term care, rather than acute-care, benefits.

These Medicaid expansions could effectively be funded with dollars freed up at the state level from the rest of the legislation that expanded the Medicare benefits. That is, when Medicare's coverage became more generous with the stop-loss and other protections, Medicaid costs for persons already covered by both programs would fall. Since Medicaid had previously filled in those gaps, states' burdens for the over-65 population would be eased. By expanding Medicaid in this way, the MCCA sought to maintain states' spending on healthcare.[4]

In the second major expansion, drug coverage was added to the package. In part, this was viewed as a way to offer benefits to higher-income enrollees who were being asked to pay a disproportionate share of the costs of the legislation (discussed in the following subsection). This was a major change, establishing an entirely new benefit. But to keep it a "catastrophic" benefit, there would be a high deductible to be met before Medicare would begin to pay. Even so, a substantial number of Medicare beneficiaries would qualify. Many advocates of this drug coverage saw it as only second in importance to long-term care, and expected many older persons to view this addition as a major improvement in Medicare.

During this period, the Senate Committee on Finance proceeded more cautiously, but within a very similar framework. Its final package looked like a scaled-down version of the House's bill, but without the drug benefit.

It was not long before the estimated costs of the various proposals began to rise. For example, a July 1987 Congressional Budget Office study indicated that the average annual benefits per enrollee would be $78 for Bowen (an increase in the estimated costs of the original proposal rather than an expansion in benefits), but $226 for the House version. The drug, SNF, home health, and Medicaid expansions added by the House of Representatives tripled the costs.

Financing

As benefit expansions substantially escalated the projected costs of the program, they created a dilemma on the financing side. Although $5 per month might not be viewed as unduly burdensome on those with modest incomes, a $20 premium (added to the already escalating Part B premium) could hurt those it presumably sought to help: the low-income elderly, who had trouble buying private supplemental insurance and meeting high out-of-pocket healthcare costs. Some other means of financing the benefit became imperative.

Under the Ways and Means Committee proposal, everyone (except those covered by Medicaid) would pay a basic premium (of $31 annually in the first year). The supplemental, income-related portion would only affect persons with adjusted gross incomes above $6,250, after which this supplemental premium would rise steeply to a maximum of $580 for those with adjusted gross incomes of $14,166 or more.[5] Although lowering burdens on those with the lowest incomes, Medicare enrollees with as little as $20,000 in income would have paid as much in total premiums as enrollees who were extremely wealthy. This premium would place the highest burden (as expressed by share of income) on middle-class beneficiaries. Wealthier elderly families would pay a smaller share of their incomes in supplemental premiums—a regressive burden for those with incomes above $20,000. Thus, this approach provided protection for those with very modest incomes, but shifted from a progressive to regressive structure for middle-class elderly and disabled persons.

The Senate addressed the issue quite differently, assessing a higher initial flat premium and then adding a supplemental premium that rose much more gradually by income. The maximum income-related premium was set at $800 per enrollee, but would apply only to beneficiaries with incomes over $60,000. In this sense, the financing behaved more like a standard surtax on the income tax, rising gradually with income. Although it too would become regressive above about $60,000, many fewer Medicare beneficiaries have incomes above that level. Figure 5.1 compares these two approaches.

The term *supplemental premium* was carefully defined to distinguish it from a tax increase. But the supplemental premium was to be administered through the Internal Revenue Service (IRS) and paid using the 1040 form. And the House version was mandatory. The Senate version of the catastrophic legislation had a greater claim to the term *premium*, since it proposed to treat this new benefit as a voluntary option. Beneficiaries could choose to enroll in the catastrophic benefit or to decline coverage. The actual choice turned out to be less voluntary than it might initially seem, however, since individuals would have to forego all of the heavily subsidized Part B coverage as well, if they opted out of catastrophic. In practice, few beneficiaries would be likely to opt out.

Figure 5.1 ADDITIONAL PREMIUMS UNDER SELECTED CATASTROPHIC PLANS
BY ADJUSTED GROSS INCOME, 1989

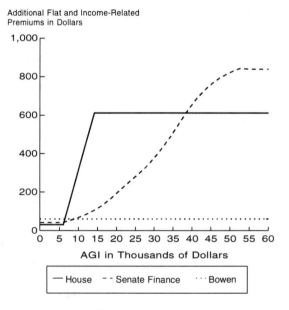

Source: Congressional Budget Office (1988).

THE MEDICARE CATASTROPHIC COVERAGE ACT: PASSAGE AND REPEAL

When the Medicare Catastrophic Coverage Act was passed in June of 1988, it was hailed as "the largest expansion of Medicare since the program's establishment in 1965" (Torres-Gil 1989). A major ceremony was held in the Rose Garden of the White House on July 1, 1988, to celebrate its signing by President Ronald Reagan. In private, the enthusiasm of the drafters was considerably lower—reflecting the long road of compromises necessary to enact such legislation. The final legislation was a complex combination of fill-in and new benefits that built on the House version, as summarized in table 5.2.

Most of the benefits added complications to the program, with the exception of the hospital coverage improvements. Regarding the latter, the legislation reduced beneficiaries' liability for hospital care to only one deductible per year. Beyond that, hospital benefits would cover the full year, eliminating the concept of spell of illness and all of the coinsurance calculations necessary under the original program. The expansion and simplification of hospital coverage represented one of the more valuable benefit changes of the act; these benefits became effective in January 1989.[6]

Also on the Part A side, the skilled nursing facility benefit (SNF) was made more generous by eliminating the requirement of a 3-day prior hospital stay, by lengthening the coverage to 150 days per year, and by reducing and rearranging the coinsurance charged. These changes also took force in 1989. Coinsurance would be required for the first 8 days—but at a much lower rate of 20 percent of the daily cost of nursing home care.[7] These changes meant that more beneficiaries would qualify for coverage and that longer stays would be covered. In retrospect, SNF changes (combined with some regulatory easing in 1988) turned out to be more substantial than originally credited and would have made important contributions to the costs of short nursing home stays over time (Liu and Kenney 1991).

Hospice and home health benefits were also modestly expanded by relaxing some of the requirements on participation in these areas. The 210-day lifetime limit on hospice benefits would have been eliminated. The home health benefits would also have been made less restrictive by relaxing the intermittency standards. Enrollees would be able to receive up to 38 consecutive days of care, 7 days a week. (Interpretation of the original intermittency requirements had stated

Table 5.2 MEDICARE CATASTROPHIC ACT BENEFITS AS ENACTED IN 1988

1989	1990	1991	1992	1993
Hospital Insurance				
Hospital Inpatient Benefits. Provides unlimited inpatient hospital care. Eliminates all copayments and deductibles except one annual deductible amount ($560 in 1989).	**Home Health Benefits.** Relaxes current requirement that limits home healthcare to intermittent visits; enrollees may receive up to 38 consecutive days of care, seven days a week.	All hospital insurance benefits in place after 1990.		
Skilled Nursing Facility (SNF) Benefits. Increases limit on SNF stays to 150 days a year and requires no prior hospital stay. Coinsurance is required for first eight days each year, at 20 percent of average SNF costs per day ($25.50 for 1989).				
Hospice Benefits. eliminates 210-day lifetime limit on hospice benefits, but retains a cost limit.				
Supplementary Medical Insurance				
No provisions take effect in 1989.	**Limitation on Part B Cost-Sharing.** Limits out-of-pocket expenses for covered Part B services ($1,370 in 1990). Adjusts the cap yearly to keep proportion of eligible enrollees constant at 7 percent.	All SMI provisions in place after 1990. **Limitation on Part B Cost Sharing.** Part B cap increases to $1,530.	**Limitation on Part B Cost Sharing.** Part B cap increases to $1,700.	**Limitation on Part B Cost Sharing.** Part B cap increases to $1,900.

Mammography. Expands coverage to include mammography screening.

Respite Care. Eighty percent of reasonable costs is paid for up to 80 hours a year of in-home personal services, to give homebound enrollees' usual caretakers a respite. Eligibility occurs after Part B copayment cap or prescription drug deduction is met.

Catastrophic Drug Insurance

No provisions take effect in 1989.	**Limited Drug Benefits.** Covers drugs administered intravenously at home, with a 20 percent coinsurance, and immuno-suppressive drugs, with a 20 percent coinsurance for the first year after transplant surgery (thereafter, the regular prescription drug coinsurance applies). Deductible in 1990, $550; coinsurance, 50 percent.	**Full Drug Benefits.** Covers all outpatient prescription drugs and insulin, subject to a deductible ($600 in 1991) that will be adjusted annually so the proportion of eligible enrollees will remain constant at 16.8 percent. Requires coinsurance of 50 percent of reasonable charges above the deductible in 1991.	**Full Drug Benefits.** Deductible, $652; coinsurance, 40 percent.	**Full Drug Benefits.** Deductible, $710; coinsurance falls to 20 percent in 1993 and subsequent years.

Source: ProPAC (1990).

that visits could be no more frequent than 5 days per week for no more than 3 consecutive weeks.) Implementation of the home health changes was set to begin in 1990.

On the Part B side, the major expansion was a limit on the amount of deductibles and copayments beneficiaries would pay for physician and other services, for the first time placing a cap on how much Medicare beneficiaries would have to pay out of pocket for Part B coinsurance and deductibles. Above the cap, Medicare would pay the full 100 percent of allowed charges.[8] This cap would have started at $1,370 in 1990 and risen each year at a rate intended to protect the 7 percent of enrollees with the highest Part B costs. The main beneficiaries of this stop-loss would be persons with surgeries or other very expensive physician procedures.

The major new addition to Medicare services was the drug benefit, covering outpatient prescription drugs above a $600 deductible. This very large deductible was designed to limit this benefit to users with unusually high liabilities. The benefit would have been phased in with only immunosuppressive drugs and intravenously administered drugs at home covered in 1990. Then in 1991, coverage would have been expanded to include all outpatient prescription drugs and insulin. Initially, enrollees would be required to pay coinsurance of 50 percent. That requirement would be reduced over time to ultimately require a 20 percent coinsurance.

Finally, Part B was also expanded to include biennial mammography screening and a small respite benefit. Under the latter, Medicare would have paid up to 80 percent of reasonable costs for up to 80 hours a year of in-home personal services to provide relief to caregivers of homebound enrollees. The coverage would only be available to those exceeding either the Part B payment cap or the drug deductible, however. Thus, it was essentially a symbolic addition to Medicare's benefit package that would be available to only a small portion of enrollees.

The Medicaid changes previously mentioned were also part of the legislation. These changes added protections for low-income Medicare beneficiaries against Medicare cost sharing and premiums and raised the income and asset protections for the spouse left in the community.

The financing package reflected a compromise between the Senate and House provisions. The flat premium was smaller than under the Senate version, but the structure of the supplemental premium looked more like the Senate's more gradual rate of premium increases. The supplemental premium would be assessed against any beneficiary whose income tax liability was at least $150. Beginning in 1989, such individuals would pay at the rate of $22.50 per $150 in liability (effectively a 15 percent surtax). The maximum liability was set at $800 per enrollee; individuals with incomes of over about $40,000 would be subject to that maximum. Couples with incomes in excess of about $70,000 would pay $1,600. Estimates indicated that only about 5 percent of older persons would be subject to these maximum tax levels, and that about 40 percent of all the elderly would pay at least some supplemental premium. But this surtax rate would rise rapidly over time to a maximum of 28 percent by 1993, or nearly double the initial rate. Over time, a larger proportion of Medicare enrollees would pay this surtax.

Another important element of the financing was that the premiums were set to begin in 1989, whereas several of the key benefits were not scheduled to go into effect until later. Revenues would thus be considerably higher than outlays in the early years of the program. This would allow for the buildup of reserves in a newly created trust fund, to ensure sufficient funds as new benefits came on line. This provision also had the short-run effect of reducing the federal deficit, and would later come under fire for that reason.

Overall Beneficiary Impact

Altogether, these changes would have increased Medicare benefits per enrollee by about 7 percent. This estimate is based on a Congressional Budget Office simulation of the impact of the MCCA, assuming that all benefits were fully in place in 1988 (Christensen and Kasten 1988b). If so, catastrophic benefits would have averaged $194 per enrollee, compared to $2,801 in "current law" benefits. Table 5.3 presents a breakdown of these components. Most of these legislative changes would have the effect of reducing Medicare copayments (89 percent of the total), whereas the rest of the $194 represented new service use or relaxation of coverage limits.

In addition, the Medicaid buy-in would have further reduced copayment liabilities by $28, on average. But this is averaged across all enrollees, whereas the benefits would be limited to a much smaller number of elderly and disabled persons. For those eligible for this buy-in, the benefits would average about $350 (Christensen and Kasten 1988a).

This simulation also illustrates the relationship of these benefits to Medigap coverage. New Medicare benefits would reduce Medigap benefit payments by a fourth, since Medicare is the first payer of services. The other three-fourths of the benefits paid by private insur-

Table 5.3 MEDICARE BENEFIT PAYMENTS, COPAYMENT LIABILITIES, AND
PREMIUMS PAYABLE PER ENROLLEE BEFORE AND AFTER
IMPLEMENTATION OF MEDICARE CATASTROPHIC COVERAGE ACT OF
1988

	Before ($)	After ($)	Change ($)
Medicare benefit payments per enrollee[a]			
Hospital Insurance	1,693	1,747	54
Supplementary Medical Insurance	1,108	1,191	83
Catastrophic Drug Insurance	0	57	57
Total	2,801	2,995	194
Medicare copayment liabilities per enrollee			
Hospital Insurance	162	118	−44
Supplementary Medical Insurance	325	262	−63
Catastrophic Drug Insurance	244	179	−65
Total	731	559	−172
Medicare premiums payable per enrollee			
Monthly premiums	290	368	78
Supplemental premiums	0	129	129
Total	290	497	207

Source: Congressional Budget Office (1988).
Note: Table shows effects of Medicare only.
a. About 22 percent of enrollees were estimated to be entitled to higher Medicare benefit payments under the MCCA when fully implemented. This reflects an unduplicated count of those affected by the Hospital Insurance provisions (4 percent), the Supplementary Medical Insurance copayment cap (7 percent), and the drug provisions (16.8 percent).

ers would remain as liabilities for Medicare beneficiaries; these would mainly include Part B coinsurance up to the cap and the Part A and B deductibles. Christensen and Kasten (1988b) projected that Medigap premiums would fall by about 20 percent in response to these changes—less of a reduction in premiums than the reduction in payments they would be required to make.

Viewed in a different context, less than one-third of the benefits from the MCCA would overlap with services covered by Medigap insurance. Some of the difference reflects the fact that only about two-thirds of Medicare beneficiaries had Medigap coverage. But even for those with coverage, over half of the catastrophic benefits would exceed what private insurers cover. These new benefits would lower the out-of-pocket spending by Medicare beneficiaries, but not eliminate the role of Medigap.

Winners and Losers

Proponents of the passage of catastrophic coverage believed they had achieved a major improvement in benefits. For example, the largest interest group representing the elderly, the American Association of Retired Persons (AARP), enjoyed accolades concerning the considerable role the organization had played in working with Congress on the MCCA (Torres-Gil 1989). Other aging organizations and organized labor had also worked hard to secure passage, and believed they had improved the program.

On the other hand, the drug industry, fearing government interference in its activities, bitterly fought inclusion of the drug benefit in the program. Although the industry could not block the legislation, it managed to water down the drug benefit provisions. For example, no reference was made in the legislation to any type of cost controls on drugs; instead, the final bill called for beneficiaries to pay higher premiums over time if costs exceeded expectations. The Pharmaceutical Manufacturers Association reportedly spent several million dollars to oppose the legislation and, failing that, to seek limitations on cost controls (Rich 1987).

Although a relative latecomer to the process, the National Committee to Protect Social Security and Medicare had attempted to derail the financing scheme of the final bill. They mounted a major lobbying and letter-writing campaign to eliminate the supplemental premium. They were unsuccessful, at least in part because their often deceptive mail campaigns were viewed by members of Congress more as a fund-raising ploy than as legitimate grass-roots organizing (Simon 1989). Opposition to the legislation from other seniors groups was only beginning to get organized about the time of passage of the legislation.

Although the final package was intended to be budget neutral from the federal government's perspective, there were clearly individual winners and losers among the beneficiaries from this legislation. Indeed, a considerable amount of debate centered on this issue. On the benefit side, additional benefits directed at low-income beneficiaries through the Medicaid program assured that many low-income enrollees would be winners. Differences in the use of health services by various groups meant that the level of benefits received varied in any given year. For example, the very old with high rates of hospital use were more likely to benefit than younger, healthier enrollees.

Table 5.4 displays the Congressional Budget Office's estimated insurance benefits (for just the Medicare portion of the MCCA) and costs

Table 5.4 NET CHANGE IN ENROLLEES' OUT-OF-POCKET COSTS BY INCOME
AND POVERTY STATUS IN RESPONSE TO MEDICARE CATASTROPHIC
COVERAGE ACT OF 1988

Enrollees' Income and Poverty Status	Percentage of Enrollees in Group	Net Change in:[a]		
		Direct Costs ($)	Premium Costs ($)	Total Costs ($)
By Per Capita Income Percentiles				
(average per capita income)				
0 to 10 ($2,881)	10.0	−237	80	−158
11 to 30 ($5,623)	20.0	−221	81	−140
31 to 50 ($8,575)	20.0	−195	89	−106
51 to 70 ($12,604)	20.0	−189	157	−32
71 to 90 ($19,579)	20.0	−171	373	203
91 to 100 ($52,291)	10.0	−161	597	436
By Poverty Status				
Poor	12.8	−232	80	−152
Near Poor[b]	19.4	−226	79	−147
Other	67.8	−178	268	90
All enrollees	100.0	−194	207	13

Source: Congressional Budget Office (1988).
a. Direct costs are Medicare benefits under the MCCA, assuming full implementation in 1988. Includes only Medicare charges.
b. Includes those with incomes above poverty line but below 1.5 times the line.

in terms of premiums paid by the income status of enrollees (Congressional Budget Office 1988). These estimates capture the impact of demographic variations. Benefits were greater for those with lower incomes. For example, the very old tend to have lower incomes on average and, hence, affect these distributions. The redistribution would be even greater if the Medicaid changes that were targeted at low-income persons had also been added to the table.

When the financing side is added in, the redistribution becomes much more dramatic. The bottom 70 percent of Medicare enrollees as ranked by their incomes would experience a net reduction in out-of-pocket costs. On average, these enrollees would pay considerably less in premiums than they would, on average, gain in increased protections. Higher-income enrollees, on the other hand, would face higher costs primarily because of the supplemental premium. Table 5.4 does not, however, take into account whether certain groups already had private insurance protection (or whether that protection was provided free of charge to those whose former employers paid the costs). Such an adjustment would result in further distinctions by level of income, since almost all high-income individuals have Medigap coverage and many of them have it subsidized or fully paid by their former employers. Such individuals would see few new benefits, only new costs.

Further, important variations by race and sex occur that are not easily explained by health status differences. For example, women tend to rely more on long-term care services than do men, whereas the relationship is just the opposite for acute-care services. Consequently, improvements aimed more at the acute-care side are likely to benefit men more than women. Men would have gained more from the MCCA than women. Black beneficiaries use fewer services than their white counterparts, perhaps because they are hampered by access to care or by low incomes. Disabled beneficiaries are also heavier users of Medicare services than are elderly beneficiaries, so they would, on average, have fared better under the legislation as well.

The actuarial projections of table 5.4 need to be understood as averaging benefits across all individuals in that income group. In practice, many individuals would have seen little change in their benefits unless they were hospitalized several times or for long periods, or unless they had very high expenses overall. It is the nature of catastrophic coverage that although the benefits can be substantial when triggered, very few individuals reach that category initially. Indeed, some of the benefits were defined to grow over time only enough to protect a certain percentage of all beneficiaries. The Congressional Budget Office (1988) had estimated that when fully implemented the MCCA would provide benefits to 22 percent of all beneficiaries. Most of the individual provisions would affect an even smaller number of beneficiaries each year, so some of that 22 percent would only receive small reductions in liabilities.

Other changes, although substantial for those who needed them, were limited to a small share of Medicare enrollees. For example, elimination of the hospital coinsurance requirements and lifting of the lifetime limits on hospitalization would each year affect only about 0.5 percent of all enrollees, or about 165,000 persons. But for those individuals, the benefits would be substantial.

Many opponents of the legislation used these small numbers of persons who would *directly* receive help in any given year to argue that the MCCA was a "bad deal." They ignored, however, the principle of insurance that everyone covered gains whether or not they trigger the caps, because all of them are at risk. And cumulated over several years, the proportion of enrollees receiving direct benefits would be higher than 22 percent. This is the principle of catastrophic coverage, but the subsequent debate implied that this was not understood or not valued by many Medicare enrollees.

The Beginning of the End

Much of the criticism leveled at the MCCA did not end with its passage in 1988. Opponents—led by the Pharmaceutical Manufacturers Association and the National Committee to Protect Social Security and Medicare—kept up a steady barrage of protest concerning the legislation and captured considerable media attention. Those in Congress who had opposed the legislation to begin with played to this protest.

Ironically, two sets of information, revising some of the estimates of the revenues and costs of catastrophic, fed this opposition. First came word in the spring of 1989 that the U.S. Treasury expected tax collections from the supplemental premium on the elderly to be higher than anticipated, generating a considerable buildup in the Catastrophic Coverage trust fund. Although some buildup had been intended in the legislation to provide a cushion for the benefits that would be phased in later but then would grow very rapidly, the Treasury Department's estimate of the size of the reserves was considerably higher than the level originally intended. Critics claimed that the new legislation was aimed at reducing the deficit at the expense of the elderly and that the new premiums exceeded benefits.

Senator Lloyd Bentsen, of Texas, already under pressure from his constituents, announced on April 20, 1989, that he would seek a reduction in the supplemental premium to counteract the unexpected surplus. This promise captured considerable media attention. Other members generally took a more cautious approach, but recognized the considerable pressure building on the supplemental premium.

Shortly thereafter, the Congressional Budget Office released a second set of numbers suggesting that the costs of some benefits had been severely underestimated. In particular, the improvements in the SNF benefit were now projected to cost more than six times the original estimate. As one of the earliest provisions to be implemented, SNF use rose dramatically in early 1989. Between 1988 and 1989, covered days per stay jumped to 34 from 27, on average, representing a 26 percent increase in length of stay in just one year. And the number of persons covered rose from 392,438 in 1988 to 591,281 in 1989, largely as a result of eliminating the three-day prior hospital stay requirement (HCFA 1991, unpublished data).

Although these numbers were not initially known, the HCFA was aware that major changes in use were occurring. The MCCA effectively allowed states to shift patients from Medicaid to Medicare, causing costs to rise even more rapidly than anticipated. States took advantage of this change, and since this affected patients already in the system, the impact was immediate. Even with no new admissions, Medicare costs would rise as existing patients were shifted from Medicaid to Medicare. In addition, nursing homes that previously had not found it in their interest to participate in Medicare, began to participate, thereby increasing the number of available SNF beds. The total number of SNF-covered days rose to over 25 million in 1989, nearly triple the amount for 1988 (Ways and Means 1991).[9]

In addition, the reestimates of the costs of the drug benefit—using newly available data—proved twice as high as the original figure (Congressional Budget Office 1989a). In this case, the change in the cost estimate resulted from the release of 1987 data showing a much greater jump in the use of drugs before the MCCA than the Congressional Budget Office had projected using much older data. The office had originally estimated that spending per enrollee on drugs grew at an annual rate of 10 percent in the 1980s; however, the new data indicated that the rate between 1980 and 1987 had instead been over 14 percent per year. Thus, the projected value of the drug benefit to Medicare enrollees increased dramatically, creating a further expected drain on the revenues.

These new figures changed the outlook; not only would there be no surplus in the trust funds for a rollback of the supplemental premium, but there would be a shortfall in the revenues needed. Senator Bentsen and others who had backed a rollback in the supplemental premium were left hanging, since all those projected surpluses suddenly disappeared.

Neither of these sets of data releases was politically motivated. Nonetheless, the timing proved disastrous for the legislation. Not only was there the prospect of out-of-control costs, but there could be no rollback of the extremely unpopular supplemental premium, and further increases in premiums might be necessary. Essentially, the stage was set in the spring of 1989 for repeal of the Catastrophic legislation. But at this point, few were willing to admit that serious modification of the law, much less repeal, was a strong possibility. The House and Senate leadership resisted any reconsideration of the legislation; they had wrestled with compromises for a year and a half before passage of the MCCA, and they were not anxious to reopen negotiations. Indeed, many thought the objections would fade.

However, the fervor against the MCCA did not die down. Continued pressure of the mail campaigns launched by well-funded opponents[10] and the generally negative tone of the media began to take their toll. Those who would benefit from the MCCA remained silent.

A major turning point came in the late summer of 1989. The discontent of a vocal minority was played out in town meetings held by members of Congress in their home districts. The most dramatic of these was a confrontation with Congressman Dan Rostenkowski that made the national news over the Labor Day weekend. A number of elderly protestors blocked Rostenkowski's departure from a town meeting in Illinois. Captured on camera was an elderly woman pounding on the hood of the car while the driver attempted to move through the crowd. Eventually, Rostenkowski "fled" on foot from view of CNN cameras. For all the world to see, an opponent of the legislation had "sent a message" to the chairman of the most powerful committee in the House of Representatives. It no longer mattered that these protesters represented only a minority of the elderly—they were vocal, visible, and seemed to be growing stronger by the day.

The Repeal

Even before the August recess, an earnest effort was begun in Congress to modify the Catastrophic legislation. The hope of proponents that the protest would prove short-lived died away, and congressional committees began to search for a compromise to save at least part of the legislation. Although some of the interest groups, such as the National Committee to Protect Social Security and Medicare, argued to keep all the benefits while changing the financing, most of the effort centered on what benefits could be retained if the supplemental premium were eliminated. There was little serious discussion of adding additional revenue sources: the original agreement to stick with a self-financed benefit package remained intact. The difficulty lay in deciding which were the more crucial benefits. Each benefit had proponents who had worked within the legislative framework during passage and who felt they had already compromised.

Through this period many options were proposed, but none seemed to capture the imagination of many members of Congress. A number of those leading the charge for repeal had been opposed to the legislation from the start, so they were unlikely to ally themselves with supporters in a compromise. Moreover, despite the lip service paid to supporting the MCCA by the Bush administration, the door to repeal was opened when the Office of Management and Budget (OMB) indicated that an exception would be granted so that repeal would not count against the deficit.[11] One of the last objections to repeal was thus eliminated.

On October 4, 1989, the House of Representatives first voted for repeal of all but the Medicaid provisions. The Senate, meanwhile, passed an amendment to salvage at least some of the benefits while eliminating the dreaded supplemental premium. However, the Senate's amendment was rejected by the House on the last night of the session. Members of the House, who literally sat with their coats on their laps, impatiently considered and then rejected the amendment. The Senate followed suit and voted repeal of all but the Medicaid low-income benefits. In the early hours of November 22, 1989, the U.S. Congress took the nearly unprecedented step of repealing a major piece of social legislation that had been so highly touted only one year earlier.

LESSONS FOR HEALTH POLICY

The issues surrounding this extraordinary turn of events and their implications for future health policy will be debated for years to come. Even at close range, a few lessons are clear. Some are insights into the political process and are discussed here only briefly. More important are the lessons for Medicare's future, not all of which are likely to be negative. Indeed, the ultimate outcome for Medicare in the 1990s may well be to embrace parts of the MCCA that helped contribute to its repeal.

Politics of the Supplemental Premium

More than any other element of the legislation, beneficiaries objected to the way the bill was financed. Medicare's Part B premium has always been a flat payment assessed on everyone except the very poorest beneficiaries, who are also covered by Medicaid. Not only did the new financing depart from the past, but it was a dramatic departure. For the first time, Medicare differentiated among beneficiaries, and at its apex, the supplemental premium represented an enormous increase in beneficiary contributions.

Although only a small share of beneficiaries—about 5 percent—would actually have to pay the maximum supplemental amount, much of the publicity generated by groups supporting repeal suggested otherwise. For example, one flyer produced by a group calling itself the Seniors Coalition Against the Tax asked in bold letters: "Will you get an $800 tax bill for Catastrophic coverage this year?" It did not spell out how to calculate the actual liability. Moreover, even for those not asked to pay the maximum, the principle—and the precedent—of setting such a high premium bothered many beneficiaries.

The supplemental premium was offered as a way to meet the Reagan administration's requirement that there should be no new taxes and that any financing should come from the beneficiaries themselves. The premium from those with higher incomes thus had to be quite large to keep the financing confined to beneficiaries. This is because the number of enrollees with high incomes is small relative to those with lower incomes. Consequently, at a top supplemental premium of $800 plus the flat premium of $48, the highest-income beneficiaries would have paid nearly four times the actuarial value of their expected benefits. Moreover, this amount was projected to grow rapidly over time, reaching a maximum combined Catastrophic premium of $1,172 by 1993—a surtax of 28 percent on top of other income tax liability (Congressional Budget Office 1988).

In practice, this very high premium would still have left an overall net subsidy under Part B even for high-income beneficiaries. Current law before the MCCA required beneficiaries to pay only 25 percent of the costs of Part B. After the MCCA, these high-income beneficiaries would have been paying about 75 percent of the overall costs of their coverage if the supplemental premiums were assumed to be directed at all Part B costs (Christensen and Kasten 1988a). However, this argument seemed to hold little comfort for those who recognized that the "price" of expanded coverage under Medicare was a substantial drop in the general revenue subsidy that high-income beneficiaries had enjoyed for many years. They would still be subsidized, but the extent of the subsidy would have been dramatically curtailed.

Added Sensitivity to Language

The supplemental premium operated in practice like a surtax to the income tax. It was to be collected by the Internal Revenue Service (IRS) through the regular income tax structure and calculated on the basis of how much income tax a beneficiary owed. Not surprisingly, it was quickly perceived by the public to be a tax.

Throughout the debate over the legislation, however, Congress and elderly organizations tried to retain the nomenclature of supplemental premium. For instance, Martin Corry, chief lobbyist for the AARP, which had supported the legislation, was quoted as saying that the fact that the IRS was involved "is simply an administrative convenience. It just happens to be the most efficient way of handling it" (Rich

1988). This semantic obfuscation backfired. Calling this tax a "supplemental premium" seemed disingenuous. The backlash by seniors stemmed both from the size of the premium and the feeling that the elderly had been deceived.

Moreover, since the litany of the Reagan administration was that no one should have to pay more taxes—and indeed the trend in the 1980s was to lower personal income tax rates—this most glaring counterexample singled out the elderly and disabled populations. Terming it the "seniors tax" (or even the "AARP tax"), opponents were able to portray the financing of the legislation in a very negative light. Why should elderly and disbled persons be the only ones to pay new taxes? And perhaps even more critical, at a time when running a deficit meant that most programs were financed by paying only 85 cents on the dollar, why should the elderly be asked to pay *more* than a dollar for a dollar's worth of benefits?

TAXES BEFORE BENEFITS

The linking of a financing mechanism to the new program in this highly visible way reflected the philosophy of Congress and the administration that no new spending should worsen the deficit. This approach, sometimes termed "pay as you go," required that new spending packages must carry their own financing. The Catastrophic legislation went even further by creating a reserve in a new trust fund so that benefits would never exceed revenues in the early years of the program.

Objections to the tax (and the subsequent debate) swamped discussion of the benefits. Was this a specific reaction to the Catastrophic legislation itself? Does it raise issues about this legislative approach in general? It is too soon to judge the long-term consequences of requiring such pairing of benefits and financing, but this episode does suggest that the financing side may get disproportionate attention and focus much of the debate on the question of gainers and losers. Any social legislation that seeks to help one group while taxing another may face formidable obstacles in achieving acceptance.

Moreover, the political environment of the Reagan administration stressed that government could be financed without raising taxes and that savings could be obtained by cutting fat out of the system. The pay-as-you-go financing of the Catastrophic legislation stands in stark contrast to that approach. Again, the rhetoric of the Reagan administration seems to have worked against its only major piece of social legislation.

Marginal Nature of the Benefits

The final MCCA legislation offered a bewildering variety of benefits to the elderly and, except for the hospital benefits, made the already byzantine Medicare program seem even more complex. Since most enrollees did not understand how benefits work under the original program, how were they supposed to interpret these changes? Additions or reforms occurred in at least eight identifiable areas: hospital care, skilled nursing care, home health care, a part B limit on copayments, hospice, respite care, mammograms, and drugs. Each of the benefit areas was likely to seem small and often not relevant to any one beneficiary. When combined, benefits totaled over $200 per beneficiary per year—an amount large enough to be difficult to finance but hard to sell as a substantial improvement in benefits.

The rising costs of healthcare make even small changes expensive—a fact of life likely to plague future health proposals of all types. Indeed, the rapid rate of healthcare inflation in recent years means that most of us are faced with "sticker shock" at the price of care. This means we are more likely to doubt that the costs of new benefits are "worth it." The Catastrophic act also seems to fit this scenario.

Benefit changes and minor reforms such as those in the Catastrophic package might fare better if added in pieces over time rather than joined into one package. For example, it might be quite reasonable to interest beneficiaries in a small premium increase to pay for all hospital benefits above the single deductible. Even the original Bowen proposal might have been more popular, given its simplicity and relatively low price tag.

Further, since there was no consistent theme or logic to these many disparate changes; the whole somehow seemed less than the sum of its parts. The lack of serious objection to the framework adopted from the Bowen Commission and the gradual addition of numerous small benefits resulted in a piece of legislation with no clear central focus. Certainly the final package did not represent as dramatic a change on the benefits side as did the financing mechanism intended to pay for the legislation. Even the term *catastrophic* evoked images of long-term care benefits that were not key elements of the law. In a sense, the Catastrophic Act was a Christmas tree bill to which ornaments had been added. The problem was that there were more ornaments than tree.

Similarly, a package of long-term care benefits might have fared better by offering a consistent theme. Indeed, many older citizens have focused much of their dissatisfaction with Medicare on the lack of long-term care benefits. Incorporating Medicaid's spousal protection and the SNF and home health changes, and adding those basic elements from the Pepper bill that would have expanded home care, could have been packaged as a first step toward long-term care—and perhaps for not much more than the cost of the MCCA if some restrictions were put on the benefits. Ironically, the SNF changes did turn out to be more significant than anticipated. The problems that this created in the estimates of spending were noted by opponents, but the other side of that coin—the significance of the benefits for elderly and disabled persons—was not appreciated. If coupled with better home health benefits, this package would be fairly similar to the Pepper Commission proposal just one year later that received relatively favorable reviews from many seniors.

Meaning of Catastrophic Coverage

The MCCA benefits were perceived as being of lesser value because they would not be directly used by many Medicare beneficiaries in any given year. But that is exactly the nature of catastrophic insurance. Rather than recognizing this as desirable insurance protection—like life insurance, for example—many Medicare beneficiaries downplayed its importance. Health policy experts agreed that this was a desirable addition to Medicare, providing protection that was missing from the program and offering relief to persons who now face financial catastrophe if they have no supplemental coverage. However, the average beneficiary simply did not see it that way; the term *catastrophic protection* seemed to promise more than it delivered.

Moreover, in practice it is difficult to offer meaningful catastrophic protection without some appreciation of the income levels of those being covered. A $2,000 limit on out-of-pocket spending is valuable for someone with $30,000 of income, but may not be meaningful for someone whose income is only $5,000 or even $10,000, for example. Long before that low-income person ever spends $2,000 out of pocket, he or she will likely have dramatically curtailed use of healthcare services. In that case the catastrophe will already have occurred before the protection is applied (Feder et al. 1987b).

Thus, the irony of the MCCA legislation was that the cutoff was too high to provide true catastrophic protection to those who needed it most; they would likely do without care or turn to Medicaid for help. And for those for whom the cap was meaningful, private purchase of Medigap protection was a viable option. Indeed, such individuals could afford to privately purchase more generous spending caps and better first-dollar coverage, particularly when compared to the level of the supplemental premium. The MCCA would have been more efficient in its coverage, but that advantage was wiped out for higher-income beneficiaries who were paying more than the actuarial cost. The act did not go far enough to discourage purchase of supplemental coverage altogether, so it did not simplify health coverage in that way either.

Role of Private Coverage

Although health policy experts often criticize Medigap, the elderly as a whole seem quite satisfied with multiple policies. Indeed, by buying such policies, they have voted with their wallets. Medigap policy-holders can choose different combinations of benefits, sometimes continuing a relationship with an insurance company that covered them before they became eligible for Medicare. They did not want the MCCA.

Moreover, since a substantial minority of elderly beneficiaries have their supplemental insurance paid for by a third party—usually an employer or former employer—they are more likely to have rich benefit packages, including drug coverage. They are the ones who would have paid the $800 supplemental premium. Not only would their tax bite have risen, but they could legitimately claim that they would benefit little from the MCCA.

The argument, however, that the MCCA was offering unnecessary benefits because so many beneficiaries already had supplemental coverage was more a testament to the elderly's enthusiasm for Medigap insurance than to informed knowledge about overlapping coverage. As noted earlier, only one-third of MCCA's benefits would have overlapped with benefits already covered by Medigap (Christensen and Kasten 1988a). But this information was not widely known or understood by Medicare enrollees.

Moreover, a side effect of the complexity of Medicare is that many older persons do not appreciate the share that the basic Medicare program pays compared to their private coverage. Statements about Medicare payments are forwarded to beneficiaries via private insurance companies who process the claims—and who are often the same companies that offer Medigap coverage. When Medigap insurers handle some of the processing for elderly clients, it is not uncommon for clients to believe that the private insurer rather than Medicare is paying most of the bill. In practice, this is not the case. When Medicare is the primary payer, its share is generally three to four times that of the Medigap company for Medicare-covered services.

During much of the debate on the legislation, proponents assumed that beneficiaries would be happy to have new coverage even if Medigap already paid, so long as there would be reductions in private premiums. Instead, many of those objecting to the coverage offered under the MCCA claimed just the opposite—that they were happy with the private coverage they had. Part of this was undoubtedly a reluctance to alter current coverage that seemed adequate. Also, many beneficiaries expressed the belief that their own plan was more efficient. Although all the evidence on the efficiency of Medicare versus Medigap runs in the opposite direction, many, if not most, beneficiaries remained unconvinced.[12] In addition, part of the objection was to subsidizing others. Some beneficiaries with good coverage were paying less than if they had to pay the average costs across all elderly persons. And many were not happy to pay a higher share to help lower-income beneficiaries.

Thus, the package of benefits offered improved security to many beneficiaries who believed they already had reasonable coverage against these circumstances. And those who would be asked to pay the most under the government plan were those who had the best coverage and at the lowest cost through their own private arrangements. The low-income elderly and many disabled persons do not have the same options for private supplemental coverage as those who objected to the MCCA. Yet, even though these groups would have benefitted from the MCCA, they were not vocal. Persons with lower incomes tend to be less politically active. Moreover, the nature of catastrophic benefits is such that many people do not appreciate them until illness strikes.

Ignoring the Need for Simplicity

One factor never seriously addressed in the legislative debate over these Medicare changes was whether they added to the complexity of the program. Yet Medicare's complexity represents one of the long-standing complaints of beneficiaries. Medicare communications from the HCFA are confusing and obscure, and it is difficult to know what benefits one has and what restrictions will affect them. By adding to the complexity of the system, the benefit package under the MCCA was almost assured of being undervalued.

As noted previously, the changes in the hospital coverage were the exception to the rule. But since these represented only a fraction of many changes, they seemed to get lost in the shuffle. Moreover, coverage of Medicare's hospital cost sharing was a benefit that almost every Medicare enrollee with any private coverage had as part of a Medigap policy.

The Part B cap and the drug benefit were both costly benefits, but they sounded complicated and restrictive. The Part B cap offered an upper bound on liability (but only for formal Medicare cost sharing), whereas the drug benefit required a substantial deductible. If it had been possible to tell beneficiaries that they would have to pay no more than, say, $2,000 or $3,000 out of pocket for hospital, physician, and drug expenses no matter what happened, the package might have been more understandable. But there were exceptions to the Part B cap, and drugs did not have any overall limit. Thus, even the notion of a "catastrophic cap" got lost in the mix of all the various pieces of the benefit.

The remaining benefits were more minor parts of Medicare—although as noted previously, the SNF expansion would have been more extensive than originally anticipated. Nonetheless, all of these benefits continued to have restrictions and limitations designed to keep them from being too expensive. As a consequence, they were dismissed by beneficiaries as too confusing or inapplicable to their situation.

Changed View of the Elderly

Part of the significance of the Medicare Catastrophic Coverage Act was that it reflected a changing attitude toward America's elderly. No longer did members of Congress view persons over age 65 as a homogeneous group in need of public support. The financing mechanism of the act alone represented a formal acknowledgment of the disparities in economic status of the elderly. Under the MCCA, the most affluent of the elderly were not seen as deserving beneficiaries of an expanded Medicare program, but rather as the source of financing for benefits to others. This major change in attitude stood in stark contrast to the views expressed when Medicare was first passed in 1965. During that debate, a generation earlier, the issue of means testing of Medicare also arose. But it was finessed by arguments that nearly all the elderly needed the health benefits and were too poor to buy them on their own (Marmor 1970). The higher average incomes of older persons made such an argument much harder to support in the 1980s. The MCCA thus signaled recognition that policy may need to differentiate groups within the elderly.

Not ready to subscribe to this view, however, older persons have resisted changes that would differentiate their ranks. Either because they reject the necessity of such a policy or perhaps because they understand its implications, older persons have sought to have Medicare remain a universal program with no distinctions by economic status or other characteristics. They may be correct, given the popularity of universal programs as compared to means-tested ones.

The MCCA was the first salvo in a potentially long and bitter debate over a changing view of older persons. Perhaps one of the legislation's greatest tactical mistakes was in moving too fast to differentiate treatment of beneficiaries. It is one thing to gradually introduce income-related premiums for Medicare and quite another to make the first step be an $848 maximum premium tied to a benefit with an actuarial value of $250—plus benefits that many already claimed from other sources.

As a result, both sides in the debate are now on the alert, hardening their respective positions. But just as surely, this issue will not go away, and it is likely to be reopened often in the future. It pits people against each other in unusual ways. For example, relating benefits to income offers one way to substantially scale back the Medicare program for those who oppose the size of government. Indeed, an income-related premium for very high-income persons was proposed by the Bush administration in its fiscal 1993 budget submission (Office of the President 1992). On the other hand, some supporters of elderly and disabled people see this mechanism as a way to protect the most vulnerable, with perhaps no overall cut in the size of the program. The contradictory goals of these two groups make for strange political posturing.

CONCLUSIONS

The MCCA provided real benefits for a majority of older Americans and filled important gaps in the Medicare program. The simplification of Part A hospital benefits, the introduciton of drug and respite benefits (even if quite limited), and the major and underestimated increase in the skilled nursing benefit would have wrought improvements in the healthcare coverage of older persons. Even many of those who already had Medigap coverage were likely to benefit. But the full measure of these improvements was not communicated well to beneficiaries.

It is, however, too easy to simply argue that older persons were misinformed. In other areas, analysts and policymakers ignored information that should have signaled problems. For years, older persons have demonstrated how much they like and are satisfied with the private supplemental policies that have grown up around Medicare. Displacing coverage that these policies now provide was not popular, and analysts could have anticipated that fact. Further, we have long known that universal programs enjoy much greater popularity in the United States than do means-tested ones. But the MCCA moved to change that formula, not to achieve major new benefits but to add marginal ones. The dramatic shift in the financing of Medicare was meaningful beyond the dollar value of the burden of the supplemental premium—it was a course change for Medicare that alarmed and angered many senior citizens. Fair or not, this was resented by many— even by those older persons who would have paid low premiums.

The Catastrophic legislation also highlighted the dilemmas that will continue to face health policy in the 1990s. It offers four important lessons for the future. First, it is expensive to make even minor expansions in programs without large cost increases. Just adding $100 worth of new benefits means $3.4 billion in new costs, and these days, $100 buys relatively little healthcare. Second, individual's perception of the value of such benefits lags behind their costs, resulting in sticker shock on the part of consumers and taxpayers. The value of these benefits was discounted by Medicare enrollees, but in truth, the average taxes that had to be raised were equivalent to the costs of the benefits. Third, the use of a flat catastrophic cap is likely to be flawed. It is too expensive to make it low enough to help those with low and modest incomes, and not as generous as higher-income individuals could afford. But if the cap is lowered for everyone, it becomes very expensive. Low-income persons need more help than we feel we can afford for all beneficiaries. Fourth, recognition of the varying economic circumstances of Medicare beneficiaries creates challenges to find a means to adapt the program to the needs of those who are still vulnerable without undermining strong public support for Medicare.

But the repeal of the MCCA did not mean the end of changes in Medicare. The 1990s will continue to present many challenges for the program, challenges that can be faced intelligently only with knowledge of the lessons that the MCCA offers.

Notes

1. Gramm-Rudman-Hollings was an attempt by Congress to limit the size of the annual budget deficit and required across-the-board cutbacks in many federal programs if federal spending was projected to exceed certain targets.

2. Dealing with long-term care or the uninsured under age 65 would necessarily require large infusions of new public monies, so these areas were not seriously examined. The report did make some suggestions for expansion of private long-term care insurance.

3. The Pepper bill would have added a Part C to Medicare to cover supportive home care services under Medicare for both the current elderly and disabled population and for children under age 18. Congressman Pepper had also proposed to expand other services and to pay for these expansions with increased premiums and a higher limit on wages subject to the payroll tax (Varner 1987).

4. Not all these expanded benefits would go to the elderly and disabled populations; the MCCA also mandated some expansion in benefits for pregnant women and children.

5. Adjusted gross income (AGI) is a term used by the Internal Revenue Service for a particular line on the 1040 form. It is income after exemptions such as income from state and local bonds and the nontaxable portion of Social Security, but before deductions and personal exemptions.

6. Before passage, Medicare hospital benefits were defined around a spell-of-illness concept. For each spell of illness a beneficiary would have to pay the deductible, which could mean multiple payments in a given year. Moreover, benefits were limited to 60 days without any coinsurance. After that, coinsurance would be charged; after exhausting both the benefits within a spell of illness and the lifetime reserve days that could be added at the end of a spell, the beneficiary would be liable for all further hospital charges themselves. (This is discussed in more detail in the appendix at the end of this volume.)

7. Previously, the coinsurance rate was tied to the hospital deductible, and the amount was higher, on average, than the full daily cost in many areas of the country.

8. Balance billing was not affected by the legislation and would not have counted toward the cap.

9. This change in SNF use was likely more dramatic than was expected from most of the other changes, because SNF use had for so long been very constrained. But even though this was likely the exception, it seemed to indicate the explosive nature of the expansion.

10. Among such opponents were the Pharmaceutical Manufacturers Association and some seniors' groups, particularly the National Committee to Preserve Social Security and Medicare and several smaller groups sometimes funded by drug companies. These more formal groups helped to mobilize the opposition, and in some cases spread a considerable amount of misleading information.

11. This was a technical issue. Because the MCCA created a trust fund that would help the federal deficit in the early years while it was building up, repeal of the MCCA would have had the unusual impact of temporarily *increasing* the federal deficit. Without this OMB exception, to remain budget neutral, taxes would have had to be raised to fund repeal of the legislation.

12. Well over 90 percent of all dollars spent on Medicare represent benefit payments to enrollees. For private insurance, average Medigap benefit payments per dollar of premium can be as low as 50 percent or 60 percent and seldom rise much above 80 percent to 85 percent (U.S. General Accounting Office 1991b).

Chapter Six

MARGINAL CHANGES AND THE FUTURE

The decade of the 1990s is unlikely to be a period of business as usual for Medicare or the healthcare system in general. Many parts of the program work well, and Medicare is often cited as a model by supporters of national health insurance. But cries for reforms of all types swirl around the program. Some of these proposals advocate major restructuring of Medicare, often with an eye to fixing the fiscal problems that Part A will confront after the turn of the century or as part of broader health reform. These proposals are taken up, respectively, in chapters 7 and 8; the current chapter explores more marginal options for change that could be enacted in the absence of other reform in the healthcare system.

Because the 1980s lowered expectations about government, because the supporters of Medicare represent formidable foes, and because the Medicare program is basically sound, many of the criticisms leveled at the program seek only marginal change, stressing shifts in emphasis rather than wholesale rearrangement or dismantling of the program. Over the course of the next few years, various options to alter Medicare will be considered. The alternatives are often contradictory—aiming at either expansions or limitations. Some proposals are motivated by the budget deficit that dominated policy in the 1980s and is continuing to have an influence during the 1990s. Other proposals seek to modestly reshape the nature of the benefits or eligibility and require at least moderately increased financial support for the program. The following options represent those that are commonly debated and that merit special attention.

RESTRUCTURING COST SHARING

The combination of deductibles and coinsurance for Medicare represents an ad hoc collection of payments with little defensible justification as points of control for the use of healthcare services. When Medicare was introduced, the deductibles for Part A and Part B were set at nearly the same level: $40 and $50, respectively. But over time the Part A deductible has grown enormously—to $652 in 1992, compared to just $100 for Part B. Home health benefits required a coinsurance payment that was eliminated in 1973. Coinsurance amounts for skilled nursing facility (SNF) benefits, on the other hand, are now higher than the value of the benefit in many areas of the country. Thus, it makes sense to consider reshaping this cost sharing even if that is not tied to any larger effort to expand or contract the size of the Medicare program.

The goal of cost sharing is to provide cost awareness and thus give beneficiaries incentives to make careful use of services. But the importance of these incentives varies by type of healthcare service. In Medicare, the most likely areas for expanding cost sharing to achieve these goals are home health services and the Part B deductible. More and more enrollees exceed the Part B deductible each year, since it has not kept up with Part B spending. It could be raised to $200 or $250 per year and still be comparable to or lower than that often found in many private insurance plans. A second area for possible expansion would be home health, although that would be a more controversial proposal, since this is a benefit used by the very old and frail. After the coinsurance requirement for home health was eliminated, use of that benefit grew rapidly, particularly on the Part A side of Medicare (Kenney 1991). Some health analysts conclude that coinsurance might be a reasonable tool for moderating use of home health services.

On the other hand, just as some cost sharing might be raised, Medicare's hospital and SNF cost sharing is already quite high. If cost sharing is used as more than just a tool for passing on a greater share of the costs to beneficiaries, some rethinking of the cost sharing is also appropriate. In practice, few advocates of cost sharing argue that hospital deductibles or coinsurance are valuable for discouraging overuse of services. Patients rarely make the decision to check in to a hospital on their own. Moreover, there are other constraints on use of hospital care, such as preadmission screening, that serve to limit inappropriate use. And in the case of current coinsurance requirements for very long stays, hospitals themselves now have strong incentives to release their patients as early as possible because of incentives established by the Prospective Payment System (PPS). Consequently, hospital cost sharing could be substantially reduced with no expected increase in the use of services. In practice, however, hospital cost sharing requirements will save the federal government about $6.5 billion in 1992 by shifting costs onto beneficiaries and/or employers who help pay a share of retirees' health insurance (*Federal Register* 1991a).

Another area of high cost sharing is the coinsurance on skilled nursing facility services. As discussed earlier, by being tied to the hospital deductible that has risen so fast, SNF coinsurance is vastly out of line with the daily costs of such services. Coinsurance that exceeds the rate of reimbursement is too high and results in a benefit that appears to last 100 days, but which, for all practical purposes, loses its value to beneficiaries after just 20 days. Coinsurance on skilled nursing care will raise about $1 billion in 1992—and actually saves considerably more than that in federal dollars, since it discourages use of this Medicare service.

Restructuring this cost sharing could improve the Medicare program by shifting cost sharing to those areas where the incentives might be more effective, while simplifying the program. The reductions in cost sharing need to occur under Part A. If done in conjunction with an increase in cost sharing under Part B, the changes could be budget neutral overall. But this creates an issue within Medicare, since the two parts of the program are now financed separately. The simplest solution would be to merge Parts A and B and create a single trust fund—a proposal that has often been made for Medicare.[1]

A number of different combinations of cost sharing are possible that would remain revenue neutral (see table 6.1). Under each of the options described in the table, both the hospital coinsurance and the concept of a spell of illness would be eliminated. Beneficiaries would be covered for up to 365 days of hospital care. In each of these options, the SNF coinsurance would also be tied to the cost of SNF care; 20 percent coinsurance would be about $20 per day in 1992. Most of the variation occurs in how the two deductibles would change. The more the hospital deductible is reduced, the higher the Part B deductible would need to be to keep the changes budget neutral. Option 3 in the table also funds part of the reduced cost sharing with a premium increase. Option 4 assumes that the Part B deductible would take into account Part A cost sharing, so that no beneficiary would face a deductible greater than $600.

Each of these options would create different winners and losers. For example, option 4 in table 6.1 would mean that an individual with a hospital stay would only be subjected to a $200 deductible for Part B services ($600 minus $400); an individual without such a stay would not receive Medicare benefits until receiving over $600 in physician

Table 6.1 BUDGET NEUTRAL OPTIONS FOR RESTRUCTURING COST SHARING
OF MEDICARE

		Part A			Part B	
		Coinsurance				
Option	Hospital Deductible	Hospital	SNF	Home Health	Deductible	Monthly Premium
Current Law 1992	$652 for each spell of illness	$163 for days 61–90; $326 for days 91–150	$81.50 for days 21–100	None	$100	$31.80
1	$500 for no more than two stays/year	None	$20 for days 21–100	Current law	$350	Current law
2	$300 for first stay only	None	$20 for days 21–100	Current law	$500	Current law
3	$500 for first stay only	None	$20 for days 21–100	Current law	$250	$39
4	$400 for first stay only	None	$20 for days 21–100	Current law	$600, but Part A cost sharing counts toward cap	Current law

Source: Author's simulations using 1987 National Medical Expenditure Survey data
and Congressional Budget Office 1992.
Note: Table assumes changes are fully implemented in 1992.

and related services. These two individuals would face a considerably
different situation under option 1, for example. A beneficiary with a
hospital stay would prefer option 4 to the situation in option 1 in
which he or she would face a $500 liability for the hospital stay and
another $350 in physician services before Medicare began to pay. The
individual without the hospital stay would be better off under option
1, where he or she would be subject to only a $350 deductible.

COST-CONTAINMENT STRATEGIES

Since Medicare now constitutes nearly 9 percent of the federal budget
(Ways and Means 1991), it is likely to remain a target of budget reduction exercises for as long as the deficit remains a problem. As

stated earlier in this volume, each year of the Reagan and Bush administrations, the February budget submission to Congress has called for substantial cuts in Medicare. Even for fiscal year 1992 President Bush called for further cuts in Medicare of $2.3 billion, in addition to the five-year $43 billion reduction agreement reached just a few months earlier as part of the 1990 budget summit (Office of the President 1991).

Ironically, although many politicians talk as though Social Security were an untouchable item in the budget, they do not seem to hold the same fear of tinkering with Medicare. Why is this so? A major explanation rests with the claim that most of the cuts are aimed at provider payments, moves that generally are viewed sympathetically by the elderly and disabled and their interest groups. Indeed, a slogan of the American Association of Retired Persons about its approach to health-care policy has been "Cut the Costs, Keep the Care." Many beneficiaries believe that hospitals and doctors are well paid for their services and sympathize with the calls for further belt-tightening. The perception, then, is that cuts can be made without a direct reduction in benefits, as would be the case with Social Security, for example. But as was emphasized in chapter 4, the cuts in Medicare have by no means been confined to providers, and even when they have been, such changes can have repercussions for beneficiaries as well. As this becomes more apparent with further provider restrictions, cost-containment efforts may meet more opposition.

Medicare is also more of a target than Social Security because Medicare is rising so fast that even substantive reductions in the program still only help to slow its rate of growth. Thus, even rather large changes have not resulted in very visible cuts. Further, even apart from the rest of the budget, lawmakers may be concerned with the continued financial viability of the program, since Part A is scheduled to face a financing crisis early in the next century.

One can safely predict that there will be at least several more rounds of cost-containment activities directed at providers. Some of the emphasis for further cost containment may shift away from the patchwork patterns discussed in chapter 3, however. Later in the decade, as fewer options are available in provider payments, more emphasis will likely be placed on minor restructuring of Medicare to better target benefits on beneficiaries most in need of help.

Hospitals

Across-the-board cuts in payments to hospitals served as the most fruitful area for achieving Medicare savings in the 1980s. For example, hospital benefits absorbed the largest share of all Medicare payments—nearly 68 percent in 1980 (Ways and Means 1991). Thus, small changes yield big savings simply because of the size of the pot. Moreover, the careful scrutiny of hospitals surrounding the introduction of PPS highlighted the strong Medicare profit margins enjoyed by hospitals, on average (ProPAC 1991). Policymakers reasoned that hospitals could afford to absorb further cuts and that the reforms in place allowed hospitals to change their behavior and avoid at least some of the negative consequences of reduced payments; they simply needed to become more efficient.

To some degree, attitudes about hospitals' abilities to absorb further broad cuts has changed. First, hospitals have proven not to equally flourish under Medicare (ProPAC 1991), and as the controls have been tightened, some hospitals have become much more financially vulnerable. More hospitals each year are losing money on services to Medicare patients, with consequences that could certainly spill over to Medicare beneficiaries and other patients as well. The discrepancies between hospitals that thrive under this system and those who face financial distress have been increasing over time. Ultimately, this disturbs more than just hospitals: other payers complain that costs are shifted to them, beneficiaries become concerned that the quality of care will suffer, and communities, which see hospitals as important employers, fear a shrinking wage base if hospitals are forced to close or severely economize.

Nonetheless, hospitals are still where the money is, and it is easier to portray these institutions as bloated or inefficient than to make similar arguments for physicians or other small-scale providers. Individuals are often more sympathetic toward their own physicians.[2] Some investigators who monitor hospitals' response to PPS feel that hospitals have not moved far enough to introduce more efficient ways of providing services. Only further financial pressure would accomplish that. Thus, hospitals will still be a target of cost-containment efforts, but the 1980s strategy of instituting broad cuts while adding some special exemptions and protections is a patchwork approach at best that may not be sufficient in the future.

Several other approaches are possible. First, PPS could be modified, perhaps as described in chapter 3, to better capture legitimate differences in costs across hospitals. Thus far, PPS has been unable to adjust for enough of the legitimate differences in costs to ensure that all hospitals receive reasonable levels of payment. One possible change in PPS would therefore be to reflect each hospital's historical costs in the payment base, rather than relying so much on national averages. Another adjustment would be to better reflect the needs of patients served by hospitals, such as adding indicators to diagnosis-related groups (DRGs) to capture severity of illness or other social factors that increase costs to hospitals of providing care. If such efforts are successful, then the burdens of further cuts would be more fairly distributed and the savings would more likely come from hospital profits. It is easier to take a tough stance on payment levels if you can argue that the system treats all hospitals fairly.

However, these types of adjustments do not eliminate the potential problem of hospitals simply avoiding making major changes by passing costs onto other payers, such as private insurers. Hospitals are often able to charge private-pay patients a higher rate and thus avoid more drastic changes in the way they provide care. The only fully effective strategy to avoid that problem is a system where all payers play by the same rules. That issue is discussed in the context of broader reform in chapter 9.

Another way to limit the inequities of cuts in hospital payments would be to focus change not on all hospitals but on a smaller scale—limiting cuts to certain categories of hospitals or specific hospital services. For example, future cuts in the hospital area could target types of hospitals, such as teaching hospitals, that now show relatively high Medicare margins (ProPAC 1991). And, in this case, since the initial adjustment giving teaching hospitals extra protection was set arbitrarily, these hospitals are a likely target for future cost-containment efforts. Even within this category of hospitals, however, some are currently struggling, so the problems of negative impacts on certain financially distressed hospitals would not be totally avoided. Further, this type of limitation also implicitly limits the amount of savings that can be achieved for Medicare, because the base is so much smaller; major teaching hospitals account for only 16 percent of all PPS payments to hospitals (ProPAC 1991). Finally, this approach would add more adjustments to PPS, furthering a trend that is undermining the basic goal of standardizing payments across hospitals.

One component that will likely change in the very near future is the hospital outpatient department. This area is one in which Medicare continues to pay, at least in part, on the basis of costs. However, cuts in this area have been ad hoc and have resulted in a crazy-quilt payment policy. Congress has already instructed the Health Care Financing Administration (HCFA) to devise a prospective payment strategy, but that effort has been proceeding slowly (Sulvetta 1992). The rapid growth in this part of Medicare suggests that even if such a payment scheme begins in a revenue neutral fashion, it is likely to serve as a major target for cost cutting in the future. Outpatient services by hospitals must increasingly compete with other settings. Ambulatory surgery centers normally receive facility payments below those offered to hospitals. Services provided in physicians' offices do not even have a separate facility payment. Thus, there are alternative standards by which outpatient services can be judged that suggest that payment levels can be brought down substantially.

Medicare has also started to seek special contracts with a few providers for high-technology services, seeking efficiency in that way. For example, liver transplants will soon be reimbursed by Medicare only if they are provided in specific settings. Such concentration may not only be less costly but better for the patients. Outcomes from such procedures are generally better if performed by those who do a high volume of such procedures, rather than by physicians and hospitals that only occasionally perform the services (ProPAC 1990). This type of specialization seems a highly likely strategy for further applications in the future. It has the potential for offering cost containment that may also improve care—achieving the best of both worlds.

Critics of hospital cost cutting, largely the hospital industry itself, point out that the cuts since 1984 that have reduced the Medicare payment updates effectively serve to punish hospitals for achieving exactly what PPS sought to do: making profits by serving patients efficiently. When hospitals do well, the administration and Congress have felt confident in reducing the rate of increase in payments to hospitals. However, we have moved a long way in this direction already. Consequently, inpatient hospital payments are not likely to be as rich a source of future cost containment as in the 1980s.

Physicians

A different problem besets those who would target physicians for major cuts. Since physicians are the point of contact of most beneficiaries with the healthcare system and the quality of care received depends enormously on these providers, policymakers have been reluctant to aggressively cut physician payments. There is fear that physicians may react by declining to treat Medicare patients. Moreover, the over 600,000 doctors in the United States represent a potentially formidable political presence. And patients, although anxious to see costs of care fall, are often reluctant to take on their own physicians.

The new Medicare Fee Schedule (MFS), which began in 1992, has triggered opposition by physicians who now see the impacts the system will have on them. There is some evidence, although the numbers are still very small, that some physicians are cutting back on accepting Medicare patients (American Medical Association 1991). Physician groups were successful in 1991 in limiting the overall payment cuts proposed by HCFA as part of the transition to the new fee schedule.

Physicians may enjoy a respite from major cuts during the transition to the fee schedule. Nonetheless, for several reasons, the recent success of physicians in rolling back some of the cuts in the initial fees proposed by the Bush administration under the new payment reform system may prove only temporary. If growth continues at a rapid pace due to greater use of services, policymakers are likely to institute broad cuts in the fee updates similar to those that have already taken place for hospitals under the PPS.

Physicians are the second largest source of expenses in Medicare after hospitals. Growth in their services has occurred at an average annual rate of 14.2 percent per year from 1980 to 1989 (Ways and Means 1991). Further, threats of refusing to take Medicare patients will be difficult for many physicians to carry out since Medicare patients account for a substantial share of patient revenues. The American Medical Association (1991) recently reported that Medicare accounts for 26.7 percent of total revenues to physicians—although this proportion varies substantially across specialties. General practitioners and ophthalmalogists will likely find it difficult to turn away patients, whereas some other specialists such as orthopedists who now see few elderly patients are in a better position to do so. If Medicare's fee schedule is adopted by other payers, Medicare may not seem as out of line as is now the case, although payment by private providers will probably remain above that for Medicare at least for the time being.

Moreover, as the MFS is introduced, a number of opportunities will be presented for marginal changes and adjustments that can result in federal savings. When specific services are identified that are "out of line," further cuts will likely be made. It is also possible that if there is a future federal budget crisis, the transition will be made "asymmetrically," instituting the cuts but not the full increases in the fees.[3]

The Volume Performance Standards (VPS) provide another probable source for savings.[4] Although the VPS currently reflect a single national standard for two groups of services, surgery and nonsurgery, the legislation left room for the VPS to be applied instead to more disaggregated groups. Many believe that if the VPS were operated on a smaller scale, physicians could more effectively be held accountable for their behavior and hence be subjected to tougher standards. Physician specialty groups might be one type of disaggregation—one that is particularly amenable to combining volume controls. Policies to hold the line on particularly rapid growth in services in some specialties such as cardiovascular disease or gastroenterology become easier with a specialty-specific VPS. Stephen Zuckerman and John Holahan (1992) have recently argued for alternative VPS based on service targets that could more effectively achieve the same ends. This would allow more careful targeting of volume standards on services that are growing especially rapidly—an even greater targeting than relying on specialties. The authors would also use a geographic adjustment to allow for finer breaks in the standards.

Also likely are changes that might be considered as eliminating abuses. For instance, we can expect additional legislative efforts to reduce the financial ties across providers that create incentives to undertake tests and services. That is, there might be further crackdowns on physicians who have financial stakes in testing centers or hospitals where they are apt to refer patients. Efforts may also be made to check bills submitted by physicians to ensure that they are not charging inappropriately for two or more services at a time. These types of payment reviews are now used by some private insurers and may well be adopted for Medicare.

HMOs and Other Managed-Care Approaches

A favorite approach of the Reagan and Bush administrations has been to promote greater use of health maintenance organizations (HMOs) and other *managed-care* arrangements for Medicare beneficiaries. *Managed care* is one of the current buzzwords bandied about in the healthcare community that promises new sources of savings. Under Medicare, the traditional approach has been to contract with provider groups to put them at risk for delivering care to enrollees. Under HMO contracts, for example, Medicare pays the HMO a flat rate per enrollee based on their characteristics (the average annual per capita cost [AAPCC, as defined in the appendix to this volume]).

After considerable growth in enrollee participation in HMOs in the mid 1980s, growth in the number of new participants has slowed considerably. As of January 1, 1991, 1.2 million enrollees—or about 4 percent of all Medicare enrollees—were in risk-sharing situations (HCFA 1991, unpublished report).[5] As more of those turning 65 each year have had HMO coverage through their employers, there may be more enthusiasm for this type of arrangement among future enrollees. But it is not likely to dominate Medicare for the foreseeable future.

Moreover, we do not know how much has actually been saved to date from the HMOs. It may seem that Medicare "saves" 5 percent on each HMO participant because the capitated rate is set at 95 percent of the expected expenditure level. However, there has been considerable controversy concerning whether the AAPCC is drawn well enough to assure that these savings are in fact real. If, for example, the HMO can selectively attract enrollees who are healthier than average, or who have less propensity to use healthcare services, they may be skimming off enrollees who would never have cost Medicare the estimated expenditure level even if they remained in the regular fee-for-service part of Medicare. If that is the case, then Medicare would not actually be saving under this program. Indeed, an analysis of the Medicare HMO demonstrations found reason to be skeptical of savings claims for just these reasons (Langwell and Hadley 1989). If the best that can be achieved is a one-time 5 percent differential, after which expenditures rise at about the same rate as for all other enrollees in Medicare, this approach will not generate substantial savings over time, unless most beneficiaries enroll.[6]

Medicare could try to further stimulate the market for managed care, but since Medicare wants to use this mechanism to save revenues, it makes no sense to do so by offering an increase in the AAPCC to HMOs. What other inducement mechanisms are possible? Could Medicare instead form its own groups of preferred providers? This does not seem likely, since HCFA does not have the personnel or experience necessary to put together effective groups on local levels. It could move in the direction of encouraging less-formal arrangements where groups such as physicians affiliated with a hospital or other network agree to take some form of capitated payment. To date, the most successful managed-care plans have been staff model HMOs rather than these less-formal organizations.

One note of encouragement, however, is offered in a study by Welch (1991), who concluded that although the AAPCC formula has little cost-saving impact, HMOs have nonetheless served to decrease Medicare expenditures. Welch found that markets with large HMO shares lower the costs of care for everyone. If HMOs help change the norms for practice of medicine, they may be successful—and may only need to capture part of the market.

Effectiveness Studies

Traditionally, new procedures or surgeries are introduced with few careful trials or tests of their effectiveness. And even if the procedures are effective for some, they are diffused to various groups or uses that may be inappropriate. Spurred by findings that some procedures are performed inappropriately in a substantial minority of cases, interest in analyzing effectiveness has grown. Studies by the RAND Corporation that suggested that procedures performed inappropriately both endanger lives and raise costs have generated enthusiasm for what some see as a magic bullet: eliminate such procedures and achieve both improved quality and a reduction in healthcare costs (Brook et al. 1989). Accordingly, since 1990, Congress and the Bush administration have extended funding substantially in these areas, and the healthcare reform package offered by President Bush in the spring of 1992 suggested that effectiveness research could play a major role in cost containment. In my view, it is unlikely that the potential cost savings from eliminating unnecessary care will prove to be the magic bullet that will halt the spiraling growth in healthcare costs; however, effectiveness research is an area where current investment could still pay dividends over time. It can contribute to cost savings, but is unlikely to be sufficient on its own.

To fully utilize any findings, a number of other steps would also need to be taken. First, the results of effectiveness research must be widely disseminated. There is some encouraging evidence that when practitioners are aware that certain procedures are not desirable or effective, those procedures fall in volume. For example, as mentioned in chapter 4, recent evidence on Cesarean section for delivery of babies led to a decline in Cesarean births in the United States, but only after an education campaign (Myers and Gleicher 1988). This may be due to physicians' awareness and/or to the patients' awareness; in either case, the dissemination of information can change behavior.

Further, we need to increase our skepticism about the introduction of new treatments and new procedures without proper analysis of their effectiveness. Once treatments are in the mainstream of care, it becomes difficult to discourage their use. Again, economic incentives might be used to change behavior. Reimbursements under Medicare for new or experimental procedures could be lowered (or the cost share to patients raised) until their effectiveness had been determined. Technically, this is the rule. But this should apply not just to high-visibility activities such as transplants but to the use of less-dramatic procedures and treatments as well. Although established procedures that cannot be shown to be effective could be treated similarly, this more dramatic step would be impossible to take without a public mandate. Enticing doctors and patients to forego accepted procedures smacks of "rationing," and even when treatments can be shown to be ineffective, some Americans may resist being barred from trying them, especially when no alternative procedures are available.

Constraints of these sorts need to be systemwide before they will be truly effective; we cannot rely on Medicare and Medicaid to discipline the whole healthcare system. Bringing more people under a public system is one approach (see the discussion in chapter 9). Short of that, the government could exert some systemwide control, perhaps by making the deductibility of insurance dependent upon insurers adopting practice guidelines. True changes in attitudes will follow only if Americans are convinced that these controls represent good *health* policy rather than merely ways of holding down federal spending. Until we, as a society, begin to accept limits on what healthcare can accomplish, government standards and regulations will be unpopular and likely unsuccessful.

Cuts Directed at Beneficiaries

It is almost inevitable that some of the effort directed at cost containment will focus on requiring beneficiaries to pay more for their care. The rising well-being of the elderly, on average, contributes to the perception that enrollees have the means to contribute. Medicare continues to be a very good deal for the elderly and disabled populations, paying substantially larger benefits than the size of workers' lifetime contributions. Of course, this could be an argument for higher tax contributions by workers as well as beneficiary contributions.

The current trend toward annual limited changes in beneficiary liabilities may well continue. A small increase in the Part B deductible or premium of a few dollars per year only modestly expands the burden on individuals. And just $30 more per year from each enrollee would save the federal government about $1 billion. However, the cumulative effects of these changes over time will prove more burdensome to individuals, particularly since higher required premiums would come on top of the increases that occur automatically each year as a result of the growth of the cost of the program from greater inflation and increased use of services.

If the stakes are raised further and the goal is to save $5 billion or more each year, it becomes more difficult to seek across-the-board increases from beneficiaries. Implicitly or explicitly, relating these payments to income becomes a more important option as part of any increase in enrollee liability. Without differentiating across individuals by ability to contribute, the feasible level of cost savings is restricted to what the lowest-income groups can reasonably afford to pay. In that case, changes in beneficiary liabilities would remain a limited source of cost containment. (This issue is discussed further in an upcoming subsection.)

INCREASES IN COST SHARING AND PREMIUMS

Rather than just rearranging the cost sharing under Medicare, beneficiaries could be asked to pay more absolutely to help reduce federal spending on the program. This could be done through selective increases in cost sharing (recognizing the high levels already in place under Part A) or through a combination of lowering some required payments and raising others enough to result in net federal savings.

A cost-sharing package to increase enrollee contributions might raise the Part B deductible to $200 per year, and add a modest coinsurance premium of 5 percent of the average costs of a home health visit. Together these could raise about $2 billion per year in savings to Medicare (see table 6.2). These changes would place added burdens on beneficiaries, particularly the oldest and frailest who use home health and more physician visits.

To achieve about $2 billion in savings *and* concurrently restructure the cost sharing would result in considerably more-dramatic increases

Table 6.2 OPTIONS FOR RESTRUCTURING COST SHARING OF MEDICARE FOR ABOUT $2 BILLION IN FEDERAL SAVINGS

	Part A				Part B	
		Coinsurance				
Option	Hospital Deductible	Hospital	SNF	Home Health	Deductible	Monthly Premium
Current Law 1992	$652 for each spell of illness	$163 for days 61–90; $326 for days 91–150	$81.50 for days 21–100	None	$100	$31.80
1	Current law	Current law	Current law	5%	$200	Current law
2	$652 for no more than two stays/year	None	$40 for all days	20%	$350	Current law
3	$500 first stay only	None	$20 for all days	Current law	$300	$43

Source: Author's simulations using 1987 National Medical Expenditure Survey data and Congressional Budget Office 1992.
Note: Table assumes changes are fully implemented in 1992.

in Part B deductibles and premiums. That is, hospital cost sharing could be limited to the payment of no more than two deductibles per year and the coinsurance for SNF cut in half. To fund this, the Part B deductible would be raised to $300 and a 10 percent coinsurance charge could be added for home health visits. Alternatively, the deductible for Part A could be reduced to $500 and limited to only once per year. If all the increases were held to the Part B side, the deductible would need to be raised to $300 and the premium to $43 (see table 6.2).

These examples illustrate the conflict between improved cost-sharing policy and generating cost savings under Medicare. To both reduce Medicare expenditures and improve cost sharing, the Part B and home health changes would need to be even greater. Although a $200 deductible might be achievable in the current policy environment, a $400 or $500 deductible would likely evoke a substantial outcry. Certainly it would be treated as more than a marginal change. And further increases in cost sharing would substantially exacerbate the burdens facing low-income beneficiaries. At least this latter part of the problem could be assuaged with income-related changes.

INCOME-RELATED BENEFICIARY CONTRIBUTIONS

Income-relating Medicare premiums or cost sharing raises several problems. It runs counter to the arguments used in setting up Medicare over 25 years ago and runs a risk of undermining the very strong public support that continues for Medicare in a period of cynicism over the worth of government programs.

To some extent we have already moved to an income-related system with the Qualified Medicare Beneficiary (QMB) program, which was passed as part of the Medicare Catastrophic Coverage Act of 1988 and survived the repeal of the overall legislation. This program, managed through Medicaid, provides relief to very low-income Medicare beneficiaries by taking over their premium and cost-sharing liabilities. As yet, participation is not very high, and the program will likely continue to have problems reaching those it intends to serve (Families USA 1992). However, it does offer a rebuttal to those who argue that cost-sharing increases will hurt poor Medicare beneficiaries.

The QMB program is limited to those with incomes under 100 percent of poverty and will only be expanded (under current law) to those up to 120 percent of poverty, and then will only pay the Part B premium for persons between 100 percent and 120 percent of poverty. A single person at 150 percent of the poverty line had an income of $9,930 in 1991. That person is likely to be devoting about 15 percent of his or her income just to Medicare cost sharing—and a higher percentage for all healthcare spending—suggesting that relief further up the income scale is needed. In addition, the QMB is not a program that was welcomed by the states. As a mandated Medicaid benefit, it effectively competes for resources that might otherwise go to low-income younger families who also need further protections.[7] Expanding the QMB program for persons up to 150 percent or 200 percent of poverty would help the first issue, but further exacerbate the second. Moreover, a large share of the elderly have incomes in that range, so that such an improvement without offsetting increases in liability elsewhere would require a substantial contribution of new revenues.

Alternatively, both Medicare cost sharing in general and the level of QMB protection could be raised, increasing the amount that cost sharing could rise before it becomes too burdensome. In that case, it would be desirable to run the QMB program through Medicare, or at least increase substantially the federal contribution for this part of Medicaid to nearly 100 percent. The advantage of the latter effort is that it keeps the income-related portion in a separate program, and hence preserves the claim that Medicare is not means-tested. On the other hand, if the program became part of Medicare, the full costs of covering the elderly and disabled populations would be retained in the same program, and the balance between the level of aggregate cost sharing and the resulting burdens on those with low incomes who need further protection could be more directly maintained.

Another option would be to explicitly income relate either Medicare cost sharing or the Part B premium. This would be simplest to do with the premium that is charged of all enrollees (at least those not covered by the QMB program or standard Medicaid). Either the income tax system or the level of Social Security benefits received could be used to determine levels of payment.

For example, if the premium were graduated on the basis of the size of the Social Security benefit, the system would change little from the current mechanism in which people's payments are deducted from their Social Security checks. The premium could simply be set higher for those with higher benefits, or even be expressed as a proportion of Social Security benefits. Although likely a more progressive system than we have now, basing payment on Social Security benefits would still create a number of inequities. Persons with the same Social Security benefit levels may have different abilities to pay. One person might have a pension and substantial savings, whereas another might rely only on Social Security. There is certainly a correlation between Social Security benefits and income, but it is by no means a direct one. Although offering the great virtue of simplicity, this option would not be as "fair" as one tied to the income tax.

But, two adjustments could be made to improve the fairness of this approach. First, Social Security recipients have some choice over the size of their benefit, depending upon when they choose to retire. If the premium were to be substantial as a share of the benefit, it might affect beneficiaries' decisions about when to retire. Early retirement results in lower benefits, which might translate into lower premium charges as well. It makes sense to have a slightly different formula for early retirees versus those who retire on or after the full retirement date, with the lower rate assessed against those who remain in the labor force longer.[8]

The second complication arises from individuals who are quite well off but who have low Social Security benefit levels—often because they were covered by another system for much or all of their working life. A highly paid public-sector employee, for example, might be able to pay much more than the premium based on what is received just from Social Security. To reconcile that discrepancy, Medicare beneficiaries with high income tax liabilities and low Social Security benefits could be required to make an additional payment at income tax time.

The alternative, to use the income tax or some other mechanism for assessing more complete abilities to pay, would likely be fairer, but considerably more complicated. If an increased premium is only assessed against those with substantial incomes, it could be done through the income tax system with little further effort. But if a sliding scale is introduced that affects enrollees with modest incomes who do not now file the income tax, the paperwork burdens on individuals would increase. Since the income tax is already an unpopular mechanism in general and also bears the baggage of the failure of the MCCA, it may be a less politically desirable approach. Requiring individuals who now do not have to file to fill out forms for *modest* premium payments seems to be a "penalty well above the level of the crime." And creating a new administrative structure to oversee a new income-related premium would be cumbersome as well.[9]

Income-related cost sharing is even more complicated to introduce. If the payment is collected by the providers, then enrollees must not only reveal their economic status to qualify for the program but make it known to their physicians and hospitals as well. One alternative is to cumulate cost-sharing liabilities, much as is now done with credit card charges, and have the government bill the individual directly. This relieves the provider and the beneficiary of some of the paperwork and would keep the beneficiary's economic status confidential. (A proposal of this sort is discussed later in this chapter as an administrative improvement.)

This means, however, that the payment by the beneficiary is not made at point or time of service, but later. Critics of this approach argue that it eliminates the crucial deterrent effect of cost sharing, which is a major justification for relying on cost sharing; point-of-service payments relate the costs to the behavior. On the other hand, a quarterly statement detailing cost-sharing expenses might be sobering for many enrollees who lose track of how many physician visits and other services they have used. At a minimum, any *hospital* deductibles and coinsurance might be collected at some other time, since these charges are not likely to influence behavior.

If cost sharing is not to be assessed to change behavior, but only to require enrollees to pay more, it may make more sense to eliminate cost sharing and raise the premium (or add a new premium for Part A). Such a premium could more readily be income related. The new premium could be set to fully offset the hospital deductible and coinsurance, and perhaps to generate additional savings. Such savings could be part of the overall cost-containment effort or could be used to buy down the coinsurance on skilled nursing facility care, for example. This type of proposal combines the concept of income relating and changing the structure of cost sharing under Medicare. It also would combine a benefit that simplifies and reduces payments in a direct way with a less-popular increased contribution. Such an effort may help assuage opposition to greater contributions from beneficiaries.

MODEST BENEFIT EXPANSIONS

Even if Medicare's finances are deemed so precarious as to preclude adding major new benefits, a number of small changes could enhance the well-being of enrollees without adding undue fiscal burdens. Cost-sharing improvements or other minor expansions might be combined with some other, less-palatable cuts in the program. One of the important lessons of the MCCA, however, would be to not oversell such changes. If, on balance, the goal is cost savings, it would be dangerous policy to suggest that a package of changes is for "Medicare enhancement," for example. Enrollees are likely to be unforgiving if they believe they are being sold a bill of goods.

A major complaint by Medicare enrollees and now a familiar refrain about the healthcare system in general is the complexity of the program and the incomprehensible paperwork. Simplifications in the program's administration would likely be welcomed by many beneficiaries. Second, at a time when choice in the use of healthcare services is declining, greater flexibility in use of services may be important, particularly if it does not add to the costs. For example, expansion of the hospice program to make it a simpler and more readily available option could enhance patients' choices, at little additional cost. Third, some modest expansions might be enacted such as adding more preventive services. More certainty about coverage for such services might result both in better policy and in only moderate cost increases—and could be viewed as a simplification.[10] Each of these recommendations is discussed in turn in the subsections following.

Administrative Improvements and Simplifications

Improved administration presents a broad area for policy change that may run the gamut from simpler, clearer explanations of benefits and reimbursement to major reform in streamlining payment of providers. It is not always a case of reducing bureaucracy and costs, as is often the cry for administrative reform. Some areas need more attention, not less.

There is no reason why Medicare could not operate with a simple enrollment card, much like a bank credit card, to be presented at the time of service. The Medicare card could work similarly to credit cards that are now scanned at the store, with information sent over the telephone wires to a central clearing house. For Medicare, this process could verify eligibility and record the charges. Medicare would pay the provider and the beneficiary could receive a monthly or quarterly bill. In an even more sophisticated version, the bill could be sent to the enrollee only after the private supplemental share was also calculated. Indeed, in the fall of 1991, Secretary of Health and Human Services Louis Sullivan met with private insurers to urge them to develop just such a billing system based on uniform reporting forms. Medicare could take the lead in this activity.

Such a streamlined system could reduce providers' hassle and paperwork enormously. Medicare could pay the full amount of the allowed charge and deal directly with the patient, rather than the provider having to seek payment from two sources. Just as improved administrative simplicity might secure some goodwill from enrollees in the face of higher cost sharing, providers might be less opposed to future cuts in their payments if some of their overhead were also reduced in this way. Medicare would also be able to track and profile use of services on a patient-specific or provider-specific basis.

Opponents of such a system would likely be alarmed at the centralized nature of the billing and information responsibilities that would be required of government, thus raising important privacy issues. The system would also take cost sharing further away from the point of service, making it less of an immediate deterrent to use of services. But this also means that all Medicare enrollees would have access to care, even if they did not have resources to pay at the time of service. These two competing goals need to be balanced; the wisdom of moving in this direction also turns on whether other methods of containing costs are successful. Further, if we move to a system of income-relating cost sharing, such a billing mechanism is particularly crucial. Some additional expenditures would be required—at least during the transition to this new system.

However, better communication with providers and beneficiaries goes beyond billing service issues. Clearing up problems and getting simple answers to questions is often time-consuming under Medicare's current structure. In fact in 1991, the toll-free line for physicians to question Medicare regarding reimbursement problems or complaints was discontinued. The proposal of similarly disconnecting the consumer information lines was also discussed by the Bush administration as a budget-cutting measure. The emphasis on scrutinizing and often disallowing claims as part of cost containment means that the providers and patients who participate in Medicare must have the ability to appeal or at least obtain information about these activities. Educational efforts to help program participants understand the rules could result in better compliance. More, rather than less, effort needs to be devoted to these activities.

Finally, improved instructions and oversight of carriers and intermediaries could improve the consistency of access to Medicare benefits. The discretion given these entities in their interpretation of different regulations results in very strict adherence in some areas to restrictions and much looser enforcement in other areas. The recent lawsuits concerning home health and SNF services have brought attention and some relief in this regard, but problems remain. Very tight budgets on these carriers and intermediaries also lead to complaints by providers and enrollees seeking help or information. Again, modest budget expansion might improve services that could pay dividends in other areas.

Hospice Care and the Last Year of Life

High-technology, expensive care for the terminally ill often makes little sense. Yet Medicare policy still treats such care as the "standard," and programs such as hospice care as less important and out of the mainstream. Elevating the status of hospice care would not be a large undertaking in terms of dollars, but an important symbolic one.

To qualify for reimbursement under the hospice benefit, patients must have a doctor certify that the patient has less than six months to live. The program then requires beneficiaries to forgo active treatments; in return, it covers more home healthcare, some drugs, and other special services. But strict guidelines and low levels of reimbursement have discouraged many hospices from participating in Medicare. Such treatment makes hospices less available to patients and keeps them "stepchildren" of the Medicare program.

When added to Medicare, hospices were viewed as a benefit expansion, and therefore the rules were made restrictive enough to prevent them from costing additional federal monies. But such a rationale may prove penny-wise and pound-foolish over time. The view of hospices as a standard alternative to healthcare is one that advocates of deemphasizing high-tech care ought to espouse. But when Medicare restricts the role of hospices and limits their expansion, patients' attitudes are also likely to reflect this vision. Also, if beneficiaries cannot participate until very late in an illness, all other treatments are likely to have been exhausted and hospice may be an added service rather than an alternative.

The Medicare Catastrophic Coverage Act would have expanded hospice by eliminating the lifetime limit on the number of days that would be covered. The Congressional Budget Office (1988) estimated the cost for that policy change at just $1 million per year—certainly not a rampant expansion. Hospice care is not an "add-on" likely to attract people who would abuse it. Similarly, patients in need of hospice care are unlikely to enter the program too early; on the other hand, restrictive policies may dissuade patients from entering a hospice program at all, or they may delay entry if they fear that at some point benefits would be cut off if they are "unlucky" enough to live longer.

Eliminating the cost sharing now required under hospice care might also encourage further use. Even though such cost sharing is limited, it sends an important message about alternative treatments.

By treating hospice not only as a reasonable alternative but as one to be encouraged, attitudes about the use of life-prolonging technology might also be influenced. Further, if payments to facilities are too low to encourage participation, or restrictive, even patients desiring such care will find it unavailable. In particular, requirements that some services must be provided by unpaid volunteers may serve as a road-block for expanding hospice programs, although use of volunteers does facilitate community involvement.

Offering hospice or similar activities alongside other care in a hospital setting (a "quasi-hospice" approach) could put alternative treatments into the mainstream and alter attitudes of providers as well as patients. By providing such services in a more traditional setting, an individual would not be making such an absolute commitment to the type of care. It might also enable earlier participation by those who wish alternative care. Patients in a "low-tech" wing might receive more nursing and social services in place of the technology, for example. Deductibles and coinsurance might be waived for this type of hospital stay.

The bottom line is that if the patient's choice is to forego treatment that would likely do little to meaningfully prolong life, the patient ought to share in the savings that could be generated. Positive economic incentives of this sort might undermine the attitude of "why not try the treatment since there is no cost to me." A careful analysis of the potential costs of alternative, lower-tech care needs to be assessed against the possible savings from foregoing high technology. At a minimum, it makes little sense to restrict access to hospice care, and it may be a cost saving to promote it. Modest expenditures to expand the hospice program make good sense.

Preventive Services

Preventive services is another area for possible modest expansion. The first steps were taken in this direction in 1988 with the MCCA, and the mammography benefit was resurrected in the Omnibus Budget Reconciliation Act of 1990 (OBRA). In theory, at least, other preventive services that the elderly and disabled populations might seek are not covered by Medicare. In practice, physicians and patients often engage in a "modest conspiracy" to obtain coverage by indicating that the physician is investigating a problem, in which case many tests and physician visits are thereby covered. Consequently, expanding coverage for preventive services is unlikely to offer as much of an expansion as it seems at first. That means that costs would not rise as much, and also that one of the outcomes would simply be to treat all patients alike rather than rewarding those who are willing to game the system.

Support for preventive services is frequently offered on the grounds of long-term cost savings to society of identifying and treating diseases at early stages. Many preventive services may well fit into that category. On the other hand, some services may identify problems, but at a very large cost. This may result because the incidence of the disease is very small and savings from prevention or early treatment are therefore small compared to the costs of routinely screening all comers. Or, it may make more sense to cover only those with characteristics that make them more likely to be at risk. In other cases, we are more effective at screening than at treating certain problems. This, then, raises the dilemma of whether we should spend resources to identify diseases that we cannot effectively treat or for which there is no advantage for early detection. Thus, not all possible preventive services should be covered.

For those who are otherwise healthy, preventive services may be the only ones received during a year. Such enrollees are unlikely to surpass even the current $100 Part B deductible. Merely adding preventive services to the list of those eligible for reimbursement thus might not improve access to them. Moreover, raising the Part B deductible is likely to be particularly incompatible with the goal of increasing coverage of preventive services. One way around this might be to specifically exempt such services from the deductible and allow them to be reimbursed at 80 percent of the fee schedule. A yearly cap could be placed on one physician visit and miscellaneous qualifying tests up to some dollar amount, for example. This option could substantially add to Medicare costs unless it was adopted in conjunction with a higher Part B deductible.

CONCLUSIONS

Aside from whether or not any of the options described here for changing Medicare are ultimately enacted, on another level they are somewhat unsettling. The cost-containment strategies promise only small savings, not nearly enough to set the program on firm financial footing into the next century. Moreover, if any of the modest expansions were undertaken, cost-containment efforts might need to be undertaken just to "stay even." Many of these changes would improve the program in important ways, but they represent only a small step in reforming Medicare.

It is tempting to make only modest changes. The success and popularity of the Medicare program relates in no small measure to its stability. Wild swings in policy such as major restructuring efforts could undermine individuals' confidence in the program. And as was the case with the MCCA, the losers may be more vocal than the winners if these changes are designed to be relatively budget neutral. And, the implicit financial constraints on enacting even some of the very modest expansion efforts discussed here dampen enthusiasm for even needed changes.

Nonetheless, more substantive changes than those described here are needed. The options considered here do not generate sufficient savings to satisfy future needs for restricting the growth of Medicare, nor do they tackle some of the bigger gaps left in the program. But the success of all these options will no doubt hinge on what happens with systemwide healthcare reform. We should not wait for such broad reforms to consider options, but should assess changes in the context of likely systemwide developments.

Notes

1. This would mean that Part B would need to become a mandatory program, however, and would necessitate a number of other adjustments. Mingling the various sources of revenue used to support Medicare—the dedicated payroll tax for Part A and general revenues and premiums for Part B—creates opportunities and challenges for financing.

2. This may be changing as well, however. A recent poll has shown that Americans are increasingly blaming physicians as well as others in the healthcare system (Henry J. Kaiser Foundation 1992).

3. In effect, this was what was done in 1989 with the overpriced procedures (Ways and Means 1990).

4. As described in chapter 3, this part of the payment reform was a first attempt to control the rate of increase in Part B resulting from greater volume and intensity of services.

5. An additional 780,000 were in other types of prepaid contracts.

6. "One-time" savings may still have a substantial impact on spending over time. And if several are combined, the trend line in spending can at least appear to slow down.

7. Monies to support this program were supposed to come from savings to Medicaid from the MCCA expansions—but these were repealed in 1989.

8. The same goal could be achieved by calculating the formula against Social Security's primary insurance amount, which is calculated before the reduction for early retirement.

9. This approach makes more sense if it is used to help fund a more substantial benefit increase such as long-term care.

10. All of these improvements could be undertaken without increasing overall spending on Medicare by more than $1 billion—and in some cases even less than that. In addition, improvements in Part A cost sharing could be undertaken with no offsetting increases elsewhere. This possibility was discussed earlier.

Chapter Seven

REDUCING THE COST OF MEDICARE

Any discussion of major options to shape the future of Medicare necessitates a delicate balancing of conflicting goals and strategies. The challenges facing Medicare in the wake of rapidly rising health-care costs and an increasing population of older persons signal the need for major changes in the program. Minor tinkering will be insufficient to hold down the costs of the program as we move closer to the 21st century.

By the time the Part A trust fund is exhausted in 2002, outlays under Medicare are projected to exceed income from payroll taxes by over $50 billion (HI Trustees 1992). At that point, this shortfall would represent about one-fourth of all Part A spending. And although Part B's funding is technically assured through general revenue support, it too is growing at an alarming rate. To bring this discrepancy back into balance will require more than minor changes in taxes and/or spending. Taxes could be increased to cover the projected shortfall in Part A, but that would require a substantial increase by the turn of the century and more thereafter. Medicare actuaries project that expenditures under Part A of the program, expressed as a percentage of taxable payroll, will total about 3.8 percent in the year 2000, and then rise to almost 4.3 percent by the year 2005 (HI Trustees 1992). If payroll taxes were increased to cover this shortfall through that period, they would have to be raised substantially from the 1.45 percent each on employers and employees to over 2 percent from each—about a 40 percent increase in taxes. This would still not account for the general revenue increases that will be necessary under Part B, nor cover the very high expenditures projected much later in the 21st century.[1]

Many of the marginal changes intended to lower payments to providers or to induce them to be more efficient have already been tried. Further action limited to Medicare provider payments will yield lower savings than those achieved so far and, if used alone, will fall short of resolving Medicare's solvency problem. Thus, more dramatic changes in the Medicare program—ones that will affect beneficiaries directly—need to be seriously debated. Both Republicans and Democrats have begun to test the waters with the suggestion that entitlements will soon "have" to be reined in. Since Medicare has been the fastest growing entitlement and second only in size to Social Security, it is the most likely candidate from a budget perspective as well. Indeed, whenever policymakers discuss cutting entitlements, Medicare is certain to be on the list.

One way or another, any major changes will shift from an emphasis on cuts in payments to providers to proposals affecting enrollees more directly than ever before. These options can be divided into three areas:

☐ Shifting risks onto beneficiaries;
☐ Reducing coverage of services; and
☐ Limiting eligibility.

SHIFTING RISKS

Options for shifting risks would initially place new burdens on beneficiaries, but more significantly, they shift the risks of higher costs *over time*. These options allow the federal government to slow growth in costs but may not similarly protect beneficiaries. The federal government could simply provide beneficiaries with vouchers to purchase qualified private plans, or it could require beneficiaries to enroll in health maintenance organizations (HMOs) or similar capitated systems.

Vouchers

Advocates of a private approach to financing healthcare for Medicare enrollees argue for a system of vouchers in which eligible persons would be allowed to choose their own healthcare plan from among an array of private options. For example, individuals might be able to opt for larger deductibles or coinsurance in return for coverage of other services such as drugs or long-term care. Since many Medicare enrollees now choose to supplement Medicare with private insurance, this approach would allow them to combine the voucher with their own funds and buy one comprehensive plan. No longer would they have to worry about coordinating coverage between Medicare and their private supplemental plan. Moreover, persons with employer-provided supplemental coverage could remain in the healthcare plans they had as employees.

To the government, this option would have the appeal of enabling a predictable rate of growth in the program. For example, the federal government could set the vouchers to grow at the same rate of growth as the gross national product (GNP) or some other factor. But most important, such options are usually developed to achieve major cost savings. The "price" of offering choice to enrollees would likely be a voucher set at 90 percent or 95 percent of the current level of government spending per enrollee. And even more important, by placing a cap on the rate of growth of the benefit, vouchers effectively shift the risk to the private insurer and/or to the enrollee. If a plan is not successful in holding down costs and Medicare's contribution is fixed, the most likely response is to raise the supplemental contribution required of enrollees.

Over time, federal savings from such an approach might be sufficient to keep within the bounds of payroll contributions, but only if this approach allows Medicare to permanently lower the growth rate in spending by 2 to 3 percentage points from its current projected average growth of about 10 percent per year. That means a 20 percent to 30 percent decline in growth—an ambitious goal for any cost-containment strategy. Thus, unless private insurers could find ways to achieve such massive reductions, the likely consequence would be a shifting of the burden onto beneficiaries. Advocates of vouchers argue that consumer opposition to paying higher prices would force insurers to hold down costs. Opponents claim that both consumers and insurers would lack the clout to achieve such cost controls.

How successful is the private sector likely to be? First, private insurers will almost surely have higher administrative overhead costs than does Medicare. Insurers will need to advertise and promote their plans. They will face a smaller risk pool that may require them to make more conservative decisions regarding reserves and other protections against losses over time. These plans expect to return a profit to shareholders. All of these factors cumulate and work against private companies performing better than Medicare unless other reforms occur. At least in the Medicare program, the government's track record at efficiently providing services is quite good, with overhead two to three times less than that in the private market (CRS 1989).

On the other side of the ledger are the possibilities that private insurers may be able to devise new cost-containment schemes that will be more effective. They may be able to bargain for good prices and adapt to changing circumstances more readily than the public sector can. For example, new types of HMOs or preferred provider organizations (PPOs) could be established. Finally, by combining coverage of those services that Medicare now covers with other medical care such as preventive services, drugs, and long-term care, the private sector may be able to find better ways to package and deliver care.

The experience from private insurers for supplemental coverage or coverage of younger populations casts doubt on the latter arguments. Healthcare costs in programs under the purview of private insurers have grown as fast or faster than Medicare costs in the last half of the 1980s (Moon 1991c). Moreover, private insurers have focused their competitive energies on policies that are at odds with the well-being of society as a whole. Insurers often hold down costs by selecting the groups that they are willing to ensure. Policies to exclude individuals with preexisting conditions or to discriminate against whole classes of individuals who may be more expensive to cover limit the insurers' risks but result in major gaps in coverage. Further, strategies of seeking discounts from providers for one group relative to others also saves costs for some at the expense of others. Larger groups with more clout implicitly penalize others. These activities are not conducive to holding down healthcare costs to society, but simply to protecting one's own turf. (Pepper Commission 1990).

Regulation would be needed to require insurers to take all comers and to guard against problems of adverse selection in which one plan may be able to compete by choosing carefully what persons to cover. Achieving this goal may be difficult, particularly if some of the features that attract people to a voucher system are maintained. That is, if Medicare enrollees are free to supplement their vouchers to enhance coverage, insurers may find that those with the most to spend on certain types of supplemental coverage may be the best risks. Covering the "extras" such as private rooms and specialized nursing care may appeal to enrollees who are relatively healthy and well-off, as compared to enrollees attracted to a supplemental package that mainly offers coverage of prescription drugs or enrollees who can only afford the bare minimum package. The challenge would be to ensure that competition would truly be managed and not allowed to put beneficiaries at risk. Are proponents of competition willing to monitor it sufficiently to prevent these practices? A voucher system could allow the government to avoid making the tough calls.

Vouchers alone offer little in the way of guarantees for continued protection under Medicare. They are most appealing as a way to substantially cut the federal government's contributions to the plan indirectly through erosion of the comprehensiveness of coverage that the private sector offers rather than as stated policy. Leaving health-care to the vagaries of the marketplace especially in the absence of other reforms, would likely create more problems than solutions. Such an approach will only be successful if it is part of a systemwide move toward managed competition.

Capitated Care Options

Rather than creating vouchers that effectively put enrollees at risk, Medicare could move to a system of requiring managed-care arrangements. The program would still be operated and overseen by the federal government, so that the government could continue to share some of the risks. But enrollees could be required to operate within an HMO, an independent practice association (IPA), a preferred provider organization (PPO), or some other similar entity paid to offer healthcare on a per capita basis. All of these organizations seek to control costs by managing the overall level of care that the patient receives, moving away from a system that pays on a per service basis where the more you use, the more the provider makes.

In a well-managed, high-quality capitated system, the individual can receive much better continuity of care. Patient records and information can readily be shared within the organization, and services will be better coordinated. Physicians have no incentives to prescribe unnecessary tests or procedures, since that only adds to the costs of care. On the other hand, they also need to perform good diagnostic and preventive services to reduce use of the big ticket items such as hospitalization. Moreover, if Medicare performs its role as a careful overseer, any propensity to skimp on care can be reduced as well. And in such a system, payments would be made on the basis of the experience of the best providers, rather than locking into some fixed rate of growth.

Such systems mainly save on the costs of care by reducing use. This may reduce unnecessary care, but may also cut into important services. Consequently, such organizations often place a substantial burden on consumers to be aggressive advocates for their own care. The barriers to care that HMOs and others establish to discourage overuse may be intimidating, particularly for the very old or frail. It may be easier to establish barriers to use of services than to carefully manage care on a case-by-case basis. Further, the restrictions on choice implicit in such a system are viewed negatively by many.

Although HMOs generally have a reasonable track record in holding down costs, some critics argue that this is more of a one-shot advantage. HMOs are able to achieve a one-time drop in use when people first enroll, but then the general trend in cost growth looks much like that for the fee-for-service sector (Newhouse 1985). If that is the case, savings would not be large enough to "solve" the financing problems of Part A, for example.

Further, savings may be easier to achieve when HMOs represent a relatively small share of the market. If HMOs "change" the way that people use services only for those who are in agreement with the capitated philosophy and employ those physicians who also agree with that approach, reaching out to the broader population may be less successful. Once enrollment is no longer voluntary, both patients and individuals who do not agree with the philosophy may resist controls on the system. Rather than change the patients, the HMOs may respond to patients' demands, leading to smaller savings than that usually observed for HMOs with limited market penetration. On the other hand, if HMOs or similar organizations become the norm for our entire healthcare system, they might change patients' attitudes toward how much care is needed.

Medicare's experience with HMOs has certainly raised some concerns. Some HMOs have found it difficult to bring the elderly and disabled populations into their programs. They have not always been able to cover patients adequately with the average annual per capita cost (AAPCC) allocations. Those that have attracted seniors have sometimes done so selectively, casting doubt on whether they are truly saving costs (Langwell and Hadley 1989). There have been some notable crises in which HMOs have suddenly dropped Medicare enrollees because of such financial difficulties (U.S. Government Accounting Office 1991a). Further, the program has had difficulty determining a reasonable payment to make to HMOs for each enrollee.

On balance, the capitated care option may be chosen on grounds of modestly improved healthcare organization and modest cost containment. By itself, it is unlikely to solve Medicare's problem of rising costs.

REDUCING COVERAGE

If we cannot find ways to provide the same benefit package at substantially lower costs, we may turn instead to options for reducing covered services or the size of the subsidy under Medicare. This approach shifts costs, rather than trying to reform the way in which care is organized.

Restructuring the Medicare Program

Medicare could become the insurer of last resort—limiting itself to protecting against truly catastrophic expenses. This would expand Medicare in some areas but result in a net reduction in coverage overall. Medicare now provides relatively good protection at the "front end" of health spending, requiring only a small physician deductible and no coinsurance for the early days of a hospital stay. But unlike most private insurance, it offers no limits on the total liability that beneficiaries may incur from hospital, physician, and other Medicare-covered services. Moreover, the coinsurance burdens increase for those with longer stays in the hospital or skilled nursing facilities— just the opposite of how most health insurance plans operate. Thus, in theory, Medicare does not operate like "insurance," which ideally seeks to spread the small probability of large losses across a population. Instead, it operates more like a prepayment system for routine expenses, covering, for example, physician office visits (above $100 per year) for over 80 percent of all beneficiaries.

A modest way to rebalance the program is to eliminate hospital coinsurance and to increase the Part B deductible. But using restructuring to save the federal government $5 billion or more per year would require a much more dramatic change. This strategy was proposed by one of President Bush's healthcare advisors, but never turned into a formal proposal. For example, one form these proposals have taken would trigger Medicare benefits only after an elderly or disabled person (or his or her private insurer) spends more than, say, $50,000 on care (essentially a lifetime deductible). Alternatively, individuals could be required to meet an annual deductible of, say, $2,500 before Medicare coverage began. After that, Medicare would step in and pay all healthcare expenses. Up to that point, individuals would likely buy private insurance as they do now, but at much higher premiums.

Under some versions of this plan, enrollees would also receive long-term care coverage—an option discussed in more detail below. But this approach could also be used just as a budget reduction plan. In that case the initial deductible might be set lower, but less would be added in "back-end" protection. Consider the case where the goal is to reduce federal outlays by about $6 billion to $8 billion annually.

One approach would be to eliminate all Part A coinsurance (as a way to improve protection at the back end), add deductibles of $750 for Part A (to be assessed no more than once per year) and $1,000 for Part B, and offer some protection for those with lower incomes. Alternatively, the two deductibles could be combined into one deductible of perhaps $1,500.

Such attempts would aid the Medigap industry—indeed, an explicit goal of some proponents of this approach. But this would not lead to great improvements in the efficiency and simplicity of healthcare for the elderly and disabled populations. Private supplemental insurance has often been subject to abuse, and those who buy such coverage pay additional amounts for marketing and profits (U.S. Government Accounting Office 1991b). Private insurers lack the market power to enforce cost controls on the healthcare system. This could place Medicare enrollees in the same disadvantageous position that younger persons in small group markets now face.

This change in Medicare would likely lead to the perception by many beneficiaries that the program had been dismantled; it would operate more like reinsurance, backing up private-sector activities. If Medicare became "invisible" in this way, support for maintaining it could erode over time, and the contributions might be further limited.

The imbalance in Medicare's coverage in which stop-loss protection is lacking, has, of course, been widely noted and was the principle behind the Medicare Catastrophic Coverage Act of 1988 that lasted only one and a half years as law. This proposal would be like catastrophic coverage, but without any of the added benefits. Efforts to reopen this issue thus understandably make many policymakers nervous.

Substantial Increases in Medicare's Premium

A more direct approach would limit what Medicare will pay per capita. One likely way to do that is to require enrollees to pay a larger share of the costs. Currently under Medicare, an enrollee is required to pay a premium equal to about 25 percent of the costs of Part B. But since this part of Medicare constitutes only about 40.5 percent of total Medicare reimbursements, enrollees effectively pay a premium of about 10 percent of the value of the total Medicare benefits they receive. If that premium contribution were raised to cover 20 percent of total benefits—a figure comparable to that often proposed in healthcare reform options as individuals' contributions—the current premium would need to be doubled.[2] That is, in 1992, the premium would have had to be about $760 per year.

If applied to all beneficiaries, this would raise almost $13 billion in premium revenues. In practice, the net saving to the federal government would be less, since those below 110 percent of poverty—approximately 5 million beneficiaries—would be eligible for protection under the Qualified Medicare Beneficiaries (QMB) program. Net savings would likely be about $12 billion after accounting for the increased Medicaid burdens.[3]

This option would represent a dramatic departure from the current system, requiring Medicare enrollees to effectively pay some of the costs of Part A for the first time. Even if the premium technically remained only on Part B, the justification for the increase is implicitly based on the full range of Medicare benefits. Since Part A is now funded fully by payroll tax contributions by workers and their employers, this change would be a recognition that through the years enrollees have drawn out much more than was contributed on their behalf—and that they will continue to do so for some time to come. As was the case with the MCCA, many enrollees are likely to view this option as a change in the rules of the game, and to strongly oppose it.

Although modest increases in premium contributions, as discussed in the last chapter, could likely be absorbed by many Medicare beneficiaries without great difficulty, increasing reliance on this mechanism to "solve" a large portion of the financing problems for Medicare would necessitate use of an income-related premium. Without an income-related approach, the burden of the Part B premium would be very high on many enrollees. A single individual with an income at 150 percent of the poverty line (about $10,000 in annual income in 1992) would be paying 7.4 percent of his or her income just for the premium alone. Even at 200 percent of poverty, the premium would still command 5.5 percent of a beneficiary's income. When other costs of care from both Medicare cost sharing and noncovered services are added to this burden, most moderate-income Medicare enrollees would be *routinely* spending 15 percent to 20 percent of their incomes on healthcare—a figure that has been used as an example of an upper bound on spending for healthcare before it becomes "catastrophic" (Feder et al. 1987b).

A major expansion of the premium is more feasible if combined with protection for those with modest incomes—up to at least 200 percent of poverty and perhaps even higher. Exempting a large share of enrollees would reduce the federal savings, however, making it tempting to recoup the losses from those with high incomes. The approach that the MCCA used, which may be an example of what *not* to do, was to recoup *all* that was lost in low-income protections from those at the upper end of the income stream. But since there are more people with limited incomes than there are individuals in the upper-income brackets, the MCCA quickly became very burdensome at the top of the scale.

This option illustrates a potential way to generate budgetary savings, and the goal of having seniors contribute 20 percent of the costs is just that—a goal and not an absolute requirement. Consequently, the 20 percent could be used to justify a contribution from those who could afford it. A full offset for the subsidized enrollees is not necessary and is likely to be undesirable from this source. How high should it be? That is likely to be both a political and a practical issue.

The QMB protection (which fully exempts some beneficiaries from the premium) might be extended to those with incomes below 150 percent of poverty and then be gradually phased out. In that case, the premium would not reach the $760 until individuals' incomes approached, say, 250 percent of the poverty level. If so, this would require approximately half of all aged Medicare enrollees to pay at least 20 percent of the costs of their Medicare benefits (U.S. Bureau of Census 1991a). For those with the very highest income, the maximum premium might be set at $1,000 or $1,200, for example. This would be greater than the amount on middle-income enrollees, but not enough to be viewed as egregious.

This variation on the premium could raise about $7 billion (if fully instituted in 1992), making a substantial contribution to reducing Medicare spending. But it would push the problem of the affordability of healthcare ever higher up the income scale for the elderly and disabled. It would do little to lower the costs of care to society, instead just shifting them to the individuals themselves. Nonetheless, going at least partway down this path is consistent with the approaches being considered for broader reform.[4]

Some advocates of an income-related program would go even further, raising a combined Part A and B premium to cover as much as half the costs of Medicare. Here the justification is based on the improved economic status of the elderly since the program's inception and the perceived need to substantially scale back programs for the elderly. A 50 percent premium would have been roughly $1,900 in 1992. But at this level, it is most feasible to apply an income-related premium only at the top of the income scale. An income-related premium of this type might start at 30 percent of Medicare for persons above an expanded QMB level and rise to 50 percent at $40,000 in income. This would mean that the premium could be limited to no more than 5 percent of the individual's income.

Savings to Medicare would be higher under this option, since it would mean effectively a fourfold increase in premiums for those with the highest incomes. But this change would be strongly resisted by high-income seniors. A more modest start with income-related premiums would seem to have a greater chance of success.

Taxing the Value of Medicare Benefits

An alternative to raising premiums would be to treat Medicare benefits—all or in part—as income and subject to the federal personal income tax. If, for example, half of the average value of benefits were added to the incomes of elderly and disabled persons, these benefits would be subject to tax rates that would vary according to other income received. This would naturally result in a progressive tax on Medicare benefits. This is analogous to taxing Social Security, although it is more complicated because these benefits are received "in-kind" and are not traditionally viewed as income by the beneficiaries.

Not only would such a tax raise revenue to help fund the current program (or expansions in Medicare), but it would make beneficiaries more acutely aware of the "value" of Medicare benefits and their rate of growth over time. If a portion of benefits were taxed, but only for those whose incomes are above some threshold, mostly high-income beneficiaries would be affected.[5] This could satisfy many who are now concerned about providing universal benefits to elderly and disabled persons regardless of their economic circumstances, yet it would not remove higher-income groups from eligibility.

Even with a very high threshold, taxation of Social Security will raise about $6.2 billion in 1992 (Ways and Means 1992). Taxes as a percentage of benefits total 2 percent under Social Security's current taxing scheme. If the same approach were used in 1992 for Medicare, this would raise between $2 billion and $2.5 billion. Lowering the threshold would increase the amount that could be raised—but this reduces the progressivity of the tax. Options from the Congressional Budget Office (1992) indicate higher savings between $4.7 billion and $10 billion in 1994.

This option results in a substantial change in policy, and one that would add considerably to the complexity of the program while raising relatively small amounts for Medicare. Critics of this approach also argue that it is unfair to tax some in-kind benefits and not others.

Consistency would mean also taxing health benefits provided by employers—another controversial policy.

LIMITING ELIGIBILITY

The third element under the control of the federal government is who participates in the program. Reducing the number of beneficiaries could also generate substantial savings. But how to do this?

Increasing the Age of Eligibility

We could simply increase the initial age of eligibility for Medicare. One of the justifications for such a change—aside from the primary one of saving the system money—is that as the life expectancy of the population has increased, the normal age of retirement should also increase. And, as people live longer, they now receive Medicare benefits for a greater share of their lifetimes. Increasing the age of eligibility could bring this proportion back to the level anticipated in 1965. In fact, this approach has already been adopted for retirement benefits under Social Security. The Social Security amendments of 1983 established a schedule by which the age of eligibility for full Social Security cash benefits would increase over time from age 65 to age 67 (although not until the year 2022).

For Medicare, the transition would need to be more rapid than established in the 1983 amendments, since the financial crisis for Medicare will come sooner than that for Social Security. For example, age of eligibility could be increased by two months every year for a period of time. Alternatively, the phase-in could begin more slowly at first and then accelerate. But moving too rapidly also creates problems for people near retirement age or who have recently retired, and who have made their financial plans based on assumptions about the availability of Medicare coverage.

Raising the age of eligibility for Medicare would create problems. Not all Americans are equally healthy at age 65. Although life expectancy is increasing over time, the health of persons in each age range has not shown similar improvement (Poterba and Summers 1985). And whereas some Americans remain in the labor force or have generous retiree benefits at age 65, others struggle to make it to that age to qualify for Medicare. Many older persons who retire earlier or are moderately disabled at, say, age 62 or 63, are in poor health and are poor candidates for purchasing insurance on their own.

To make this option less burdensome on those individuals, Medicare could change in other ways, allowing for at least partial eligibility for all those aged 65 and above. This option could be analogous to early retirement under Social Security that is now available at age 62—an alternative that will be retained after the full retirement age rises, albeit with greater reductions in benefits. For example, full eligibility might be retained at age 65, but a higher premium charged to enrollees between the ages of 65 and 67. In that way, Medicare would be available for those who must retire early. If this is also combined with some low-income protections and phased in slowly, the objections of critics could be effectively addressed. The disadvantage of this more modest approach is that it limits and postpones savings to the federal government.

Age Rationing

Another option that would effectively restrict eligibility by age—but one unlikely to be enacted—is the proposition by Daniel Callahan (1987) that beyond a certain age, only palliative care should be offered. This means no heroic efforts to sustain life for persons above an age limit such as 75 or 80. Proposals for age rationing of healthcare stem from the economic arguments that we are spending too much on medical services and that something must be done beyond the usual tools of cost containment. And age is viewed as a proxy for determining who is not a good candidate for certain types of services.

However, age rationing of healthcare would not work. The problem of excessive use of medical care by the elderly is overstated. Moreover, the evidence does not support holding the elderly totally responsible for spending decisions. Adopting a cure such as age rationing may prove to be worse than the disease.

Who is responsible for the high costs of healthcare? For all types of care and for individuals of all age groups, use of healthcare services has risen dramatically over the last 20 years, although healthcare spending has grown faster per capita for the elderly than for other age groups (Meyer and Moon 1988). Studies of the growth of spending generally cite a number of contributing factors: healthcare price inflation, the aging of the population, technology, and a general increase in the number of services. Inappropriate use of health services and the impact of technology on spending in healthcare rate as the most logical areas for focusing attention. It has become fashionable to associate such expenditures with the last year of life. Are we devoting an increasing share of our health resources in vain attempts to forestall death—often through new technology? Certainly, few statistics sound as compelling as Lubitz and Prihoda's (1984) widely quoted finding that 28 percent of Medicare spending is concentrated on the 5 percent of enrollees in their last year of life. This finding and other similar ones are cited by those who believe that a key to controlling healthcare spending will be to limit spending on the very old.

But is such rationing a magic bullet that would reduce healthcare spending in the United States? A careful look at the data suggest that the answer is not nearly so simple. First, if technology is being used extensively in futile cases involving the very old, the share of resources devoted to healthcare in the last year of life should be rising. The evidence, however, does not support these claims. Anne Scitovsky (1984) pursued this question and found that high expenditures were not a new phenomenon; they certainly preceded the introduction of Medicare in 1965, for example. More recently, Lubitz (1990), updating the 1984 Lubitz and Prihoda study, found that between 1976 and 1985 (a period of enormous cost growth in healthcare), there was no increase in the share of Medicare resources going to those in the last year of life. The proportion of decedents increased slightly, but the proportion of Medicare dollars fell slightly.

Further disaggregation of Medicare data also reinforces this analysis. If we look first at expenditures by age in Medicare (figure 7.1), the familiar pattern of more spending on the very old emerges, seemingly supporting claims of disproportionate spending on this age group in hopes of sustaining their lives just a bit. But the data show exactly the opposite pattern by age for persons in their last year of life (figure 7.2). In this case, we spend considerably more on the 65 to 69 year olds than on those age 85 and older. Effectively more is spent on younger Medicare beneficiaries who are more likely to recover—a result consistent with reasonable healthcare policy. Since life expectancy at age 65 is now about 17 years, (U.S. Public Health Service 1990), spending on the younger old is not necessarily just cheating death for a few months but, rather, treating patients with many useful years left.

These findings suggest several things. First, physicians do not always know that death is imminent when making healthcare spending decisions. And since people die often after being ill or requiring medical treatment, it is only natural to see extraordinary spending on those who die (as well as on those who survive a major illness). The issue more appropriately is whether it appears that we disproportion-

Figure 7.1 MEDICARE SPENDING BY ALL ELDERLY BY AGE, 1986

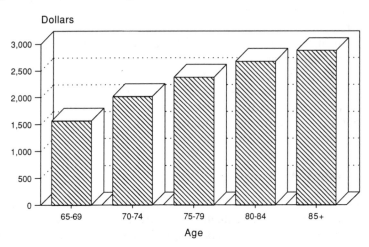

Source: Health Care Financing Administration (1990).

Figure 7.2 MEDICARE SPENDING BY DECEDENTS BY AGE, 1985

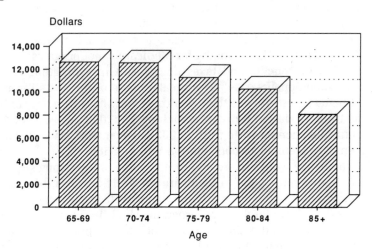

Source: Lubitz (1990).

ately spend on those with no chance of survival and whether that contributes substantially to the problem of the growth in healthcare spending. Here the evidence is much weaker. There does seem to be a drop-off in spending on the very old compared to the young in their last year of life, suggesting that, at least on average, decisions are being made to resist heavy acute-care expenditures.

Given these caveats, it is difficult to imagine how to design a reasonable policy that would save substantial dollars for the federal government. Age rationing is certainly not a magic bullet; indeed, it would likely prove to be a quagmire.

Means-Testing Medicare

A more feasible and equally dramatic alternative would be to fully means-test Medicare—that is, make it available only to persons whose resources are below some prescribed limit. This is the ultimate extension of income-related cost sharing. Higher-income elderly and disabled persons could be offered the option of either buying into the system at a nonsubsidized rate (such as is now done for persons over age 65 who are not eligible for Social Security benefits) or of being precluded from participating altogether. The former is likely to be the more desirable approach, however, since there might be savings to participants from the economies of scale and low administrative costs of Medicare, even if no formal federal subsidy is involved.

The main justification for moving in the direction of means testing would be for budgetary savings. Advocates of a means-tested approach also argue that Medicare is not a sufficiently progressive program, since everyone eligible has access to the same benefits. On the other hand, whereas the financing for Medicare is not progressive, the combination of benefits and taxes does result in a program where higher-income beneficiaries pay a greater share of the costs through payroll taxes assessed over their working lives. For example, contributions from a salaried individual making $100,000 per year totaled $2,900 in 1992, compared to the $20,000 per year worker whose combined employee-employer contribution will be $580.

Such a change would likely undermine some of the strong support that has traditionally gone to Medicare precisely because it is a universal program. It would constitute a major shift in philosophy from a universal to a "welfare"-based program. Medicare would no longer be viewed as a "middle class entitlement," and support would only be targeted on those most in need of services. As discussed in chapter 2, the drafters of the legislation were very cognizant of what they were doing when they stipulated that the program would include all of the elderly.

A major practical concern with such an option is where to set the cutoff for eliminating the federal subsidy. At what income is an elderly person capable of footing the bill for the full costs of Medicare? Consider 1990 levels of spending. In this case, the average Medicare subsidy was $3,230 and the enrollee's liability was $1,002 (Ways and Means 1991). Together this total of $4,232 would consume a substantial share of the income of most enrollees. And, at least for the elderly, Medicare out-of-pocket costs tend to represent about half of the total out-of-pocket liability they have each year. Other expenses such as prescription drugs also account for a substantial portion of their incomes. Thus, per capita liabilities just for acute care were about $5,000 in 1990. In that same year, median per capita income—that is, the income level for the average elderly person—was about $10,000. Certainly, at least half of the elderly would not be good candidates for paying for all their own care.

If policy were set so that the average expenditures on healthcare should not total more than 15 percent of an individual's income, the cutoff for eligibility for Medicare would be set at about $35,000. If the figure used instead were 12 percent, the income cutoff would rise to about $43,300. These levels would mean that very few elderly persons would be excluded from Medicare. In 1990, 7.2 percent of the elderly had per capita incomes in excess of $35,000 and only 4.3 percent had incomes in excess of $45,000 (U.S. Bureau of the Census 1992a).[6] Eliminating eligibility for those with incomes above $35,000 would likely save the federal government between $7 billion and $8 billion— about the same amount as the premium changes discussed earlier. To avoid the problem of an enormous "notch" where people just above an income cutoff receive nothing and people just below receive the full subsidy, a phaseout would be needed. For example, the subsidy could be reduced beginning with those whose incomes were $35,000 or more, and then eliminated at, say, $50,000. The subsequent federal savings would be substantially lower—totaling only $3 to 4 billion.

CONCLUSIONS

To achieve savings in excess of 10 percent of Medicare spending in any given year, several of the preceding options would need to be enacted. For the most part, each of the options described would save less than $10 billion if fully implemented (in 1992 dollars). With any political compromise, the amount of savings would be less. The resulting "moderate" versions of various options, as well as rough cost savings estimates, are summarized in table 7.1.[7] Not all are equally desirable, however.

To fully means-test Medicare is a less appealing approach than others, since it fundamentally alters the nature of the program. Unless adopted in its most draconian form, its savings would be limited. The same results, with less angst, could be achieved by increasing—and income relating—the Part B premium. These examples indicate the effects of varying stringency in income cutoffs, and show that means-

Table 7.1 OPTIONS FOR ACHIEVING MEDICARE SAVINGS

General Approach	Specifics	Approximate 1992 Savings[a] ($ billions)
Increasing Medicare premium	Raise premium (combined Parts A and B) on sliding scale reaching 20 percent of costs of Medicare. Premium would start at 10 percent of costs at 200 percent of poverty and rise to the maximum for persons with incomes over $40,000.	7
Restructuring to make Medicare more catastrophic	Eliminate Part A coinsurance and limit deductible to one per year ($750). Raise Part B deductible to $1,000. Increase QMB protection.	7
Limiting Medicare through vouchers or HMOs	Pay 95 percent of AAPCC toward costs of healthcare premiums. Beneficiaries would enroll in private plans and be at risk if costs grow over time.	5
Means-testing eligibility for Medicare	Restrict eligibility to persons with incomes below $50,000 (or charge premiums of 100 percent of cost). Phase out eligibility with higher premiums on those with incomes over $35,000.	4
Taxing the average value of Medicare benefits	Tax one-half of Medicare benefits for persons with incomes over $25,000 (and couples over $32,000) by adding to income subject to personal income tax.	3
Increasing the age of eligibility for Medicare	Raise eligibility by one month per year until eligibility age reaches 67.	0.4[b]

a. These rough estimates were extrapolated from data from the Congressional Budget Office 1992, the Health Care Financing Administration 1990, and the U.S. Bureau of the Census 1991a.

b. Savings would grow faster than other options over time, but would be small initially.

testing could raise *less* than the other options. Income relating the premium or taxing the value of the benefit reduces subsidies gradually, rather than simply eliminating them.

Raising the age of full eligibility for Medicare constitutes a reasonable approach, but it needs to be phased in over time. This makes it a less-than-satisfying option for those who wish to see large savings right away. Increasing the age of eligibility could be combined effectively with premium increases to achieve greater beneficiary-based savings. But a higher age of eligibility may come into conflict with other reform proposals (see chapter 9). It is also important to note that most of these savings to the federal government translate directly into higher costs on those required to pay them. These proposals, then, are not so much cost containment as cost shifting.

Just as there are advocates of doing less under Medicare, many supporters of the program would like to see it expanded, perhaps funded by some of the reductions described here. These proposals for expansion are the subject of the next chapter.

Notes

1. Actually, it is probably not useful to focus on the figures after about the year 2010. If we do not find ways by then to hold down healthcare costs for everyone, a major crisis of greater proportion than that faced by Medicare will be under way.

2. If such a policy were adopted, it would make sense to combine the two parts of Medicare and require participation in Part B. This could also ease some of the pressure on the Part A trust fund.

3. Some of the increased Medicaid burdens would be borne by the states, unless the Qualified Medicare Beneficiaries (QMB) program were to be shifted to Medicare. In that case, only about $11 billion would be saved. This option is discussed in chapter 8.

4. One important difference, however, is that 20 percent of the costs of care for elderly and disabled persons is a substantially greater dollar amount than the same proportion for younger families. Consequently, an argument could be made for using a lower percentage in setting the premium.

5. Again, this is comparable to how Social Security is now treated in the tax code. In that case, the thresholds are $25,000 for single individuals and $32,000 for couples. These thresholds limit substantially the number of elderly and disabled persons who are taxed on their Social Security benefits.

6. Options to eliminate Medicare for the very well off are effectively symbolic gestures that save little, at least initially. For example, just 2 percent of households with the head over age 65 have incomes above $100,000 (U.S. Bureau of the Census 1991a).

7. The only option missing is that of age rationing, which would not raise sufficient funds to justify such a controversial cost-containment approach.

Chapter Eight

EXPANDING MEDICARE

Unmet needs for services now excluded by Medicare can only be accommodated by substantial increases in spending. In the current environment, where the costs of healthcare are very high and over 33 million persons are covered by Medicare, even relatively minor expansions of the program implicitly become major options for change—particularly if the overall goal for Medicare is to grow less rapidly in the future. To slow the growth in Medicare and at the same time absorb the costs of an additional $5 or $6 billion in expansions would be a formidable task.

Nonetheless, proponents of expanding Medicare can make a strong case that there are gaps that could be filled in to better serve beneficiaries. But even the most ardent supporters of such change generally temper their options with modifications that result in less than fully comprehensive expansions. Incremental improvements are more likely to be sought in today's environment, by limiting the types of new benefits or eligible enrollees, or requiring offsetting changes elsewhere in the program. These options cover both acute- and long-term care concerns.

IMPROVING ACUTE CARE

Despite the concerns about the cost of Medicare and the fiscal crisis ahead for Part A, there remains serious discussion about expanding Medicare's coverage and eligibility. The possibility of adding coverage of prescription drugs was discussed at the time of Medicare's passage, was included in the Medicare Catastrophic Coverage Act of 1988 (MCCA), and remains on the wish list of groups such as the American Association of Retired Persons. Further, there are as many advocates for reducing the eligible age to 62 as there are for raising the age of eligibility for Medicare benefits from 65 to 67. Some also seek to expand eligibility to newly disabled persons, who must now wait 29 months to receive Medicare. And on an even broader scale, some reformers push to expand Medicare to include children, or the population as a whole.

Moving an Expanded QMB Program to Medicare

The Qualified Medicare Beneficiary (QMB) program was established as part of the Medicaid program in the Medicare Catastrophic Coverage Act and was one of the few elements retained after repeal. Its goal was to extend protection for low-income Medicare enrollees against the costs of Medicare's cost-sharing and premium liabilities. Medicaid has traditionally reached only about half of the elderly poor. The MCCA required that everyone up to the poverty line receive at least the fill-in protection for Medicare-covered services.[1] Funding for states to meet these new responsibilities was to come from a shifting of costs from traditional Medicaid beneficiaries to Medicare as a result of the expanded coverage under the MCCA. But when the Medicare portions of MCCA were repealed, state Medicaid programs were left with increased responsibilities but no offsetting decrease in demands elsewhere.

Particularly during the recession of the early 1990s, some states found these new responsibilities to be burdensome, and argued that they were thus forced to underserve other important groups such as mothers and children. Perhaps because of the resistance of states, the QMB program got off to a slow start, with low enrollments by eligible Medicare beneficiaries.

One option for addressing the issue of pressures on Medicaid from the QMB program and for extending relief up the income scale would be to shift it formally into the Medicare program. This could provide important relief to Medicaid, and would make it more difficult for Medicare to shift future burdens of healthcare for the elderly and disabled onto that program. It also would make Medicare responsible for all acute healthcare for elderly and disabled persons, reducing fragmentation and confusion. As part of the Medicare program, it might be easier to raise the participation rates and ensure that low-income persons receive protection against cost-sharing burdens. Moreover, at current levels of cost-sharing, protection probably needs to be set higher than 120 percent of poverty. This is particularly important as other changes to increase premiums and cost sharing are debated in the future.

Since Medicaid is partially state funded, it is tempting to shift costs away from Medicare using this mechanism. Moving the QMB program formally into Medicare would raise federal costs just to maintain the existing level of effort. Costs would also likely rise if rates of participation increased as well. One recent study estimated that as many as 2 million beneficiaries were eligible but not participating in the QMB program (Families USA 1992).

Adding Stop-Loss Protection

One of the areas of greatest concern to health policy professionals in assessing the quality of health insurance is whether it offers good stop-loss protection—that is, the guarantee that above a certain threshold, the individual should not have to continue to pay out-of-pocket for Medicare-covered services. This is one of Medicare's greatest weaknesses; there is no limit on the amount of cost sharing that beneficiaries are theoretically liable to pay.

Ironically, however, this is not likely to be the greatest concern of many beneficiaries. Traditionally, Medicare enrollees have been more concerned about choosing supplemental policies on the basis of first-dollar and not last-dollar coverage. Further, objections to the MCCA were that the benefits were not the ones most desired or valued by enrollees. Nonetheless, adding good stop-loss protection to Medicare would be an important improvement in the program.[2]

A proposal to limit liability on the Part A side was already described in chapter 6, and was combined with an option to finance it. If a cap on Part B services were added to the Part A improvements of eliminating the coinsurance, covering all hospital care for up to a year, and limiting the deductible to one per year, the cost of the two components would rise dramatically, however. These benefits, which were part of the MCCA, were estimated by the Congressional Budget Office (1988) to cost $5.7 billion in 1992.[3] In this case, the Part B cap would have been set at about $1,700 per enrollee in 1992. The net increase in spending would be less today, however, because, at least in theory, the QMB program now provides stop loss for those with the lowest incomes. That means that about 10 percent to 12 percent of Medicare enrollees now have this protection, reducing the costs of the program by a similar proportion. That still means that federal outlays would rise by about $5 billion.

These relatively expensive benefits were, of course, part of the package that many elderly and disabled persons opposed. Moreover, even at this level of expense, the protections are not very generous for low-

and moderate-income beneficiaries who are above the QMB protection levels, but who would still find out-of-pocket expenses of up to $2,300 catastrophic (Feder et al. 1987b). Since higher-income beneficiaries are the ones who opposed these protections as unnecessary, a limited alternative would be to simply move the QMB program higher up the income scale.

Expanding Eligibility for Medicare

The two groups most closely related to existing Medicare beneficiaries are early retirees between the ages of 62 and 65 and newly disabled individuals who have qualified for Social Security but must now wait another 24 months to receive Medicare. Both these groups receive Social Security, and in that sense are recognized as needing public support. And both may have special healthcare needs that render private insurance either expensive or unavailable at any cost.

Persons Aged 62 to 65

Most Americans under the age of 65 receive their health insurance through the workplace. But workers aged 62 to 64 are less likely to have such coverage, and those who retire before age 65 are at additional risk of being uninsured. Many of these individuals and their families live on modest incomes and may not receive retirement benefits from former employers. In 1988, 10.2 percent of all persons aged 62 to 64 had no insurance from any source, and another 16.9 percent relied on private, nonemployer coverage.[4] Women are disproportionately likely to have no insurance (10.9 percent) or to have only nonemployer coverage (20.1 percent) (Moon 1991a).

This age group may get some relief from legislation passed in 1985 to require employers to allow employees who leave the firm or dependents who have a change in status (such as a divorce or being widowed) the option of buying into the group health plan (referred to as "COBRA protections"). There are limits on how long persons can keep such coverage, ranging from 18 to 36 months. But most important, even when available, these benefits may be too expensive for departing workers, who must pay the full costs of the coverage. Survey data from the Health Insurance Association of America indicate the average monthly premium for a conventional group plan was $148 for individuals and $319 for families in 1990 (Sullivan and Rice 1991). Employees eligible for COBRA protections would have to pay 102 percent of these costs.

Privately purchased nongroup coverage is usually more expensive than group plans. People aged 62 to 65 have substantially higher health expenditures on average than younger families and individuals, and the cost of individually purchased policies normally varies by age. Thus, if nongroup insurance is experience rated, costs to early retirees for individual coverage could be $250 to $350 per month. Affordability issues can thus extend to families with incomes well above the official poverty thresholds. And individual nongroup insurance is not just expensive, it also often excludes coverage for preexisting conditions for a period of time (for example, a year or in some cases indefinitely).

Several different groups of Americans in their early 60s are particularly at risk.[5] A majority of early retirees have little choice in the timing of retirement and receive neither pensions nor good health benefits. These individuals may have faced a period of unemployment before deciding to take reduced Social Security benefits, or they may have health problems that make continuing in their current jobs untenable. They may have had only sporadic periods of employment or have worked in jobs without insurance. For involuntary early retirees, Social Security benefits will be less than if they had postponed retirement. They are also likely to lack private pension coverage, further limiting their retirement incomes. In 1988, over one-third of all early retirees had benefits of less than $350 per month (U.S. Social Security Administration 1991).

DISABLED PERSONS

Persons who qualify for Social Security disability must still wait for 24 months to obtain eligibility for Medicare. During that waiting period, the lucky ones may have private coverage or be eligible for Medicaid. COBRA protections, for example, are guaranteed not to run out during the waiting period. But for those who do not have access to COBRA or other group insurance, finding insurers who will cover a totally and permanently disabled person may be difficult indeed. Almost by definition, such individuals will have important preexisting conditions that may preclude them from buying coverage or from getting insurance to cover their problems. Experience from Medicare indicates that such individuals have very high levels of health expenditures.

Further, disabled individuals tend to have low incomes; to qualify for Social Security they must be unable to work, so unless other family members work, Social Security benefits may be the main source of income for many disabled persons. Median monthly Social Security benefits for older disabled workers (aged 55 to 64) were $558 in 1985 and represented over half of the income received by typical recipient families. Consequently, elimination of the waiting period for Medicare would relieve these individuals of an important burden.

EXPANDING COVERAGE TO THESE GROUPS

Medicare is potentially a logical source of coverage for disabled and older Americans who are without employer-based coverage. Early retirees, spouses of Social Security beneficiaries, and recently disabled persons have much in common with current Medicare beneficiaries. Health expenditures for 60- to 64-year-olds look much like those for 65- to 69-year-olds, for example. And newly disabled persons would likely have health expenses comparable to long-term disabled persons. Thus, the needs of these groups are quite similar to those of current beneficiaries. Moreover, the rationale for coverage is much the same: these are people outside the mainstream of employer-covered insurance who will ultimately receive Medicare coverage. It makes sense to create a reasonable transition to Medicare benefits for these persons.

Options to extend coverage could require either a full or partial premium contribution by individuals. At one extreme, if individuals were required to pay the full actuarial value of the coverage, not only would the number of people being helped be limited, but such a policy could create problems of adverse selection. Medicare coverage would undoubtedly be less expensive than individual coverage, given Medicare's low administrative costs. Moreover, for those who have health problems and cannot get reasonable coverage, this proposal would be particularly helpful. However, persons who would buy in to Medicare under this type of proposal would likely represent a more expensive group to insure than many employee groups. Not only are they older than average employee groups, but this option would likely attract high-risk persons, further raising the actuarial costs. For many, COBRA options, if available, would be more desirable, leading to further adverse selection of the Medicare buy-in group.

At a minimum, it thus makes sense to offer some subsidy to those who buy in to limit the adverse selection problem and ensure that the public option will be at least as affordable as many employers' group premiums. A limited subsidy starting at age 62 and extending to, say, age 67 would be consistent with the new structure of Social Security. Federal savings from raising the age of full eligibility might be used to help finance this liberalization for those under age 65. But a limited subsidy would not be sufficient if affordability is the major problem.

Without substantial subsidies, many of the poorest members of this group will continue to find insurance unaffordable. And most disabled persons would not be able to afford coverage unless it were generously subsidized. Thus, the members of this group most at risk would likely still be uninsured.

On the other hand, a very generous subsidy creates other problems. If it induces those who now have insurance to turn instead to Medicare, increased coverage for the group that needs help will come at the expense of also insuring many who now have reasonable coverage. Employers who now offer coverage may decline to do so in the future if the Medicare option is available. Relatively well-off early retirees may prefer subsidized Medicare coverage.

These expansions of Medicare make most sense in the context of broader health reform. For example, if reforms call for mandated employer participation in offering insurance, relieving them of the burdens of older and disabled workers could help hold down the costs of coverage.

Adding Prescription Drug Benefit to Medicare

The major uncovered service on the acute-care side is prescription drugs, which are covered only if administered to patients in a hospital or nursing home. In all other cases, regardless of how essential the drugs are to a patient's course of treatment, Medicare does not pay. This lack of coverage is one area where Medicare coverage remains substantially less comprehensive than the standard policies available for most Americans through their employers.

Many, but not all, elderly persons who have Medigap coverage are able to get private supplemental insurance for drugs. Often the best drug benefits are available to the relatively well-off elderly who have retiree coverage that brings their insurance up to the level of what was available when they were working (NCHSR 1989). Plans purchased directly by the elderly may offer drug benefits, but usually at a premium. Such coverage is inherently expensive, since the elderly are disproportionately large consumers of drugs. Moreover, prescription drug coverage is also often sought by those who know they need it, creating additional pressures on price from adverse selection.

In addition, some states offer special drug programs for low-income elderly persons that help fill in some of the coverage gaps. These are in addition to the drug benefits provided through the regular Medicaid program (all but two states offer drugs under Medicaid) (Soumerai and Ross-Degnan 1990).

Lack of coverage for prescription drugs can actually raise the costs of Medicare-covered services. If individuals do not fill their prescriptions or cut back on the amount they take, conditions may worsen for them and lead to more acute problems that require hospitalization and additional medical expenses. For example, one recent study on a Medicaid program that limited prescriptions for enrollees found that such a policy resulted in additional admissions to long-term care facilities and ultimately much higher costs than if all the necessary drugs had been available (Soumerai et al. 1991). In those cases, not covering drugs certainly constitutes a penny-wise but pound-foolish policy.

Adding prescription drug coverage to Medicare would substantially raise overall costs to the federal government. Many individuals now are able to pay for their prescriptions, so any savings in avoiding complications from not taking drugs will certainly not be sufficient to account for making that coverage available to everyone. The prescription drug program that would have been available under the MCCA would have been quite expensive. The final estimates for the drug benefit were $2.2 billion in 1991, despite a $600 deductible and 50 percent coinsurance (Congressional Budget Office 1989a). In 1992, that number was projected to double to $4.4 billion (with 40 percent coinsurance and a $652 deductible). Reducing the deductible or coinsurance would further increase the annual costs.

ADDING LONG-TERM CARE

The hardships that the costs of long-term care impose on individuals and their families can be staggering. It is hardly surprising, then, that the strongest candidate for expansion of Medicare in the eyes of the beneficiaries is long-term care.[6]

Medicare began as an acute-care program and as yet covers very few of the long-term care needs of the population over age 65. Periodically, groups concerned about the elderly and disabled populations note the inadequacies of Medicaid, which is the primary public source of support for long-term care, and call for Medicare to offer a broader benefits package in this area. However, proposals to expand long-term care coverage through Medicare tend to be very expensive. If coverage were to be provided under the same terms—universal coverage only partially paid for by the recipients themselves—costs might range as high as $60 billion. Thus, a full-fledged long-term care plan could be nearly as large as the existing acute-care program.

At present, long-term care is funded mainly by Medicaid, individuals, and their families. Medicaid provides mostly nursing home coverage, with eligibility limited to individuals who have spent down their income and assets to very low levels.[7] It essentially offers protection after the catastrophe has already occurred. Middle-income people benefit from the program, but only once they have already devoted most of their resources to paying for care. Medicaid has been characterized as insurance where the deductible is your lifetime savings and the coinsurance is your annual income. For most American families, this represents a very unpalatable option.

It also makes little sense for individuals to rely only on their savings to meet long-term care needs. Not everyone will require such care, but when they do it can be very expensive. In a sense, this is the perfect "insurable" event, in which the risks ought to be shared across a large group. But the private sector has been slow to develop such insurance policies, despite a well-demonstrated need.

Why can't individuals simply seek long-term care insurance products through the private market? Insurers are understandably cautious about marketing products where the liabilities will not be known for many years. This conservativeness, combined with the costs of marketing and selling to a largely nongroup market, may make the price too high for many persons aged 65 and over.

Further, private insurers often offer coverage only to individuals in good health at the time of enrollment. In addition to current disability, individuals with hypertension, arthritis, any history of heart disease, diabetes, or recent hospitalizations may be screened out. As yet, there is little evidence that such factors are actually good indicators of later need for long-term care, but, nonetheless, individuals with such medical histories are unlikely to be able to purchase individual long-term care insurance policies.

In addition to a comprehensive social insurance approach, a range of options are possible that would limit overall public costs. Only some services might be covered, such as home healthcare, while leaving nursing home coverage under the Medicaid program. Alternatively, coverage could be broad, but limited in scope to only lower-income Medicare enrollees. Or, long-term care services could be added, but in exchange for reduced benefits on the acute-care side. Over a longer time frame, long-term care services could be added as an insurance benefit with only modestly subsidized premiums—although this approach is less compatible with the rest of Medicare. Finally, any or all of these programs could be made optional.

Comprehensive Long-Term Care Coverage

In the aggregate, the financial resources required to provide long-term care services to all those in need sobers even the most sympathetic legislators. In an era of fiscal austerity and concern over reducing the federal budget deficit, enacting a public, comprehensive long-term care system is often viewed as a goal beyond our collective means. Nevertheless, there is considerable public support, backed by reasonable arguments, to move in that direction. National polls indicate that the American public strongly favors a universal, public-sector approach to solving the problem of long-term care (Moon 1989). In addition, even strong advocates of private "solutions" to the problem recognize that there will always be gaps and unmet need. A comprehensive approach, which by definition is universal is seen by many as offering the best possibility of achieving: 1) equitable treatment for those in need, 2) control over administrative costs, and 3) the orderly development of a reasonable delivery system.

Society as a whole is now bearing much of the cost of long-term care, but in ways that place enormous burdens on a few. Some of these are very visible costs: the $22 billion that Medicaid spends on long-term care each year, and the even larger amount that individuals and families pay. There are also invisible costs in the sacrifices that families make and in the unmet needs that result in suffering and reduced quality of life for those with unmet needs.

A universal program could also help ensure access to quality care. Leaving the current system intact or encouraging private insurance will result in two distinct worlds of long-term care services and delivery. Already many providers concentrate on the "private" market, discriminating against Medicaid patients. Medicaid, as a welfare program, provides low payments in many areas, and providers know that private-pay patients will bring in more revenues and greater profits. Naturally, private-pay patients are preferred to Medicaid patients, often resulting in the seemingly contradictory findings of empty beds and waiting lists under Medicaid. Although a two-class system of care is, to some extent, inevitable, making the largest tier be the public program would limit the problems with quality.

A comprehensive program could also be efficient. Social Security and Medicare have both proven to be very effective in holding administrative costs to a minimum. For example, Medicare is able to return about $0.97 in benefits for every $1 of financing. A public system would clearly benefit from having the largest possible risk pool over which to spread both risks and costs. Moreover, a public program like Medicare has no marketing or advertising expenses. Finally, the delivery system for any long-term care program will be an essential element in determining whether needs are met at a reasonable cost. A single system for reimbursing providers offers opportunities to mold an as-yet-undeveloped delivery system and to use prudent purchasing to hold down costs of care.

A system relying on private insurers plus Medicaid would continue the patchwork system that has developed over time in the long-term care area. Form is likely to follow reimbursement; if private insurance continues to focus on nursing homes, for example, home care will continue to lag. And if the emphasis in private insurance is on more formal home care (as seems likely for purposes of accountability), we may have a more medically oriented long-term care system than anyone believes is desirable.

A universal system would undeniably result in increased costs of long-term care. Those who now postpone or avoid getting services because of the fear of being on welfare or the inability to qualify would become eligible. In addition, expansion of covered services into community and home-based settings would encourage users who wish to avoid institutionalization at all costs. Although such expansion may be politically difficult, it should not be decried as bad simply because costs would rise. Indeed, meeting unmet needs should be a goal of an expanded system, and some increase in expenditures on nursing home and home and community services should be welcomed. Nonetheless, as stated earlier, the issue of cost is compelling. It is hard to advocate spending an additional $60 billion under a program that is facing severe financial constraints. Many proponents of other Medicare expansion options advocate expanding the acute-care side before turning to long-term care. Moreover, since the elderly are increasingly viewed as a "privileged" group, expanding benefits to this population before solving other problems may be politically untenable. Indeed, many critics of expanded long-term care protection contend that it would serve mainly to protect the assets of the upper middle class and preserve inheritances. If so, this would not be the most efficient or desirable use of public dollars.

Moving to a national universal system could also lead to inflexibility. Services now vary dramatically from location to location in the United States; what works well in Buffalo, New York, may not be easily transported to a small town in Arizona. Long-term care likely does not need to be as standardized as the acute-care system to be efficient and of high quality. Thus, fitting everything into one mold may not be the best approach, and could lead to added costs over time.

An Income-Related Benefit

As mentioned previously, another major argument against comprehensive long-term care is that it would serve largely to protect the assets of the wealthy, and that since the elderly person being cared for may never return to the community, any income or asset protection would largely help the heirs. A fully comprehensive program is not likely to be popular politically, nor is it perhaps the best use of scarce public dollars. Consequently, there may be more sentiment for an income-related approach to long-term care.

Such an approach would cost substantially less, depending, of course, on what cutoffs are set. If the limit allows for protections that would be meaningful to many middle-class elderly or disabled families, even maintaining a spend-down type of program may be acceptable. For example, if asset protection levels were set at $30,000 and $60,000 in 1990 for singles and couples, respectively, nearly 60 percent of the elderly would not have to spend down any assets before becoming eligible (Moon forthcoming). Once eligible, the individual or couple could be assessed a substantial copayment of perhaps 40 percent or 50 percent of the costs of their care if their incomes are above a certain level. This type of income relating would leave most individuals eligible for at least partial benefits. The other approach is to totally exclude those with incomes above a certain level, but such a direct move away from universal coverage might prove unpopular.

The major barrier to an income-related long-term care benefit to be added to Medicare is that it points out the inconsistency of protecting the assets of a rich older woman facing gall bladder surgery but not those of her neighbor who must be sent to a nursing home to recuperate from a broken hip. To the beneficiary, these are likely to appear to raise the same issues, making the discrepancy in coverage under Medicare seem inequitable. Thus, if the benefit is to be highly income related, but similar changes are not incorporated on the acute-care side, it may make more sense to create a separate program for long-term care, or to continue to use Medicaid for providing long-term care.

Limited Expansion of Medicare Benefits for Long-Term Care

Perhaps the simplest small-scale expansion of Medicare would extend the existing skilled nursing and home health benefits to cover a broader range of needs for elderly and disabled people. These two programs are now carefully restricted to ensure that they do not offer true long-term care benefits. Skilled nursing facility (SNF) coverage requires that the patient need either skilled nursing care or rehabilitation services. In addition, it is limited by a three-day prior hospitalization requirement and a very high coinsurance payment after 20 days that effectively makes that benefit worthless after that time for many enrollees. Home healthcare is also a skilled benefit, limited to certain services—it does not cover simple homemaker services essential to a comprehensive home care program, for example. It does not have the same limits on days of coverage as SNF, however, and has grown more rapidly over time than SNF services.

Several simple changes could substantially expand the help that Medicare offers to enrollees with chronic care needs. First, the SNF changes that were part of the MCCA could be reinstated. Eliminating the prior hospitalization requirement, expanding coverage to 150 days per year (with perhaps a lifetime limit of 300 or 450 days), and reducing substantially (or eliminating) the coinsurance would likely extend coverage to many more persons. Early analysis of the impact of those changes suggested an immediate response by providers and beneficiaries (Liu and Kenney 1991). In addition to these changes, some increases in reimbursement might also be necessary where those payments are too low to induce participation by nursing homes.[8]

These benefits would largely aid those who will have short nursing home stays and eventually return to the community. For such individuals, the burdens of having to spend down to become eligible for Medicaid are particularly harmful, since they will return to the community with fewer resources to meet other needs. But without changing the skilled care requirements, not all beneficiaries needing long-term care, even for short stays, will be covered. Thus, another approach might be to cover the first 100 or 150 days of a nursing home stay for any Medicare beneficiary. This would encompass those who need skilled care for rehabilitation, but would also offer some initial relief to all nursing home residents. Only those with longer stays would have to "spend down" through the Medicaid program. This is effectively the approach suggested by the Pepper Commission (1990). It also could help smooth the transition between acute and long-term care. Under our current system, acute care is sometimes used inappropriately to compensate for the lack of good long-term care coverage.

On the home health side, benefits could be extended to cover home care services that supplement the medical benefits now offered. This would involve less skilled, homemaker types of services. The requirements for intermittency of the benefit would also need to be relaxed somewhat. This benefit would fill in a gap not now covered consistently under the Medicaid program. But without some careful limits, this "moderate" expansion could become a very expensive part of Medicare. Particularly if nursing home care coverage were limited in duration, the pressures on the home care side would be great as individuals who ought to be institutionalized tried to remain in the home using these Medicare services.[9] Thus, some limits and/or cost-sharing requirements are likely to be necessary if this benefit is to constitute only a modest expansion of the Medicare program. Again, cost sharing might be varied by level of income.

The costs of these two expansions are difficult to predict with accuracy. When the costs of the SNF catastrophic benefits were originally estimated, they were projected to increase spending modestly, costing about $260 million more in 1989—up to about $1.5 billion. In practice, SNF expanded to $4.5 billion in that year. The net new costs would not be so great a jump now, however, since some of the 1989 expansion has been retained—probably because providers who did not participate before are now accepting Medicare beneficiaries (Liu and Kenney 1991). But if the skilled requirement were relaxed, ultimately the level of SNF use could be substantially higher than that projected for overall SNF use under the MCCA. Thus, new SNF costs might be much higher—albeit partially offset by lower Medicaid spending. A full-fledged home health benefit has been estimated to cost approximately $15 billion for just the elderly in 1990 (Pepper Commission 1990). A more limited program might be kept to a portion of that total.

How would this expansion be justified? First, it runs the danger of being viewed as "only" a marginal change (comparable to the changes contained in the MCCA). Thus, it could both be expensive and undervalued by beneficiaries, since it avoids taking on the expenses of truly long-term nursing home stays. In addition to modest premium increases, or perhaps in lieu of such increases, the composition of the Medicare benefit might be changed, reducing the comprehensiveness of the acute-care benefit. Using a "trade-off" approach might enhance the chances for achieving these changes.

Changing the Composition of Medicare Services

Many variations of an approach to reorder Medicare benefits are possible, but one option often suggested would be to increase the Part B deductible and/or premium, to pay for expanded long-term care benefits.[10] The long-term care expansion could be all or part of the SNF/ home health changes described previously. SNF and home health services could be shifted to Part B or to a new Part C, if that is where the offsetting funding was to be generated. The key issue is how high the Part B deductible or premium would have to go to fund these additional benefits.

Since so many beneficiaries now exceed the Part B deductible, raising it just a little will yield considerable revenues. As the deductible amount increases, however, the "return" from this process declines. Fewer and fewer beneficiaries are likely to have such high physician expenses. For example, to raise enough revenues to contribute an average of $500 per year per enrollee for expanded long-term care would likely require that the deductible be raised to the range of $800 to $1,000. At that level, coverage for acute care places many beneficiaries at considerable risk. To finance a *comprehensive* long-term care plan, Part B would have to be prohibitively high and combined with Part A increases as well. Thus, this trade-off approach is only viable for small-scale expansions or in combination with a premium increase.

Medicare enrollees would likely turn to the private sector to purchase additional coverage to replace these acute benefits. And if the long-term care coverage that this trade-off would support would be less than comprehensive, individuals could end up buying two separate private supplemental policies, each with its own loading and administrative costs. This "solution" might then make financing healthcare even more complicated than it is now. Thus, a trade-off approach alone is probably an insufficient response to easing in new benefits.

An Optional Long-Term Care Benefit

What about the prospects for saving money by making any added long-term care benefits an optional, and self-financed, part of the program? It makes most sense to think of such a benefit as an insurance program, although some policymakers also have suggested allowing beneficiaries to choose a long-term care track or an acute-care track when they initially enroll in Medicare. Both of these options are briefly considered here.

OFFERING PUBLIC INSURANCE FOR LONG-TERM CARE

If no new resources are to be added to Medicare to subsidize long-term care services, why offer such a program? As already mentioned, many individuals are excluded from enrolling in private insurance plans, either because they are too old or have some preexisting medical condition. Thus, one rationale for public insurance is to assure access to individuals through a government insurance program. In addition, Medicare could use its potential market power and its lower administrative costs to make long-term care coverage more affordable to older persons. And it can take a less conservative approach on risks than do private insurers, because its pool would be very large and miscalculation of future events could be addressed with later subsidies. Supporters of an optional government program also suggest that it could set the standards for coverage and eligibility against which private insurers would compete. Over time this competition might lead to better products in the private insurance market.

If public insurance were offered in this way to all comers, Medicare might, however, be at a disadvantage as compared to private insurers. What is not clear is whether the increased costs associated with taking all who wish to enroll would be offset by savings from better pooling and lower administrative costs. These two advantages might cancel out the higher costs from adverse selection, but it seems more likely that without some government subsidies, public insurance might still be more expensive than in the private sector if exclusionary practices are allowed.

The sicker, more disabled population who would be be attracted to the public program could be substantial. Each year approximately 180,000 persons who are receiving Social Security disability benefits turn 65. In addition, others who may not have qualified as totally and permanently disabled under Social Security may also have some disability that is likely to result in eligibility for long-term care benefits over time. It would be unfair to prevent such individuals from participating; indeed, giving such persons access to coverage would seem to be a goal of the program. Nonetheless, if these individuals chose the long-term care option, the group could start out with a very adverse risk pool that could quickly escalate costs and discourage others from participating. Private insurers who could exclude such individuals could offer better plans to those in good health, further affecting adverse selection. Thus, even before the program started, it might attract such a poor risk group that it could never be financially viable.

Strict regulations requiring private insurers to take all comers as well would substantially reduce this problem, but might drive most such companies out of business.[11] Thus, if we make optional public insurance viable, it is unlikely that many private insurers would remain in the market. Many consumer advocates are in favor of just such a response, but when optional approaches are discussed, they often pay lip service to retaining the option of buying private insurance.

ALLOWING A TWO-TRACK OPTION UNDER MEDICARE

A second way to make long-term care available on an optional basis would be to allow individuals to choose whether to be on an acute-care "track" or a long-term care "track" under Medicare. The acute-care track would retain the same services now available through Medicare, whereas the long-term track would reduce acute-care benefits in order to extend some long-term care benefits under the program. The major advantage of a two-track approach is that it would allow individuals to choose a different mix of coverage without having to pay more for Medicare.

This type of program could appeal particularly to individuals whose employers or former employers offer supplemental acute-care coverage, but not long-term care insurance. For the working elderly, Medicare is a secondary insurer, so less coverage on the acute-care side and more on the long-term care side would likely mean improved coverage for the worker. Retiree benefits could similarly fill in some of the gaps in acute coverage for those who chose a long-term care option.

A number of critical issues would have to be addressed under such a proposal, including: (1) the trade-offs between acute and long-term care, (2) how frequently, if ever, individuals could switch options after the first election, (3) how the system would be adjusted over time to keep it actuarially fair and financially sound, and (4) whether any beneficiaries would be subsidized to help them afford long-term care coverage.

Those who chose a long-term care track might have to forgo considerable acute-care benefits for many years to "buy" the long-term care benefits. For example, the annual premium for even a modest long-term care benefit would likely total about $600 per year for an average Medicare beneficiary aged 65. To achieve that solely through changes in the acute-care coverage would be difficult. As was the case with the trade-off option described earlier, this might require at least a $1,000 Part B deductible and potentially an increase in Part A's deductible as well. For example, unofficial Congressional Budget Office estimates in 1989 indicated that increasing the Part B deductible to $800 would have freed up only $314 on average that could be used for long-term care. The danger here is that the resulting combination of acute- and long-term care coverage would be inadequate for both types of benefits.

To offer stability to the program, considerable limits would have to be placed on how often, if ever, an individual would be able to switch between the programs. A one-time-only decision would certainly be the simplest to administer and might result in the least amount of adverse selection. That is, individuals at age 65, most of whom are healthy, would have to decide which plan they wish to participate in so that a reasonable risk pool might result for the long-term care option.[12] More frequent switching—for example, offering the choice every five years—would raise the likelihood of much greater adverse selection, driving up the costs of the program and making it unstable.

The third issue of actuarial fairness arises because acute health and long-term care insurance represent very different types of insurance risk and require different streams of benefits over time. Payouts under the long-term care option would likely rise slowly at first, but then increase steadily in later years. It would be difficult to initially set an appropriate trade-off between the acute- and long-term care options so as to ensure actuarial fairness. Considerable windfalls or shortfalls could be created for Medicare over time, requiring adjustments that could throw the system out of balance. The premium for long-term care insurance might rise much more rapidly than anticipated, for example, generating not only a crisis for Medicare but also for beneficiaries. This problem could occur even if there were no adverse selection, if prices rise differentially under the two options.

Even if the financial balance could be maintained, pressures to expand coverage might be great from individuals in one option who "guessed wrong" to be allowed to switch or at least to receive some relief. In the early years of such a program, pressure would probably come for acute-care relief from those with high deductibles but who are not drawing their long-term care benefits. Later, those in the acute-care option may object when they see their peers receiving long-term care benefits. These pressures might result in allowing switching of options at critical points that could destabilize the financial soundness of Medicare.

Ultimately, the disadvantages of choice outweigh the advantages of moving in this direction. An unstable Medicare program pleasing no one would be the most likely result.

CONCLUSIONS

Stop-loss protection, prescription drug coverage, improving low-income protection, and adding some long-term care benefits—each of these areas has been identified in this chapter as worthy of inclusion or expansion under Medicare. But to do any one of these would require a substantial commitment of resources. (To fully evaluate them, we should also consider how they would be financed.)

How do we reconcile simultaneous expansion and contraction? Can cuts in the program exist side by side with increases in other areas? In theory, coordination of these critical goals ought to be possible. The prospects for obtaining so much in savings that both the financial stability of Medicare *and* limited expansions in the program can be achieved with no added revenues are slim, however. What is more probable is that major cuts will occur along with some reordering of priorities for change. It seems inevitable that beneficiaries will be asked to contribute more for their care, but the composition of that care may not remain the same. A good example of how these two goals could be reconciled is the issue of age of eligibility. The age of eligibility for participating in the program (with a less-generous public subsidy) could potentially be combined with requiring greater premium contributions from those aged 65 and 66, for example.

Nonetheless, it is crucial to establish some priorities for any expansion. Because of the disparity in the economic status of Medicare beneficiaries, expanding the QMB program should constitute a particularly high priority. Ranking the remaining options for expansion of the acute-care side creates a dilemma: drug coverage is likely to be favored by beneficiaries, whereas many analysts would push for stop-loss protection. This was one of the struggles undertaken in the MCCA where limited approaches to each satisfied no one. Drug coverage may be the most difficult for Medicare beneficiaries to obtain because of the problems of adverse selection. Since drugs are such an important part of many treatment plans, good care often depends on access to prescription drugs. Moreover, with extended coverage would likely come more oversight of drug pricing, which could be beneficial in other ways as well. Thus, adding prescription drugs to Medicare ought to also rank high.

Regarding long-term care, expanding Medicare to include such care cannot be funded by marginal changes on the acute-care side—the stakes are simply too high. Even a limited long-term care program would require a new financing mechanism and should effectively be considered a separate program. For that reason, rather than for the importance of such coverage, it should carry a lower priority.

One of the ironies of the Medicare Catastrophic Coverage Act was that the benefits were criticized as being too insignificant while the costs—at least in terms of higher per enrollee contributions—were faulted for being too high. But the total cost of the benefits offered was essentially equal to the revenues that needed to be raised. The enrollees only wanted the changes if they would be financed by others. The failed catastrophic legislation proved that it is difficult to please the parties that must sign on to any such change—the taxpayers and the beneficiaries. What pleases one side may doom a proposal to failure with the other side. Although advocates of change will continue to seek ways to reshape the Medicare program, unless policymakers can become alchemists or unless beneficiaries alter their appreciation for the costs of providing services, this dilemma will be difficult to overcome.

A key ingredient for making some of the changes work for Medicare will be its role in the broader context of health system reform. (This is particularly important for decisions regarding age of eligibility, for example.) Better economies and modest expansions could be achieved along with greater public participation in healthcare for persons of all ages. The need to reshape Medicare reaches beyond marginal changes and into the arena of total reform. We can only go so far with incremental adjustments; a new healthcare system is needed to facilitate the full range of changes in Medicare. These issues are addressed next, in this volume's final chapter.

Notes

1. This is a less-generous benefit than traditional Medicaid, which covers such non-Medicare services as prescription drugs.

2. Stop-loss protection is likely to be a part of comprehensive healthcare reform for the younger population, so it might be added to Medicare to ensure consistency in coverage of benefits.

3. This figure assumes that these changes were fully implemented and is based on a 1988 cost estimate (Congressional Budget Office 1988).

4. Medicaid and Medicare are generally not available to these older individuals, unless they have disabilities and qualify for either Supplemental Security Income or Social Security.

5. Spouses and dependents of Medicare beneficiaries under age 65 may also be at risk if they have no independent source of health insurance. If these spouses are not employed or are employed in jobs that offer no insurance, they would only be able to purchase insurance in the individual market.

6. Long-term care could be the subject of a whole book of its own; this discussion merely touches on some of the issues relevant for Medicare. For more discussion of this issue, see Ball (1989); Moon (1989); and Rivlin and Wiener (1988).

7. "Spend down" is a term used to refer to the requirement that before becoming eligible, individuals must spend all of their assets above a certain cutoff to pay for care. Then after becoming asset eligible, they must spend essentially most of their income each period before Medicaid will pay the balance.

8. However, a major stumbling block—the small number of Medicare eligibles compared to other types of nursing home payments—does seem to be an important factor in nursing homes' decisions to participate in the program. Moreover, if longer stays were covered and eligibility loosened somewhat, the average cost per day of care for Medicare SNF patients would likely fall.

9. Criticisms of the current Medicaid program stress the bias toward institutional care that exists, since that part of long-term care services is better funded. The bias in the other direction under Medicare could be even stronger, since most individuals would prefer to remain in their homes if given the choice.

10. Alternatively, a new Part A premium could be introduced. Either way, some adjustments recognizing the need for combining A and B, would be necessary.

11. Another approach would be to develop a less-comprehensive plan—and at considerably lower cost. The public plan could be viewed as a very basic one to give moderate-income individuals better access, rather than competing directly with more generous or comprehensive private insurance offerings. Medicare could carve out one portion of the market, leaving the high end (either as complete packages or supplemental offerings) to the private sector. But again, it would be necessary to set strong standards for the private market to prevent "cream skimming." Through some type of subsidy, this optional program could also be modestly expanded to those with lower incomes. By putting the coverage in a single package, the pool of persons in a public plan would be increased, probably lessening adverse selection that would occur without any subsidized participation.

12. Another approach might be to only permit a one-time choice but offer some flexibility by allowing individuals to postpone the decision until age 70, for example. In that case, everyone would start out in the traditional Medicare program, but would be able to switch to the long-term care option until they reach age 70. The premium cost and/or deductible trade-off would rise over time to reflect the greater actuarial costs of allowing such a choice.

Chapter Nine

HOW SHOULD MEDICARE CHANGE?

In considering what Medicare should look like in the future, we are inevitably influenced by the characteristics of the program in the past and present. There are lessons to be learned about the system, both good and bad. At the same time, we should realize that these achievements and failures constrain our future choices. Bold strokes have appeal, but in getting from "here" to "there," we need to be guided by the fact that we are now "here."

Medicare will remain an important program for the elderly and disabled. It should not be eliminated, unless it is folded into a broader healthcare plan that covers all Americans. And even after healthcare reform, it may make sense to maintain Medicare as a separate, but coordinated, program.

How should we proceed? First, we need to retain some of the basic tenets of Medicare. It makes sense both to provide insurance against healthcare expenses and to fund such coverage for elderly and disabled persons largely through contributions by working-age individuals. Americans have not proven to be farsighted financial planners and are unlikely to save enough to fund these expenses at retirement. Furthermore, disability often occurs unexpectedly, making insurance even more important.

Second, it also makes sense to finance the program with contributions that bear a relationship to ability to pay. Although the payroll tax is not progressive, raising the cap on what is subject to the tax ($135,000 in 1993) has resulted in what is effectively a proportional tax, and the combination of taxes and benefits is progressive. Moreover, the payroll tax remains a stable and popular source of revenue. New revenues might more appropriately come from other sources, but, because of its popularity and reasonably progressive nature, the present payroll tax should continue in place.

Third, Americans believe that healthcare is a right, and Medicare is now a well-established program offering equal access for nearly all elderly and disabled persons so long as they contributed during their working years and "played by the rules." At least for these population groups, universal coverage is thus well accepted.

These elements should be recognized and built upon. But other aspects of Medicare will likely need to change over time, particularly in the context of broader reform. Proposals made for our healthcare system as a whole need to be part of the debate over changes for Medicare.

MEDICARE AND BROADER REFORM

At the same time, Medicare ought to play a key role in discussions of healthcare reform.

Various parties in the debate over healthcare reform often cite Medicare as an example—sometimes positively, sometimes negatively. But in addition, some of the changes needed in Medicare are likely to be possible only if made in the context of broader reform.

Lessons from Medicare for Reform

All but the most extreme approaches to healthcare reform would generally keep Medicare intact or fold it into a broader system that would itself emulate Medicare. That is, some members of Congress—including Congressman Pete Stark—have proposed extending Medicare to the entire population. Alternatively, Medicare could be expanded to include a larger part of the population; the most well known of these proposals would lower the eligibility age or expand disability coverage. Not only does that help those population groups directly, but it could be used to make employer-based reforms less burdensome on business. If employers are required to offer healthcare coverage (mandates) or to either pay a tax or offer coverage ("pay-or-play" proposals),[1] the costs to employers will be considerably reduced if older workers are covered under the Medicare program.[2]

In addition to expanding Medicare coverage to groups that are similar to current Medicare enrollees, some proposals would add children to Medicare's roles. The reasons are at least twofold. First, covering dependents in a public plan rather than through employers relieves businesses of that burden and reduces incentives to eschew married employees. This could help in a pay-or-play plan, or might be used as an incentive to get more employers to voluntarily cover their employees. Second, uninsured children may be the most logical place to incrementally expand coverage if universal plans are desired but deemed too expensive or controversial. As a universal program, Medicare could simply be broadened to include all children up to the age of 18.[3]

Many healthcare reform proposals also cite pieces of the Medicare program as lessons for the future.

For example, proponents of a Medicare-type approach cite its low administrative overhead as an example of the savings that could be obtained from a similar national system. Medicare's administrative costs are about 3 percent of expenditures, compared to about 10 percent for private health insurance. Proponents of a fully public system of healthcare use these administrative cost differences to calculate what could be saved by moving away from private insurers. Such savings could help finance coverage of the currently uninsured. Although these comparisons can be overblown, it is noteworthy that Medicare is singled out for attention as a positive model for the rest of our healthcare system.

Medicare's cost-containment innovations include new payment mechanisms for providers. Medicare has been relatively successful in holding down costs, particularly of hospital services in the late 1980s. The Prospective Payment System for hospitals has been widely accepted as an improvement over the old cost-based system. And the new Medicare Fee Schedule for physicians, although now controversial, is likely to become a standard for payment of physicians as well. Some reform proposals would adopt Medicare's cost-containment efforts and apply them universally.

Several reform plans offered in various circles base their benefits on the Medicare package, citing it as good standard coverage that is now well-accepted (see, for example, the Pepper Commission 1990). Medicare's coverage used to be criticized as less generous than that found in private insurance packages offered through employers (Congressional Budget Office 1983). However, as employers have raised deductibles and coinsurance, limited their coverage of certain services, and increased employee contributions, the charge that Medicare's benefits are too limited has been substantially eroded. This is less in praise of Medicare's benefit package than in recognition that coverage is now less generous elsewhere. Medicare coverage still lags behind the private sector in several respects, however. For example, although cost sharing is not much higher overall under Medicare than private plans, it is not well balanced (as argued in chapter 6). And Medicare now has no stop-loss protection to limit the total liability that beneficiaries may face from cost sharing for covered services.

Critics of Medicare's benefit package also argue that if the standard for health insurance benefits for younger families are limited to those offered by Medicare, a thriving supplemental insurance industry will develop (similar to the heavily critized Medigap policies), retaining the inefficiency of the private sector and the potential for serious abuse of the healthcare system. Although older Americans seem to be more averse to taking risks than younger families and thus more likely to purchase supplemental coverage, this could certainly be a serious concern.

Finally, opponents of a government approach to health reform properly fault Medicare for the often confusing paperwork it bestows on patient and provider alike, its rigidity, and its micromanagement of doctors and hospitals. Low administrative costs sometimes translate into lack of services to enrollees. And the payment reforms used by Medicare interfere in provider decisions, often alienating the provider community.

One of the major controversies over how to structure cost containment revolves around how much micromanagement is desirable. Some critics even go so far as to blame Medicare for the growth in healthcare prices over the last 20 to 25 years. Those most critical of Medicare would move to a system of vouchers, with everyone choosing his or her own healthcare insurance plans,[4] whereas others would retain a public program but manage the system through global budgets to hospitals or other groups of providers.

It is appropriate that, as the largest single insurer in the United States, public or private, Medicare is watched closely for lessons for the future. On balance, its lessons are positive.

Enhancing Cost Containment through Health Reform

For the purposes of this volume, even more important than what can be learned from Medicare is the issue of what broad-based reform can and should do for Medicare. Reform of the overall system will give Medicare a better chance of holding the line on healthcare costs even if the program remains essentially unchanged. The most obvious example of this is in payment of providers. If the rules apply equally across all payers of healthcare, providers cannot shift costs from one source of payment to another.[5] Hospitals, for example, would have to seek greater efficiencies in the provision of care, rather than charging private insurers more to compensate for Medicare's restrictive payments. This would place more stress on providers, but it would allow more direct control and understanding of the impact of payment policies.

Similarly, attempts to control the volume of physician services can never be very effective if they only influence a portion of a healthcare professional's business. For example, by limiting volume increases for Medicare enrollees, the system may do more to encourage physicians to discriminate against the elderly and disabled populations than to change their style of medical practice. Rather than adding discipline to the healthcare market, we would be providing yet another possibility for gaming the system.

The application of practice guidelines or limits on ineffective treatments will also be substantially more effective if done concertedly. Since such activities will be most effective if they change the attitudes of both providers and patients, efforts to influence practice must be viewed as systemwide changes and not just as a gimmick by one public program to hold down its own costs. Patients are more likely to accept constraints if they feel they are being equitably applied rather than singling out one group for special treatment. It is easier to make the case that a change will lead to better healthcare if it is applied to everyone. Moreover, it may be easier to change attitudes of younger, healthier individuals than those of the typical Medicare beneficiary.

Thus, one necessary step for successfully implementing the "next generation" of cost controls will likely be the presence of more universal requirements. Payment standards applied equally regardless of the third-party payer will be more effective, and rules about what to cover will only be considered fair if applied across the board. If global budgets or spending caps are imposed, they should include the Medicare population as well as younger families and individuals.

Determining the Comprehensiveness of Healthcare Coverage

Another way in which the future of Medicare is linked to health system reform involves the scope of benefits offered to the rest of the population and what that implies for Medicare. For example, proposals by the Pepper Commission (1990) would require more generous coverage for those under 65 than that available now under Medicare. Consequently, the Pepper Commission explicitly proposed to expand some of Medicare's benefits as well. When a universal package of acute-care benefits is developed, stop-loss protection and prescription drug coverage are likely to be included—both of which are now missing from Medicare.[6]

Debate over proposals to expand acute-care coverage to the younger population may help forestall major cutbacks in the Medicare program in the interim as well. Although there is certainly a lack of consensus on how to achieve universal coverage and pay for it, there does seem to be strong agreement that such action is desirable. Thus, to reduce insurance protection for the elderly at the same time would seem inconsistent with the trend in public policy. For example, proposals that would fully means-test Medicare are particularly at odds with the goal of achieving universal coverage.

Further, the more ambitious general reform proposals, such as that by Senator Robert Kerrey, of Nebraska, include long-term care coverage as part of the package. Yet even many of those whose main focus is expanded long-term care coverage often argue that these benefits should be added only concurrent with or subsequent to reforms that improve acute-care coverage for the population as a whole. The problems of the younger uninsured may need to be tackled before adding yet another major benefit that would largely help the elderly. But concurrent treatment of the two problems might result in broadening the base of support for change.

To the extent that these options also come with financing packages, a major stumbling block to more progressive financing of Medicare improvements can also be eased. That is, one of the objections to the Medicare Catastrophic Coverage Act was that a relatively small group of elderly and disabled individuals was being asked to subsidize the poor in their own group. When the entire population is involved and new financing mechanisms are being considered, it is likely to be easier to make a case about fairness and spread the burden across all age groups so that no one group feels unfairly singled out.

The most basic issue for universal coverage is the problem of affordability for those of modest means. Subsidies to low-income families represent an essential element of acute-care reform for the under-65 population. Hence, any plan must include special protections for low-income groups and perhaps some scaling of benefits by income level. If these subsidies rely on income or excise taxes for financing, older and disabled persons will be paying for the young. Consequently, it makes sense to reorient benefits for all age groups if all groups are paying. What may not be possible with Medicare alone might be inevitable in broader reform, and would sweep Medicare along with the tide.

Similarly, proposals to tax enrollees for part or all of the insurance value of their Medicare benefits make more sense if we also tax the fringe benefits that individuals receive from their employers in the form of health insurance contributions. Enrollees benefit from the subsidy that Medicare provides, and employees receive nonwage compensation from employer-subsidized insurance. Both of these subsidies could be treated as income and subject to the income tax. Logically, it makes little sense to treat one as income but not the other. Both of these proposals are controversial, however, basically for the same reasons. Individuals do not tend to view these subsidies as income in the same way that tax experts often do. Although taxation of all or part of these benefits may be an option for helping finance a reformed healthcare system, their controversial nature makes them poor candidates for changes aimed only at reducing the federal deficit. There is little value in introducing marginal changes in this area. On the other hand, taxation of private insurance and of Medicare might be part of a major revenue-raising scheme to achieve healthcare reform.

RECOMMENDATIONS FOR GETTING FROM "HERE" TO "THERE"

Many of the options discussed thus far can add to the effectiveness of Medicare and enhance the quality of life of disabled and older Americans. But these proposals also should be viewed in the context of setting priorities. Perhaps the fiscal austerity of the 1980s has created a smokescreen impeding change; nonetheless, the size of the deficit and the importance of many competing demands on the federal government suggest that it is foolish to argue for adopting all possible expansions in Medicare at once. If done in the context of broader healthcare reform, more options are possible as we exert control over the system and sort out priorities for health spending across all age groups. Moreover, raising taxes is essential for broader reform, a fact that opens further possibilities for Medicare as well. That still, of course, leaves the competing needs for other services to be reckoned with.

My recommendations here are influenced not just by what is "good policy" but also by a sense of what Medicare beneficiaries themselves have demonstrated preferences for, particularly in light of the Medicare Catastrophic debate. And even if, on balance, the program will be expanded, a number of the cuts discussed thus far may also be important elements for change.

The first set of changes, as outlined here, could be done immediately without waiting for reform elsewhere in the system (many of these were discussed in chapter 6). They should be combined with modest continued efforts at cost containment involving providers. On balance, they would result in savings to the federal government.

☐ Revise cost sharing;
☐ Expand the Qualified Medicare Beneficiary (QMB) program;
☐ Modify the Part B premium to make it income related;
☐ Expand the hospice program; and
☐ Streamline billing and administration.

Revise Cost Sharing

We ought to bring a better balance and logic to Medicare's cost sharing. This implies not increasing the overall costs of the program much, if at all. Any shortfall from these changes could be recouped by the premium changes discussed later here. The most important reductions in cost sharing should be the elimination of hospital coinsurance, limiting the Part A deductible, and reductions in skilled nursing facility (SNF) coinsurance.

Hospital coinsurance and multiple deductibles do little to discourage unnecessary use of services, particularly given the other strong controls on hospital use in the Medicare program. Rather, these cost-sharing mechanisms are essentially used to cut federal costs by shifting the burdens onto beneficiaries. The hospital deductible is considerably higher than that normally found in the private sector. And the coinsurance is not only inordinately high, but it unnecessarily complicates the program. It does not begin until after 60 days; individuals with such long hospital stays (or multiple stays) are unlikely to be in a position to respond to economic incentives. Further, hospital cost sharing is based on an arbitrary spell-of-illness concept, which was adopted as a means for limiting costs in the program and not based on any sound medical rationale.

SNF coinsurance effectively limits the program to a 20-day benefit rather than a 100-day benefit because of coinsurance rates above the average costs of care in many areas. Since the coinsurance is linked to the costs of hospital care, it bears no relationship to costs of providing skilled nursing care.

Reductions in Part A cost sharing could be at least partially offset with an increase in the Part B deductible, since, at $100 per year, this part of Medicare's cost sharing is low relative to the private sector. Raising the Part B deductible and indexing it over time might also discourage some unnecessary use of routine physician visits. Thus, this deductible might not only require beneficiaries to pay more, but it might be a tool to influence use of services—actually achieving the stated goal of cost sharing.

A number of combinations of changes in Part A and B are reasonable, but I would restrict cost sharing in the hospital to no more than one deductible per year (or institute a premium in lieu of the deductible), initially set that deductible at about $500, eliminate hospital coinsurance, and reduce the SNF coinsurance to 20 percent of the costs of SNF care (about $20 per day in 1992). The Part B deductible could be increased to $350 per year to offset most of the costs of the Part A changes. The net costs of this change would be less than $0.5 billion—an amount that could be made up with the premium changes described later here.[7]

One complication of raising the federal government's liabilities under Part A and reducing them under Part B would be a worsening of the Part A trust fund balances. It makes sense, consequently, to combine these two parts of the program and make explicit decisions about how much of the additional revenues for Medicare (over and above the payroll contributions) should come from premiums and how much from general revenues.

Expand the QMB Program

Improved protection for those with low and moderate incomes should occur simultaneously with changes in cost sharing. The QMB program now pays the premiums, deductibles, and coinsurance of Medicare beneficiaries whose incomes are below poverty. By 1995, it will also cover premiums for those up to 120 percent of poverty. QMB protection should extend higher up the income scale than just to the poverty line. That is, it should reduce the cost-sharing burdens for low-income beneficiaries, and it should protect more than just the poor. Those with modest incomes now have difficulty paying this cost sharing, which reduces their access to the program. Initially, persons with incomes below at least 125 percent of poverty should be protected—with expansions added later, as will be discussed here.

This additional protection for cost sharing under Medicare ought to be part of the Medicare program, shifting the QMB program out of

Medicaid. This would help ensure that beneficiaries would participate in the QMB program and that QMB would be a full-fledged part of Medicare. Many beneficiaries are either unaware of the program or are reluctant to apply for it through Medicaid. This shift would also help ease some of the pressures on Medicaid, but to keep the costs low initially, it might need to be done in stages.

These changes would raise the costs to the federal government by about $3 billion to $4 billion. Some of this would come from shifting to the federal government burdens now placed on the states through Medicaid, some from increased participation from eligibles likely if QMB is part of Medicare, and part from expanding protection to those up to 125 percent of poverty.

Create an Income-Related Premium

The third element of rebalancing beneficiary contributions under Medicare would be to make the premium income-related. Beneficiaries should be asked to contribute more for their care, but in a way that protects those with few resources. It also should deemphasize any welfare stigma in doing so.

The simplest way to introduce a sliding scale premium would be to use the Social Security system. Part B premiums are already taken out of individuals' checks, and that could be continued. But instead of a flat payment, the premium could be tied to the size of the Social Security benefit. This could work on a sliding scale up to a cap. The steps would be relatively gradual so that the maximum payment would not be dramatically higher than the overall average. For example, the premium might average $450 per year if implemented in 1992 (compared to current law of about $382) and rise to a maximum of $700. The total revenue obtained in this way could be adjusted to fully cover the costs of other small-scale expansions described here and still result in net savings. As outlined here, gross federal savings would total about $5 billion. This would result in net savings from these three sets of changes of approximately $1 billion.

The formula should not penalize those who do take their full Social Security benefit by delaying retirement (as discussed in chapter 6). Moreover, those with high incomes but low Social Security payments could be required to pay an additional amount through the income tax to adjust for inequities from using Social Security to income-relate the benefits. Elderly and disabled persons with incomes over, say, $40,000 to $50,000 per year could be required to pay the full $700 regardless of the level of Social Security payments they receive. Reconciliation would be required only of those beneficiaries with small Social Security payments and high incomes (for example, above $25,000). In this way, the program could minimize the disruption caused by an income-related premium (such as that passed under the MCCA).

The combined impact of these three changes could result in modest net savings for the Medicare program combined with a more reasonable cost-sharing framework. It would recognize the diversity of Medicare beneficiaries—that is, the need to protect some beneficiaries while asking higher contributions of others, but to do so unobtrusively.

Expand the Hospice Program

Changes in the hospice program to raise its status as an acceptable option to more aggressive types of treatment at the end of life could be done at little additional cost to Medicare. For example, restrictions requiring the physician to certify that life expectancy is less than six months could be eased. Providers could be encouraged to participate rather than be subjected to the stringent requirements now on the books. Some of the changes would be largely symbolic; others to attract more patients would likely save costs elsewhere in the system. Some resources could be spent to promote hospice care—for example, by funding demonstrations to bring it more into the mainstream of care. Such demonstrations should stress that this is a reasonable choice and one that is easy for patients to make.

This effort ought to be combined with an aggressive attempt to educate patients and their families about alternatives and choices. Promotion of living wills and of durable powers of attorney that allow Medicare enrollees to make their wishes known could be coordinated with these efforts. Too often, less care is associated with inferior care or a withdrawal of support. Attitudes of patients, families, and providers about alternatives need to change. These efforts should focus on *choice* and not on requirements for types of care.

Streamline Billing and Administration

A low-cost change that could substantially improve Medicare in the eyes of the beneficiaries and providers would be to simplify billing and administration of the program. The cost-sharing changes just outlined would help ease some of the complexity of the program, but streamlining should go further.

Medicare beneficiaries could also be given a card to be presented to providers. All billing could go through the card, which could also be coordinated with any Medigap plans, so that beneficiaries would not have to file separately or deal with multiple forms. The government could require that all doctors use the same forms for billing patients, thus ensuring uniformity. As described earlier in this volume, imagine an environment in which the patient presents a card to the physician in the same way people now use credit cards. A simple computer link—similar to the scanners now used to approve credit cards—would provide information on how much would be paid by insurance and how much would be owed by the patient. The patient would not have to file a separate insurance claim, the physician would only have to fill out a simple form signed by the patient concerning what services were delivered, and the system could track use of health services in a uniform way.

The billing system would require only a centralized clearing mechanism and standardized cards and computer equipment. It could track the plans and requirements of multiple insurers, much like systems now in place that accept credit cards regardless of type or issuer.

Beneficiaries could receive one bill per month or bimonthly, in which they would pay just once for any cost sharing owed. Clear language would indicate what Medicare contributes—helping to underscore the substantial amount that Medicare provides—and what is paid by private insurers. Streamlining the billing process could lead to substantial administrative savings, both in terms of lower healthcare spending when less paperwork is needed, saving time and frustration for both patients and healthcare providers. If Medicare can truly claim that it reduces those burdens, future payment cuts will certainly be more palatable as well. It is likely that any costs incurred in making these changes could be recouped with lower payments elsewhere in the system.

NEXT STEPS

Other changes will likely take more time to implement. But more important, they should be part of broader healthcare reform. They include:

☐ Adopt all-payer regulation;
☐ Improve acute-care coverage;

☐ Add an income-related long-term care benefit; and
☐ Pay for expansions with progressive financing.

All-Payer Regulation

The next steps in controlling costs—beyond incremental adjustments to current efforts—are not likely to be painless for providers; in some cases they will require sacrifices by patients as well. Such painful restrictions will only be effective if they spread the pain across all providers and all individuals, however. The healthcare system needs a consistent set of rules applied to all payers of healthcare. This can be done either in an all-payer context where there are multiple payers of healthcare (insurers), all of whom use the same fees and rules, or a single-payer context where the federal government processes all claims. All-payer systems require at least careful regulation of the current system; such a system would likely work better if combined with other healthcare reforms, but it could also be a standalone change—so long as it is not simply a Medicare-only policy. A single-payer system is usually imagined in the context of major healthcare reform and adoption of a Canadian-style healthcare system.[8]

The immediate result would be to reduce gaming of pricing and discounts and the resultant shifting of costs across payers. Powerful insurers will not be able to compete by striking deals with doctors or hospitals for special discounts while less-powerful insurers pay more than their fair share. Moreover, physicians and hospitals will not have incentives to discriminate against patients who happen to be covered in plans that pay less well. These controls could go beyond fees and rates of payment; volume controls and determinations of appropriate treatment could be implemented in a consistent manner. Since the same set of rules will apply and the information required will be uniform, less administrative machinery will be needed, and the response of providers could be more readily ensured and monitored.

A fully comprehensive effort to bring about an all-payer system would include global expenditure targets, at least as regards rates of growth over time. This implies making explicit decisions about how much of our economy should be devoted to healthcare.

All-payer regulation offers the best prospect for controlling healthcare costs. This type of approach could be modified to incorporate and test some of the principles of managed care as well, since the struggle to reduce the rate of growth of healthcare costs is likely to be ongoing and never easy. Health maintenance organizations or other formal groups of providers could be given waivers to opt out of the rates and volume controls if they can achieve comparable limits on spending growth.[9] Such a mixed system could result in a true test of approaches for limiting growth in healthcare spending.

Improve Acute-Care Coverage

Expansion of Medicare to cover prescription drugs or preventive services, or to provide stop-loss protection ought to be done in the context of standards of coverage for the population as a whole.[10] Medicare enrollees should be treated on the same basis as younger insured groups. Although some Americans may have additional coverage through supplemental policies or perhaps more generous employer-based coverage, we need some consensus on a national minimum standard. (For elderly and disabled individuals, the costs of such coverage will still be higher than those of providing equivalent insurance to other groups.)

Prescription drugs are one of the important benefits that should be viewed in this context. Drugs are an instrumental part of the treatment of many health problems, and lack of coverage can lead to poor health outcomes and ultimately higher costs. But for the elderly in particular, the costs of prescription drugs are high and would increase substantially the costs of the Medicare program. If as a society we decide we cannot afford to cover all prescription drugs, it would be fairer to cover part of them for everyone (using a high initial deductible, for example) than to offer coverage to the young but argue that we cannot afford it for the old.

This would, of course, mean higher Medicare spending. Final cost estimates for Medicare's drug benefit indicated that it would reach $4.4 billion by 1992 (with 40 percent coinsurance and a $652 deductible).

Although stop-loss protection was undervalued by the elderly when it was covered by the MCCA, it is part of any good insurance program and should be provided under Medicare. All major healthcare reform proposals contain some stop-loss provisions. For Medicare beneficiaries, an individual limit of $2,500 or $3,000 is likely sufficient, *if* low-income persons have protections from cost sharing. This is in the range of the stop-loss protection offered under the MCCA—and might cost about $5 billion. But the level chosen should be consistent with that contained in plans for younger families.

Finally, the low-income protection under Medicare should also be adjusted to be at least as generous for Medicare beneficiaries as for the population as a whole. If more-generous protections are available to the general population than those proposed previously here as a first step, the program should be further expanded. For example, most reform plans provide protection up through at least 150 percent of poverty. This is particularly important for Medicare beneficiaries whose out-of-pocket costs are likely to be higher than younger families with the same levels of income. Altogether, these acute-care expansions could add $12 billion to $15 billion to the annual costs of Medicare.

Expand Long-Term Care Coverage

Improved long-term care coverage makes sense on several grounds. First, the current system of relying on Medicaid and individuals' own resources results in great hardships and inequities. Long-term care coverage could substantially improve the quality of life of many who do without needed care or get by with less. Second, the problem of long-term care is amenable to a shared-risk approach, and it makes little sense to retain our current system. Third, the acute-care system is currently misused to compensate for the much better coverage available for acute-care problems than for long-term care. Medicare is the major insurer affected by this misuse and likely has higher costs because of it.

But even an income-related long-term care program will be expensive. It must be funded with additional public revenues; it is not feasible to fully fund it by shifting resources from Medicare or even from Social Security—although this could certainly be part of the financing scheme. The elderly and disabled populations can and should be asked to pay a substantial share of any new burdens from expanding long-term care. But since these burdens are now shared with the young, the young should also help to support such programs.

Several approaches are possible. I favor a comprehensive program of nursing home and community-based care with substantial, but income-related, cost sharing. Those who can afford to do so would be asked to pay much, but not all, of the costs of their care. This gives them a stake in the program and ensures that all or most care falls under a system that can be subjected to cost controls. Other approaches, such as that offered by the Pepper Commission (1990) or mandatory insurance coverage where people pay premiums on a sliding scale, could also achieve the goals of protection for disabled people, and at a lower price than that of full social insurance.

But any of these limited approaches are still likely to result in a substantial increase in tax burdens for Americans—perhaps in the range of $40 billion to $50 billion.[11] Expansion of long-term care coverage merits a more careful and detailed analysis on its own. And in an era when many policymakers are reluctant to take on this problem until we achieve universal access on the acute-care side, the program needs to be coordinated with other healthcare reforms. It likely would not, and perhaps should not, be adopted until universal coverage of acute care is available for all Americans.

Require Financial Contributions Based on Ability to Pay

One of the greatest sources of controversy under the MCCA was the supplemental premium that effectively required enrollees with higher incomes to pay a surtax through the income tax to support the expansions. Objections were raised on several grounds, including the unfairness of asking only elderly and disabled individuals to pay to subsidize those with lower incomes. In principle, this is a sound objection. It makes little sense to require only female-headed families to pay for welfare benefits for poor female-headed families, for example. But, it is not unfair to ask high-income beneficiaries to pay directly at least the full share of their own costs for expansions in the program. And as a society, we should be willing to subsidize the purchase of goods deemed essential by persons who otherwise could not afford them. That is, after all, what the discussion of universal health insurance for the under-65 population is all about.

Asking that Medicare beneficiaries contribute on the basis of ability to pay is thus not only consistent with other healthcare reform but is likely to be an essential element. Expanding coverage under Medicare to be consistent with coverage for the young would require additional resources. It is not only reasonable but necessary to include elderly and disabled persons in revenue raising for such expansions. This does not mean the elderly must be singled out on the revenue side; rather, it suggests, for example, that income tax increases will likely be needed in addition to payroll tax changes (that effectively exempt most elderly and disabled persons). Broadening of the base of the income tax might also target this group, by subjecting more of Social Security to the income tax, for example, to make up for lower payroll tax burdens on this group. This would be particularly appropriate if long-term care were part of a healthcare reform package.

Further, premium and cost-sharing requirements under most health reform proposals vary by income, and it makes sense to change Medicare in that direction as well. Indeed, that goal was one of the first changes advocated here. But when combined with other reforms, the premium could be further expanded. For example, the Medicare premium should rise to require about a 20 percent contribution (based on the combined costs of Parts A and B of Medicare) from the elderly and disabled populations, if that is the requirement on the young. Compared to current contributions, that would mean a doubling of the Part B premium—that is, a premium of about $763 per year in 1992. And it could rise even more for those with very high incomes. This is a broader increase in the premium than that described earlier, which could be done in the nearer term. The difficulty, of course, arises because in the case of Medicare, it means cutting benefits for the wealthy elderly, but for the young it means offering less-generous new benefits for well-off younger families. It is always more difficult to retrench on existing policy than to add new benefits.

The combined impact of higher taxes and higher premiums needs to be carefully assessed. Old and young alike will need considerable reassurance concerning the fairness of these changes as we move in the direction of substantial reform.

CONCLUSIONS

How likely are any of these changes? If one reads too much into the lessons of the MCCA, one might expect little change. Indeed, some in Congress and in the Bush administration have practically made this a rallying cry. But it is equally plausible to argue that the MCCA failed to go far enough and address the broader concerns of its beneficiaries. Moreover, the push to reform the broader healthcare system seems to be on a fast track. Perhaps reform will not come in 1993 or 1994; but certainly by later in the decade, dissatisfaction with the healthcare system by the average citizen is likely to impel further change. Medicare could and should be swept along with the tide.

In the meantime, there are changes that can be made in the system. Improved cost-sharing requirements, some increase in premiums, better low-income protections, improved administration, and an expanded hospice program are consistent with reform, but should not be dependent upon it. Those who might otherwise push for such reforms are reluctant to open the program to change that might get out of hand, as seemed to happen with the MCCA. If other major change seems imminent, even these proposals are likely to be put on hold. In that case, what we are likely to see in the next few years will only be marginal cuts for budgetary reasons, often with little in the way of improved policy in mind.

In my view, the greatest hope for major improvement in Medicare is that it will occur secondarily to, rather than center stage with, reform legislation. Whether Medicare remains a separate program or is folded into a broader system, Medicare changes should be part of healthcare reform. Supporters of the program should keep it in the systemwide debate and take advantage of opportunities to enhance its offerings while ensuring that Medicare remains in the mainstream.

Notes

1. Many of the healthcare reform proposals popular in the early 1990s, including those of the Pepper Commission and the Democratic leadership, have been of the "pay-or-play" variety. These require employers to either offer and pay a share of insurance coverage for their workers or pay a tax, usually a share of payroll, which would then put their workers into a public plan. The advantage of this over a strict mandate for offering coverage is that employers with low-wage workers or small businesses will likely find it cheaper or simpler to pay the tax and enroll their workers in the public plan.

2. Eliminating the more expensive older workers from this requirement lowers costs to employers and likely would take away any incentive not to hire such individuals.

3. Politically, such an option may also be appealing to groups interested in the plight of elderly and disabled persons because it disarms the argument that we are not doing enough for children *because* of the existence of programs like Medicare. Once both the young and the old are in the same system, explicit trade-offs between these two groups can be made as a matter of policy.

4. Perhaps the "purist" form of this approach is that proposed by the Heritage Foundation (Butler 1992).

5. Obviously the simplest form of coordination would be through a single program with a single administrative entity overseeing the system. But so-called all-payer systems could also provide coordination in a world of multiple insurers. What is needed is regulation that requires all of these payers to play by the same rules.

6. One complication is that these benefits are more expensive for elderly and disabled people than for younger families because of the former's higher use of services.

7. I am not proposing to add coinsurance on home health services, but that would be another way to also offset these higher net costs.

8. Even here, however, there could be lesser reforms to institute a single-payer system. Such a proposal has been developed in the state of New York, which would retain private insurers and hence a less than fully public system.

9. An alternative approach would be to emphasize managed care organizations with a smaller fee-for-service sector controlled by all-payer rate setting.

10. This is not to say that coverage has to be identical. For example, if appropriate medical care requires more visits for well babies and less screening for other groups of the population, then differences could be established. But the standards ought to be based on appropriateness or effectiveness and not on source of insurer.

11. Such estimates are subject to enormous variation and, not surprisingly, are very controversial. The Pepper Commission (1990) proposal carried an estimated price tag of $42.8 billion in 1990 dollars. That amount would be considerably higher if expressed in 1993 or 1994 dollars.

APPENDIX

THE MECHANICS OF MEDICARE

The Medicare program was established by legislation in 1965 as Title XVIII of the Social Security Act and first went into effect on July 1, 1966.[1] The program is divided into two basic parts: Part A is Hospital Insurance (also referred to as HI), and Part B is Supplementary Medical Insurance (SMI).

Eligibility

Medicare covers three groups of individuals: persons aged 65 or over who are also eligible for any type of Social Security benefit, persons who have been receiving Social Security disability benefits for two years, and insured workers, their spouses, or children with end-stage renal disease (ESRD). Dependents and widows or widowers of retired workers are covered, so long as they are at least age 65. Disability coverage is limited to the covered worker or an adult disabled child of a covered worker. Eligible persons are enrolled in Medicare Part A at no charge.

When Medicare was first passed in 1965, it covered only elderly persons, and initially everyone over the age of 65 was eligible. That blanket eligibility included all persons who reached age 65 by 1968. Consequently, all persons aged 89 and over in 1992 have Medicare coverage regardless of their Social Security status. Subsequently, only those over age 65 who were eligible for some type of Social Security benefit were eligible for Medicare. But even without blanket coverage, over 98 percent of all persons aged 65 and over are covered by Medicare either as a worker or dependent. In 1991, approximately 30.5 million elderly persons were enrolled in the Medicare program.

Anyone over the age of 65 who is not otherwise eligible may elect to enroll in Medicare by paying an actuarially fair premium. That premium was $192 per month in 1992, and about 19,000 persons elected such enrollment. These are generally persons who have had little or no labor force attachment or who have immigrated to the United States from other countries.

The two-year waiting period for Medicare coverage for disabled persons, coupled with a five-month waiting period for eligibility for Social Security, means that individuals with disabilities do not receive Medicare coverage until 29 months after the onset of the disability. They may also continue to receive benefits for up to 36 months after Social Security cash benefits end, so long as they are still disabled. Persons disabled as children may also qualify once they reach age 18 if their parents were eligible for Social Security. In 1991, 3.4 million disabled persons were covered by Medicare. Dependents of disabled beneficiaries are not eligible for Medicare unless they are age 65 or older.

ESRD patients are covered once they file for benefits and if they are entitled to monthly Social Security benefits or are children or spouses of covered workers. In 1990, there were 144,000 HI ESRD beneficiaries.

All persons enrolled in Part A of Medicare and all persons over the age of 65 may also elect to join Part B, which requires a monthly premium contribution to pay some of the costs of the Part B benefits. When persons enroll in Medicare or turn age 65, the Part B premium is automatically deducted from their monthly Social Security check. Enrollees must inform the Social Security Administration if they do not want to enroll in Part B. If an eligible individual elects to delay joining Part B, a penalty (of 10 percent for each year of delay) is added to the premium to discourage individuals from joining only when they are sicker. (The premium is discussed later in this appendix.)

The generosity of the subsidy means that most, but not all join. Most elderly beneficiaries elect this option, but a smaller percentage of disabled persons do so. In 1991, over 98 percent of elderly and 91 percent of disabled Part A beneficiaries elected Part B coverage.

Legislation in the 1980s made Medicare the secondary payer in cases where enrollees aged 65 to 69 were still in the labor force and had private health insurance. The private insurance company is liable for the bulk of acute-care expenses, and Medicare will pay only for services not covered by this private insurance. Although this provision has been poorly enforced, in theory it limits eligibility for working enrollees. An individual may decline to take private coverage from an employer, for example, if a large premium contribution is required. In that case, the worker would receive full benefits from Medicare.

Yet another dimension of eligibility is the creation of Qualified Medicare Beneficiaries (QMBs) under the Medicare Catastrophic Coverage Act (MCCA) of 1988. These special beneficiaries, whose incomes must be below 100 percent of the federal poverty level and whose resources are under the amount specified for Supplemental Security Income in 1991, are entitled to have the Medicaid program pick up the costs of Medicare's premium, deductibles, and coinsurance.[2] Although most of the MCCA was repealed in 1989, this provision remained in force. These protections were partially expanded under the Omnibus Budget Reconciliation Act (OBRA) of 1990. Beneficiaries can have Medicaid pay for their Part B premiums if their incomes are between 100 percent and 110 percent of poverty in 1993. Eligibility limits for that protection will rise to 120 percent of poverty in 1995. Thus far, only a portion of those eligible for the QMB protection have signed up; many beneficiaries seem to be unaware of the program.

Benefits

Medicare coverage is limited to acute-care services, particularly physician services and acute hospital care. This basic benefit package has changed little since Medicare's inception.

PART A

Under Part A, hospital coverage is limited to 90 days within a "spell of illness," plus a one-time supply of 60 "lifetime reserve days" that can be used to extend the covered period within one or more spells of illness. The first 60 days of the spell of illness are fully covered (after payment of a deductible). After that, the beneficiary is liable for coinsurance for the next 30 days (see the discussion upcoming).[3] The lifetime reserve days, which would then begin, also require beneficiary cost sharing. A spell of illness begins when the patient receives hospital or extended care services and ends when 60 days have elapsed between such periods of treatment. Thus, a spell of illness is not really related to a particular illness, but, rather, refers to a period of time elapsing before the next spell begins. Inpatient psychiatric services are limited to 190 days over a patient's lifetime.

Another Part A benefit is skilled nursing facility (SNF) care for up to 100 days in a qualified facility per spell of illness. This is a very limited benefit, however, that must follow a three-day period of hospitalization and is restricted to enrollees who require the skills of technical or professional personnel for skilled nursing or rehabilitation. This is not a general nursing home benefit, but is intended to be an extension of acute-care treatment. Coinsurance is charged beginning on the 21st day of the stay.[4]

Home healthcare, like SNF, is a restricted benefit, largely provided under Part A.[5] Coverage is limited to skilled nursing or rehabilitation benefits provided in the home. Unlike SNF, no prior hospitalization is required, and there is no limit on the number of days that can be covered. But home health services must be prescribed by a physician with the expectation of rehabilitation for the patient. The care must be "intermittent," usually defined as less than daily, but recent guidelines permit a period of daily visits of up to eight hours per day. Finally, the patient must be confined to the home—a requirement somewhat at odds with the stipulation that the care received be intermittent.[6]

Hospice care was added to Part A as a benefit in 1983. It includes nursing care, physical and occupational therapy, medical social services, home health aide services, continuous home care if necessary, medical supplies, physicians' services, short-term inpatient care, and counseling. Persons electing hospice benefits face limitations on what other Medicare services are covered that relate to the terminal illness, however. For example, if a person elects to be in the hospice program, only inpatient care for alleviation of pain, respite care, or acute symptom management is permitted. Aggressive treatment for the terminal illness would not be covered. A physician must certify that the patient is terminally ill and is expected to die within 6 months. After an initial eligiblity period of 210 days, benefits may be extended for a second 210-day period if patients are recertified by their doctors. Services must be performed by a certified hospice program and must reflect a written plan of care.

PART B

Part B of Medicare pays 80 percent of physicians' "reasonable" charges (also called "allowed" charges) for surgery, consultation, and home, office, and institutional visits after the enrollee meets a $100 deductible. These reasonable charges are established by a complex payment calculation that was replaced in 1992 by the Medicare Fee Schedule (discussed in chapter 3). Routine physicals are not covered. Restrictions are placed on certain nonphysician providers of care such as dentists, chiropractors, and podiatrists. Mental health services are also limited to the lesser of $562.50 per year or 62.5 percent of actual service costs. Other covered services include x-ray and radiation therapy, ambulance services, physical and speech therapy, and rural health clinic services. Physicians are also permitted, within limits, to charge beneficiaries more than the reasonable amounts established by Medicare—a practice referred to as "balance billing" (described in more detail later here).

Part B also covers 80 percent of the reasonable charges for laboratory and other diagnostic tests, home dialysis supplies, durable medical equipment, and artificial devices. The budget summit of 1990 also added biennial mammography screening coverage—one of the few preventive services offered by Medicare.

Facility charges for hospital outpatient services and ambulatory surgery centers are also covered, again with coinsurance requirements.[7] An individual treated in a hospital outpatient department or emergency room or an ambulatory surgery center will receive at least two bills—one for the facility and one for the physician.

HMOs

Medicare also allows its beneficiaries to enroll in health maintenance organizations (HMOs) and similar organizations called "competitive medical plans" that meet certain conditions. The HMO must provide all the services that Medicare covers. The Medicare program pays the HMO directly for the costs of the beneficiary according to a formula designed to pay 95 percent of the benefit payments for a similar beneficiary in the fee-for-service portion of Medicare, referred to as the average annual per capita cost (AAPCC). Beneficiaries who wish to participate must enroll in Part B. The HMO may also charge a premium in lieu of the deductibles and coinsurance amounts the beneficiary would pay if not in the HMO. The HMO premium may be higher to cover services beyond what Medicare normally provides. For example, HMOs also often offer drug coverage. Beneficiaries electing to enroll in a Medicare-approved HMO must abide by the rules of the HMO and will not be covered for any services performed outside of the HMO, but they may disenroll at any time. Beneficiaries do not have to file any claims forms. HMOs are at risk if the costs of care exceed their AAPCC payments, and they must share at least part of any savings with beneficiaries in the form of improved benefits.

Cost Sharing and Premiums

Enrollees in the Medicare program are required to share some of the costs of their own care—both through a premium for coverage under Part B and payment of a portion of the costs of services received in the form of deductibles and coinsurance. Most of these contributions grow each year as healthcare costs increase under Medicare. All enrollees (not in HMOs) are liable for these payments, although Medicaid pays for certain low-income enrollees, and others may receive or purchase private insurance to cover these liabilities.

PART A

For Part A, this cost sharing is organized around the concept of "spell of illness," as previously defined here. Consequently, rather than an annual deductible, the deductible is assessed at the beginning of each spell of illness. If a patient is hospitalized several times during a spell of illness, only one deductible is assessed. On the other hand, if a patient has multiple spells of illness in any given year, several deductibles may be charged. For example, about 7 percent of beneficiaries pay two or more deductibles in any given year (Congressional Budget Office 1988). The size of the deductible increases each year at the same rate as Medicare payments to hospitals. In 1993 the deductible is $676. The historical trends in this and other beneficiary cost sharing are shown in table A.1.

Similarly, coinsurance is assessed on the basis of the number of covered days during a spell of illness. (The calculation of number of days may cumulate across multiple admissions to the hospital.) The first 60 days of hospital care require no coinsurance. Between days 61 and 90 of the spell of illness, the individual is assessed coinsurance of one-fourth the hospital deductible for each day (or $169 in 1993). After 90 days of hospitalization during a spell of illness, the Medicare beneficiary must draw upon a lifetime reserve of 60 additional days of coverage, while paying coinsurance equal to one-half the deductible ($338 in 1993) for each day. After exhausting that reserve, the Medicare beneficiary is liable for the full costs of any additional days in the hospital. About 0.5 percent of all Medicare enrollees exhaust their lifetime reserve days in any one year, usually because they have experienced several periods of hospitalization.

Coinsurance is also assessed on days 21 through 100 of a skilled nursing facility stay. The amount is set at one-eighth of the hospital deductible. At $84.50 in 1993, this amount is larger than the amount that Medicare pays daily for SNF care in many areas. Consequently, many beneficiaries simply do not file for Medicare reimbursement for more than 20 days of SNF care, since the cost to beneficiaries is higher than the value of the benefit.

In addition to the hospital deductible, there is another deductible equal to the cost of the first three pints of whole blood received by a beneficiary as part of covered inpatient services. This deductible is also calculated on a spell-of-illness basis. The patient can avoid this deductible by arranging for replacement of the blood by donors.

Table A.1 MEDICARE DEDUCTIBLES, COINSURANCE, AND PREMIUMS, 1966–92

| For Benefit Periods Beginning in Calendar Year | Inpatient Hospital | | 60 Lifetime Reserve Days ($) | Skilled Nursing Facility, 21st-through 100th-Day Coinsurance ($) | Supplementary Medical Insurance Deductible ($) | Supplementary Medical Insurance Premium ($) |
	First 60 Days' Deductible ($)	61st through 90th Day, Coinsurance per Day ($)				
1966	40	10	—	—	50	3.00
1967	40	10	—	5.00	50	3.00
1968	40	10	20	5.00	50	4.00
1969	44	11	22	5.50	50	4.00
1970	52	13	26	6.50	50	5.30
1971	60	15	30	7.50	50	5.60
1972	68	17	34	8.50	50	5.80
1973	72	18	36	9.00	60	6.70
1974	84	21	42	10.50	60	6.70
1975	92	23	46	11.50	60	6.70
1976	104	26	52	13.00	60	7.20
1977	124	31	62	15.50	60	7.70
1978	144	36	72	18.00	60	8.20
1979	160	40	80	20.00	60	8.70
1980	180	45	90	22.50	60	9.60
1981	204	51	102	25.50	60	11.00
1982	260	65	130	32.50	75	12.20
1983	304	76	152	38.00	75	12.20
1984	356	89	178	44.50	75	14.60
1985	400	100	200	50.00	75	15.50
1986	492	123	246	61.50	75	15.50
1987	520	130	260	65.00	75	17.90
1988	540	135	270	67.50	75	24.80
1989[a]	560	NA	NA	25.50	75	31.90
1990	592	148	296	74.00	75	28.60
1991	628	157	314	78.50	100	29.90
1992	660	165	330	82.50	100	31.80

Source: Data from Health Care Financing Administration, Office of the Actuary, Office of Medicare Cost Estimates.
a. Includes MCCA legislation.

Finally, the hospice program requires several coinsurance payments. Beneficiaries must pay 5 percent coinsurance (up to $5) for each palliative drug and biological prescription furnished by the hospice when the beneficiary is *not* an inpatient. A 5 percent coinsurance payment is also required for each day of respite care, capped at the level of the hospital deductible.

Home health services do not require any cost sharing. A 20 percent coinsurance payment was required until 1973, when the bulk of home healthcare services were shifted to Part A from Part B.

PART B

Under Part B, the deductible is a set amount—now $100 per year—which does not rise automatically over time. It has been increased three times by legislation from an initial level of $50 per year. For physician and certain other services, the coinsurance is set at 20 percent of the amount that Medicare establishes as its "allowed" charge. The two major exceptions to the coinsurance requirement are laboratory services, for which Medicare usually reimburses 100 percent of the fee schedule, and home health services. Most other services under Part B are subject to the coinsurance requirement. Since physician fees generally rise each year, the amount that Medicare beneficiaries pay in cost sharing consequently goes up even when the same level of services is used from year to year.

The Part B premium is also tied to the costs of Part B services. Enrollees must pay approximately 25 percent of the costs of care for an elderly enrollee. That amount was first introduced as a temporary change in 1982 and has periodically been extended since then. In 1990, premiums of about 25 percent were established using projected spending through 1995. In 1993, the Part B premium is $36.60 per month.

The original share that enrollees paid was higher, set at 50 percent in the enacting legislation. But over time, the premium grew much faster than Social Security payments, resulting in a Part B premium deduction from Social Security that was consuming an ever-increasing portion of monthly Social Security checks. The 1972 amendments to Medicare changed the premium so that thereafter it would grow no faster than the rate of the Social Security cost-of-living adjustment (COLA). Then the reverse problem arose. With high rates of healthcare spending in the 1970s, the share paid by beneficiaries gradually eroded to about 25 percent of Part B costs by 1981. The 1981 legislation essentially froze the premium share in place at 25 percent of the costs of an elderly enrollee as a federal budget reduction measure.

Normally the premium is automatically deducted from the beneficiary's Social Security check. Each January, both the Social Security COLA and the premium increase go into effect. An additional protection for beneficiaries with small monthly payment amounts is that for each enrollee, the Part B premium is not allowed to rise (in dollars) by an amount greater then the Social Security COLA. Consequently, whereas a few enrollees effectively have their COLA adjustment each year eliminated by the increase in Part B premiums, no one actually receives less in nominal dollars from one year to the next because of Medicare premium increases. And in practice, unless the Social Security COLA is very small and the Part B premium increase very large, only a few beneficiaries have their full COLA eliminated.[8]

GROWTH IN ENROLLEE LIABILITY

Since most of the cost sharing under Medicare is linked to expenditures, enrollees' liabilities have risen sharply over time. This is shown in figure A.1. Most of the liability comes from Part B, through coinsurance and the premium. Thus, although Part B is less expensive from the standpoint of federal dollars, it is the more costly program as far as beneficiaries are concerned. Ironically, hospital expenditures, which are less important for cost sharing, constitute the bulk of Medicare spending (figure A.2).

Paying Providers

Medicare providers must generally be certified as meeting certain standards. They then bill Medicare on a fee-for-service basis. Hospitals and other major providers do not, however, file each claim separately. Rather, they are paid periodically, with adjustments to reconcile the actual amounts they are owed. These periodic interim payments (PIPs) were originally established to smooth the cash flow for hospitals. In the 1980s, they became a convenient, albeit bogus, device to achieve Medicare "savings." By delaying the payment from one fiscal year to the next, it can appear that Medicare had been cut.[9]

Physicians may ask patients to pay in full at the time of service, rather than seeking reimbursement from Medicare.[10] Physicians who directly bill Medicare are said to "accept assignment." If they accept assignment for all their Medicare patients, they are termed "participating providers" and are eligible for somewhat higher payments (allowed charges) for services. This distinction was made to encourage physicians to take assignment. If physicians decline to take assignment, they deal directly with the patient, who then must be reim-

Figure A.1 MEDICARE ENROLLEE COSTS, 1975–90

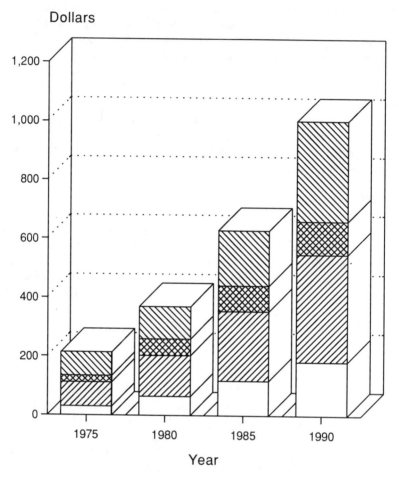

Source: Ways and Means (1991).

bursed by Medicare. When such physicians bill their patients for more than the allowed charges, they are said to "balance bill" the patients, effectively asking patients to pay more than the formal coinsurance of 20 percent of allowed charges. The number of physicians seeking to balance bill their patients has declined rather dramatically over time. In 1980, 48.7 percent of all covered charges were balance billed; that percentage declined to 15.2 percent by 1990. The extent of balance billing varies considerably by location of practice and specialty, however. Moreover, before 1992, those physicians who did balance bill could charge their patients substantially higher amounts—often as much or more than the 20 percent coinsurance. This feature will change dramatically under the new Medicare Fee Schedule that began in 1992, since physicians who balance bill will face strict limits.

Over time, the calculations for paying hospitals, physicians, and other providers of Medicare services have become more and more complicated. Initially, payment policy for hospitals and other large providers was based simply on reported costs. In the case of physicians, payments reflected "reasonable charges," defined as the lower of either a physician's own usual or customary charge, or the prevailing charge for physicians in a particular area. This is where policies to control costs have concentrated; these issues are discussed in detail in chapter 3.

Financing the Program

Medicare Part A is financed almost entirely by a 1.45 percent tax on the first $135,000 of earnings, assessed of both employees and em-

Figure A.2 SHARE OF MEDICARE BY CATEGORY OF SERVICE 1967, 1980, 1990

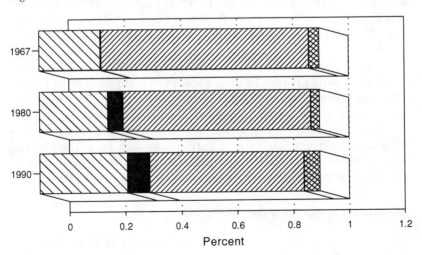

Source: Ways and Means, 1991.

ployers (and thus is a 2.9 percent tax on overall payroll up to the limit). It is part of the Federal Insurance Contributions Act (FICA) tax that most individuals see as a deduction in their paychecks each pay period. It is assessed regardless of wage level (up to a cap) on persons of all ages, but is paid mostly by persons under the age of 65 (since few persons over that age remain in the labor force). The upper limit on earnings was increased as part of the budget summit in 1990, a change that more than doubled the amount subject to tax. The 1993 Medicare limit of $135,000 compares to a limit of $57,600 applicable to the other parts of the FICA tax. The payroll tax rate was last increased in 1986 as part of the 1983 Social Security amendments and is not currently scheduled to rise further.

Together, the earnings limit and the combined employer/employee tax rate yield a maximum contribution of $3,915.00 on behalf of a worker in 1993. That compares to an initial tax rate of 0.7 percent (combined) against a base of $6,600 in 1966—for a maximum payment of $46.20. Converted to an average over the 26 years, this represents an annual growth rate of 18.5 percent, reflecting not only the increasing tax rate but an expanded tax base as well.

This payroll tax generates the bulk of the revenues for Part A. These revenues are combined with premiums (paid by those elderly not otherwise eligible), small general revenue transfers to cover beneficiaries such as railroad retirees, and interest from previous balances to form the Federal Hospital Insurance Trust Fund. Under the law, payments are made only so long as there is a positive balance in the trust fund. The HI trustees report for 1992 indicated an increasing balance in the near term, offset by payments exceeding revenues beginning in 1996 and total exhaustion of the trust fund by 2002 (see table A.2).

Part B's funding comes from the premium contributions of beneficiaries and general revenue contributions by the federal government. Although there is a trust fund for Part B as well as Part A, it is much less important since, by law, the U.S. Treasury must make up the difference between premium contributions and Part B spending. Thus, whereas general revenue contributions may be large, there is no crisis in funding requiring legislation, as is the case with Part A.

Administering the Program

The Health Care Financing Administration (HCFA) is in charge of overseeing the Medicare program, and promulgates rules and regulations governing its operations. The administrative costs of the program are quite low overall—about 2.5 percent of program outlays.

Table A.2 ESTIMATED OPERATIONS OF FEDERAL HOSPITAL INSURANCE TRUST
FUND, 1991–2002 ($ billions)

Calendar Year	Total Income (Billing, $)	Total Disbursements ($)	Net Increase in Fund ($)	Fund at End of Year ($)
1991	88.8	72.6	16.3	115.2
1992	92.7	79.4	13.3	128.5
1993	98.5	86.4	12.1	140.7
1994	104.4	95.5	8.9	149.6
1995	110.1	105.5	4.6	154.2
1996	116.2	117.4	− 1.1	153.0
1997	122.1	129.2	− 7.0	146.0
1998	128.1	141.6	− 13.5	132.5
1999	133.9	155.2	− 21.3	111.2
2000	139.8	170.0	− 30.2	81.0
2001	145.5	184.5	− 39.0	42.0
2002	149.0	200.3	− 51.3	0.0

Source: HI Trustees (1992).
Note: Data are based on Alternative II assumptions, which are usually considered
intermediate assumptions regarding factors such as life expectancy and healthcare
inflation.

Day-to-day processing of claims and oversight of providers is done at
a much more disaggregated level, however. HCFA contracts with "fiscal intermediaries" to process Part A claims and contracts with "carriers" to process Part B claims. These groups, usually insurance companies, deal directly with hospitals and physicians, respectively, to
determine the appropriate levels of payment and then pay those providers. These entities also check claims for accuracy and fraud, and
provide summary records of healthcare use to HCFA.

Carriers and intermediaries have always had considerable latitude
in interpreting HCFA instructions, often resulting in inconsistent enforcement of regulations. In turn, these actions affect whether beneficiaries have access to certain benefits. A good example is the skilled
nursing benefit, which has been the subject of court cases to try to
resolve some of the disparities. Even after such pressures, however,
availability of skilled nursing facilities varies substantially across the
country, likely reflecting differences in intermediaries' treatment as
well as other factors.

In practice, HCFA's data have been rather incomplete in terms of
what services have been provided and how much has been paid to
providers, limiting the agency's ability to oversee the work of the
carriers and intermediaries. Only in the last few years have carriers
even been required to meet uniform reporting requirements. HCFA,

however, has tried to improve data collection and reporting. For example, a new common working file project attempts to ensure that data are reported in a more consistent and reliable fashion. Regional centers now process information directly that used to be processed by the carriers and intermediaries and then passed on to HCFA.

HCFA also contracts with Peer Review Organizations (PROs) for further oversight of the use of services and quality control, particularly for hospital care. These organizations assess the appropriateness of care delivered, determine whether hospitalization was required, and, to a much lesser degree, assess the quality of that care. HCFA defines the mix of these activities in its scope of work for contractors, and these descriptions have changed over time. For example, in the third scope of work for the period 1988 to 1990, more attention was directed to assessing the quality of care. The tools for quality oversight are limited, however. For instance, when hospitals or physicians are found at fault, the main penalty available is exclusion from the Medicare program, leaving little room for intermediate remedies for less serious offenses. Further, many of the PROs' activities still center on cost-containment efforts. For example, retrospective reviews of a sample of inpatient hospital cases include generic quality screening, discharge review, admission review, review of invasive procedures, diagnosis-related group (DRG) validation, coverage review, and determination of the application of the waiver of liability provision (Lohr 1990). The fourth scope of work is now being phased in, with even more emphasis on quality.

Other activities to oversee the quality of care include certification of providers. For example, HCFA has its own process of certifying hospitals. In addition, it accepts certification of hospitals by the Joint Commission on Accreditation of Healthcare Organizations (JCAHO) in lieu of its own hospital certification process. This is referred to as "deemed status." Other providers have also sought deemed status if they meet accreditation standards established by their provider organizations.

Funding for research has always been part of HCFA's responsibilities as well. Recently, HCFA has broadened its interests to improve data, develop new measures for analysis, and spend additional funds on activities such as effectiveness research that may influence both the quality and cost of Medicare over time.

Notes

1. Unless otherwise noted, material for this appendix is drawn from several sources that detail the workings of the Medicare program. For more information, see Ways and Means (1992); Commerce Clearing House (1988); U.S. Social Security Administration (1991); HI Board of Trustees (1992); and SMI Board of Trustees (1992).

2. Several states are allowed to limit protection to persons with incomes below 95 percent of the poverty level until 1992.

3. Coinsurance is a charge assessed against the user of a service that is defined as a percentage of the cost of that care. The term *cost sharing* normally refers to coinsurance and deductibles—the costs of care that beneficiaries are required to "share."

4. Technically, this is not coinsurance—although it is the term that Medicare uses— since it is not tied to the cost of SNF care, but, rather, to the cost of hospital services. This is described later in this appendix.

5. Home healthcare is also covered under Part B, but the only enrollees who receive home health through Part B now are those not also enrolled in Part A.

6. The dual, and essentially conflicting, requirements of intermittency and confinement to the home were criticized in the 1980s by elderly advocates as providing a "Catch 22" that precluded eligibility for many Medicare enrollees. Easing of the intermittency guidelines has lessened this problem somewhat and expanded use of this benefit.

7. The coinsurance requirements are extremely complicated in the case of hospital outpatient services. Although Medicare pays outpatient departments on the basis of costs, coinsurance is calculated on the basis of charges, which are generally higher. Consequently, most beneficiaries effectively pay more that 20 percent coinsurance for hospital outpatient facility services.

8. For example, the Part B premium rose by just $1.30 per month between 1990 and 1991. The COLA increase in that year was 5.4 percent, so only persons with benefits of less than $24 would have had their COLAs fully eliminated. Only about 4 percent of retired workers receive payments of less than $200 per month.

9. In the budget agreements of 1981, 1982, and 1986, shifting of the timing of the (PIP) served as a major source of projected Medicare savings. In actuality, these efforts served to shift the timing of spending from one fiscal year to another and had no lasting effects on the federal budget deficit.

10. Even after the recent requirement that physicians must file claims for their patients, they can ask for payment directly from the beneficiary, rather than being paid by Medicare.

REFERENCES

Aaron, Henry, Barry Bosworth, and Gary Burtless. 1989. *Can America Afford to Grow Old?* Washington, D.C.: Brookings Institution Press.

AHA. *See* American Hospital Association.

American Healthline. 1992. "Clinton: What He's Been Saying on Health Care Reform." APN publication, 1 (November 4): 3.

American Hospital Association. 1990. *Hospital Statistics: 1990 Edition.* Chicago: Author.

————. 1988. *Socioeconomic Characteristics of Medical Practice, 1988.* Chicago: Author.

Andersen, Ronald, Joanna Lion, and Odin W. Anderson. 1976. *Two Decades of Health Services: Social Survey Trends in Use and Expenditure.* Cambridge, Mass.: Ballinger Publishing Co.

Andersen, Ronald, Joanna Kravits, Odin W. Anderson, and Joan Daley. 1973. *Expenditures for Personal Health Services: National Trends and Variations, 1953–1970.* Washington, D.C.: U.S. Department of Health, Education & Welfare.

Anderson, Martin. 1978. *Welfare.* Stanford, Calif.: Hoover Institution.

Ball, Robert. 1989. *Because We're All in This Together: The Case for a National Long Term Care Insurance Policy.* Washington, D.C.: Families USA Foundation.

Beebe, James, James Lubitz, and Paul Eggers. 1985. "Using Prior Utilization to Determine Payments for Medicare Enrollees in Health Maintenance Organizations." *Health Care Financing Review* 6 (Spring): 27–38.

Berenson, Robert, and John Holahan. 1990. "Using a New Type-of-Service Classification System to Examine the Growth in Medicare Physician Expenditures, 1985–1988." Draft. Washington, D.C.: Urban Institute, October.

Berki, S.E. 1986. "A Look at Catastrophic Medical Expenses and the Poor." *Health Affairs* 5 (Winter): 143–145.

Board of Trustees, Federal Hospital Insurance Trust Fund. 1992. *1992 Annual Report of the Board of Trustees of the Hospital Insurance Trust Fund.* Washington, D.C.: U.S. Government Printing Office.

————. 1991. *1991 Annual Report of the Board of Trustees of the Hospital*

Insurance Trust Fund. Washington, D.C.: U.S. Government Printing Office.

———. 1981. *1981 Annual Report of the Board of Trustees of the Hospital Insurance Trust Fund.* Washington: U.S. Government Printing Office.

Board of Trustees, Federal Supplementary Medical Insurance Fund. 1992. *1992 Annual Report of the Board of Trustees of the Federal Supplementary Medical Insurance Trust Fund.* Washington, D.C.: U.S. Government Printing Office.

———. 1991. *1991 Annual Report of the Board of Trustees of the Federal Supplementary Medical Insurance Trust Fund.* Washington, D.C.: U.S. Government Printing Office.

Brook, Robert H., Caren J. Kamberg, Allison Mayer-Oakes, Mark H. Beers, Kristiana Raube, and Andrea Steiner. 1989. "Appropriateness of Acute Medical Care for the Elderly: An Analysis of the Literature." Report R-3717-AARP/HF/RWJ/RC. Santa Monica, Calif.: RAND Corp.

Burkhauser, Richard, Karen Holden, and David Myers. 1986. "Marital Disruption and Poverty: The Role of Survey Procedures in Artificially Creating Poverty." *Demography,* 23: 621–31.

Butler, Stuart M. 1992. "A Policy Maker's Guide to the Health Care Crisis, Part II: The Heritage Consumer Choice Health Plan." Washington, D.C.: The Heritage Foundation, March 5.

Bye, Barry V., and Gerald F. Riley. 1989. "Eliminating the Medicare Waiting Period for Social Security Disabled-Worker Beneficiaries." *Social Security Bulletin* 52 (May): 2–15.

Callahan, Daniel. 1987. *Setting Limits: Medical Goals in an Aging Society.* New York: Simon Schuster.

Campion, Frank D. 1984. *The AMA and U.S. Health Policy since 1940.* Chicago: Chicago Review Press.

Chassin, Mark, J. Kosecoff, D. H. Solomon, et al. 1987. "How Coronary Angiography Is Used." *Journal of the American Medical Association* 258: 2543–47.

Chesney, James D. 1990. "Utilization Trends before and after PPS." *Inquiry* 27 (Winter): 376–81.

Christensen, Sandra. 1992. "The Subsidy Provided under Medicare to Current Enrollees." *Journal of Health Politics, Policy and Law* 17 (Summer): 255–64.

———. 1991. "Did 1980s Legislation Slow Medicare Spending?" DataWatch. *Health Affairs* 10 (Summer): 135–42.

Christensen, Sandra, and Rick Kasten. 1988a. "Covering Catastrophic Expenses under Medicare." *Health Affairs* 7 (Winter): 79–93.

———. 1988b. "The Medicare Catastrophic Coverage Act of 1988." Staff Working Paper. Washington, D.C.: Congressional Budget Office, August 1.

Clark, Robert, George Maddox, Ronald Schrimper, and Daniel Sumner. 1985. *Inflation and the Economic Well-Being of the Elderly.* Baltimore: Johns Hopkins University Press.

Commerce Clearing House, Inc. 1988. *1988 Medicare Explained—Including Medicare Catastrophic Coverage Act of 1988.* Chicago: Commerce Clearing House.

Congressional Budget Office. 1992. *Reducing the Deficit: Spending and Revenue Options.* Washington, D.C.: U.S. Government Printing Office, February.

————. 1991. *Universal Health Insurance Coverage Using Medicare's Payment Rates.* Washington, D.C.: U.S. Government Printing Office, December.

————. 1990. "Managed Care and the Medicare Program: Background and Evidence." Staff Memorandum, Washington, D.C.: Author, May.

————. 1989a. "Background Material on the Catastrophic Drug Insurance Program." Washington, D.C.: Author, July.

————. 1989b. *The Economic Status of the Elderly.* Washington, D.C.: Author, May.

————. 1988. "The Medicare Catastrophic Coverage Act of 1988." Staff Working Paper. Washington, D.C.: Author, August 1. Photocopy.

————. 1987. "Background Information on Out-of-Pocket Costs under Medicare." Washington, D.C.: Author, March 18. Photocopy.

————. 1983. *Changing the Structure of Medicare Benefits: Issues and Options. A CBO Study.* Washington, D.C.: U.S. Government Printing Office, March.

Congressional Research Service. 1989. *Health Insurance and the Uninsured: Background Data and Analysis.* Senate Committee on Education and Labor, Print 100-2, 122–23.

Coulam, Robert, and Gary Gaumer. 1991. "Published Research on the Effects of PPS: A Critical Appraisal." Cambridge, Mass.: Abt Associates. Photocopy.

Council of Economic Advisors. 1964. *Economic Report of the President.* Washington, D.C.: U.S. Government Printing Office.

Danziger, Sheldon, Jacques van der Gaag, Eugene Smolensky, and Michael Taussig. 1984. "Income Transfers and the Economic Status of the Elderly." In *Economic Transfers in the United States,* edited by Marilyn Moon. Chicago: University of Chicago Press.

Davis, Karen. 1975. "Equal Treatment and Unequal Benefits: The Medicare Program." *Milbank Memorial Fund Quarterly* 53 (Fall): 449–88.

Davis, Karen, and Diane Rowland. 1986. *Medicare Policy: New Directions for Health and Long-Term Care.* Baltimore: Johns Hopkins University Press.

Davis, Karen, and Cathy Schoen. 1978. *Health and the War on Poverty: A Ten-Year Appraisal.* Washington, D.C.: Brookings Institution Press.

Derthick, Martha. 1979. *Policymaking for Social Security.* Washington, D.C.: Brookings Institution Press.

Doty, Pamela, Korbin Liu, and Joshua Wiener. 1985. "An Overview of Long Term Care." *Health Care Financing Review* 5 (Spring): 69–78.

Epstein, Arnold, and Edward Cumella. 1988. "Capitation Payment: Using

Predictors of Medical Utilization to Adjust Rates." *Health Care Financing Review* 10 (Fall): 51–69.

Epstein, Arnold M., Jonathan Bogen, Paul Dreyer, and Kenneth E. Thorpe. 1991. "Trends in Length of Stay and Rates of Readmission in Massachusetts: Implications for Monitoring Quality of Care." *Inquiry* 28 (Spring): 19–28.

Families USA. 1992. "The Medicare Buy-in: Still a Government Secret." Washington, D.C. Author.

Feder, Judith M. 1977. *Medicare: The Politics of Federal Hospital Insurance.* Lexington, Mass.: Lexington Books.

Feder, Judith, Marilyn Moon, and William Scanlon. 1987a. "Catastrophic Health Insurance for the Elderly: Options and Impacts." Georgetown Center for Health Policy Studies Working Paper. Washington, D.C.: Georgetown University.

————. 1987b. "Medicare Reform: Nibbling at Catastrophic Costs." *Health Affairs* 6 (Winter): 5–19.

Feder, Judith, John Holahan, Randall R. Bovbjerg, and Jack Hadley. 1982. "Health." In *The Reagan Experiment*, edited by John L. Palmer and Isabel V. Sawhill. Washington, D.C.: Urban Institute Press.

Federal Register. 1991a. "Medicare Program: Fee Schedule for Physician Services." Vol. 56, November 25, 59502–59819.

————. 1991b. "Medicare Program: Fee Schedule for Physicians' Services; Proposed Rule." Vol. 56, June 5, 25792–25978.

Feinglass, Joe, and James J. Holloway. 1991. "The Initial Impact of the Medicare Prospective Payment System on U.S. Health Care: A Review of the Literature." *Medical Care Review* 48 (Spring): 91–115.

Fitzgerald, J. F., L. F. Fagan, W. M. Tierney, et al. 1987. "Changing Patterns of Hip Fracture Care before and after Implementation of the Prospective Payment System." *Journal of the American Medical Association* 258: 218–21.

Freudenheim, Milt. 1992. "Doctors Dropping Medicare Patients." *New York Times*, April 12: 1, 26.

Gerety, M. B., V. Doderholm-Difatte, and C. H. Winograd. 1989. "Impact of Prospective Payment and Discharge Location at the Outcome of Hip Fracture." *Journal of General Internal Medicine* 149: 1392–97.

Ginsburg, Paul, and Grace Carter. 1986. "The Medicare Case Mix Index Increase." *Health Care Financing Review* 7 (Winter): 51–65.

Grad, Susan. 1989. "Income and Assets of Social Security Beneficiaries by Type of Benefit." *Social Security Bulletin* 52(1): 2–10.

————. 1988. *Income of the Population 55 or Older, 1986.* U.S. Social Security Administration, Office of Policy. Washington, D.C.: U.S. Government Printing Office, June.

Hadley, Jack, Stephen Zuckerman, and Judith Feder. 1989. "Profits and Fiscal Pressure in the Prospective Payment System: Their Impacts on Hospitals." *Inquiry* 26(3): 354–65.

Hadley, Jack, Robert Berenson, David Juba, and Judy Wagner. 1986. "Alternative Approaches to Constructing a Relative Value Scale." In *Medicare Physician Payment Reform*, edited by John Holahan and Lynn Etheredge. Washington, D.C.: Urban Institute Press.

Health Care Financing Administration. 1990. *Program Statistics: Medicare and Medicaid Data Book, 1990*. Washington, D.C.: U.S. Government Printing Office.

Health Insurance Association of America. 1991. *Source Book of Health Insurance Data, 1991*. Washington, D.C.: Author.

————. 1989. *Source Book of Health Insurance Data, 1989*. Washington, D.C.: Author.

HIAA. *See* Hospital Insurance Association of America.

HI Trustees. *See* Board of Trustees. Federal Hospital Insurance Trust Fund.

Henry J. Kaiser Foundation. 1992. "Survey Says Widespread Public Concern About Health Insurance and Costs." News Release, Washington, D.C., April 8.

Holahan, John, and John L. Palmer. 1988. "Medicare's Fiscal Problems: An Imperative for Reform." *Journal of Health Politics, Policy, and Law* 13 (Spring): 53–81.

Holden, Karen, Richard Burkhauser, and D. J. Feaster. 1987. "The Timing of Falls into Poverty after Retirement: An Event-History Approach." Madison: University of Wisconsin, Madison. Photocopy.

Hsiao, William C., and William B. Stason. 1979. "Toward Developing a Relative Value Scale for Medical and Surgical Services." *Health Care Financing Review* (Fall): 23–38.

Hsiao, William C., Peter Braun, Edmund Becker, Nancyanne Causino, Nathan Couch, Margaret DeNicola, Daniel Dunn, Nancy Kelly, Thomas Ketcham, Arthur Sobol, Diana Verrilli, and Douwe Yntema. 1988. "A National Study of Resource-Based Relative Value Scales for Physician Services." Final Report. HCFA Contract No. 17-C-98795/1-03. Cambridge, Mass.: Harvard University.

Kahn, Katherine, Lisa V. Rubenstein, David Draper, Jacqueline Kosecoff, William H. Rogers, Emmett B. Keeler, and Robert H. Brook. 1990. "The Effects of the DRG-Based Prospective Payment System on Quality of Care for Hospitalized Medicare Patients." *Journal of the American Medical Association* 264(15): 1953–55.

Kenney, Genevieve. 1991. "Understanding the Effects of PPS on Home Health Use." *Inquiry* 28 (Summer): 129–39.

Kosekoff, Jacqueline, Katherine Kahn, William Rogers, et al. 1990. "Prospective Payment System and Impairment at Discharge: The "Quicker-and-Sicker" Story Revisited." *Journal of the American Medical Association* 264 (Oct. 17): 1980–83.

Langwell, Kathryn, and James Hadley. 1989. "Evaluation of the Medicare Competition Demonstrations." *Health Care Financing Review* 11 (Winter): 65–79.

Lave, Judith. 1990. "The Impact of the Medicare Prospective Payment System and Recommendations for Change." *Yale Journal on Regulation* 7: 499–528.

Leader, Shelah, and Marilyn Moon. 1989. "Medicare Trends in Ambulatory Surgery." *Health Affairs* (Spring): 158–170.

Liu, Korbin, and Genevieve Kenney. 1991. "Impact of the Catastrophic Coverage Act and New Coverage Guidelines on the Medicare SNF Benefit." Urban Institute Working Paper. #4710. Washington, D.C.: Urban Institute, October.

Lohr, Kathleen N., ed. 1990. *Medicare: A Strategy for Quality Assurance*, vol. 1. Institute of Medicine. Washington, D.C.: National Academy Press.

Lubitz, James. 1990. "Use and Costs of Medicare Services in the Last Year of Life, 1976 and 1985." Washington, D.C.: Health Care Financing Administration, May 11. Photocopy.

Lubitz, James, and Ronald Prihoda. 1984. "Use and Costs of Medicare Services in the Last Two Years of Life." *Health Care Financing Review* 5 (Spring): 117–31.

Marmor, Theodore R. 1970. *The Politics of Medicare*. Chicago: Aldine Publishing Co.

McIlrath, Sharon. 1991. "HCFA Issues Final RBRVS Rules." *American Medical News* (December 2): 1, 5, 6.

Merrick, N. J., Robert Brook, Arlene Fink, and David Solomon. 1986. "Use of Carotid Endarterectomy in Five California Veterans Administration Medical Centers." *Journal of the American Medical Association* 256: 2531–35.

Meyer, Jack, and Marilyn Moon. 1988. "Health Care Spending on Children and the Elderly." In *The Vulnerable*, edited by John Palmer, Timothy Smeeding, and Barbara Torrey. Washington, D.C.: Urban Institute Press.

Michel, Richard C. 1991. "Economic Growth and Income Equality since the 1982 Recession." *Journal of Policy Analysis and Management* 10(2): 181–203.

Mitchell, Janet, and Terri Menke. 1990. "How the Physician Fee Schedule Affects Medicare Patients' Out-of-Pocket Spending." *Inquiry* 27 (Summer): 108–13.

Moon, Marilyn. Forthcoming. "Women and Long Term Care." In *The American Woman: A Status Report*, 5th Edition. New York: WW Norton.

————. 1991a. "Expanding Medicare to Cover At-Risk Older Americans." Testimony presented to Subcommittee on Health, House Committee on Ways and Means, One Hundred Second Congress, First Session, March 19.

————. 1991b. "Measures of Health Care Spending and the Elderly." Urban Institute Project Report 6132-01. Washington, D.C.: Urban Institute, March.

————. 1991c. "Medicare's Future: Increasing Pressure for Radical Reform." *Internist* 32 (March): 14–16.

————. 1989. "Taking the Plunge: The Arguments for a Comprehensive Approach to Long Term Care." *Journal of the American Geriatrics Society* 37 (December): 1165–70.

————. 1988. "The Economic Situation of Older Americans: Emerging Wealth and Continuing Hardship." In *Annual Review of Gerontology and Geriatrics*, vol. 8, edited by George Maddox and M. Powell Lawton. New York: Springer Publishing Co.

————. 1987. "The Elderly's Access to Health Care Services: The Crude and Subtle Impacts of Medicare Changes." *Social Justice Research* 1(3): 361–75.

————. 1979. "The Incidence of Poverty among the Aged." *Journal of Human Resources* 14 (Spring): 211–21.

Moon Marilyn, and Isabel Sawhill. 1984. "Family Incomes: Gainers and Losers." In *The Reagan Record*, edited by John Palmer and Isabel Sawhill. Cambridge, Mass.: Ballinger Publishing Co.

Myers, Robert J. 1970. *Medicare*. McCahan Foundation Book Series. Homewood, Ill.: Richard D. Irwin.

Myers, Stephen A., and Norbert Gleicher. 1988. "A Successful Program to Lower Cesarean-Section Rates." *New England Journal of Medicine* 319 (Dec. 8): 1511–16.

National Center for Health Services Research. 1989. "Health Insurance Coverage of Retired Persons." Research Findings 2, National Medical Expenditure Survey. Washington, D.C. U.S.: Department of Health and Human Services.

————. 1987. "A Summary of Expenditures and Sources of Payment for Personal Health Services from the National Medical Care Survey." Data Preview 24, Public Health Service, U.S. Department of Health and Human Services. Washington, D.C.: Author, May.

National Center for Health Statistics. 1991. *Health, United States, 1990.* Hyattsville, Md.: U.S. Public Health Service.

————. 1987. *Family Out-of-Pocket Expenditures for Health Care United States, 1980.* Ser. B, Descriptive Report #11, Public Health Service, U.S. Department of Health and Human Services. Washington, D.C.: U.S. Government Printing Office, August.

NCHSR. *See* National Center for Health Services Research.

NCHS. *See* National Center for Health Statistics.

Newhouse, Joseph, William Schwartz, Albert Williams, and Christina Witsberger. 1985. "Are Fee-for-Service Costs Increasing Faster than HMO's Costs?" *Medical Care* 23 (August): 960–966.

Newhouse, Joseph et al. 1982. *Some Interim Results from a Controlled Trial of Cost Sharing in Health Insurance.* Santa Monica, Calif.: RAND Corp.

Newman, Howard N. 1972. "Medicare and Medicaid." *Annals of the American Academy of Political and Social Science* 399 (January): 114–124.

New York Times. 1966. "Doctors' Fees Up as Much as 300% under Medicare." Aug. 19: 1.

————. 1965. "Medicare Caution Given Physicians." Aug. 12: 15.

Office of National Cost Estimates. 1990. "National Health Expenditures, 1988." *Health Care Financing Review* 11 (Summer): 1–41.

Office of Technology Assessment. 1986. *Payment for Physician Services: Strategies for Medicare.* OTA-H-294. Washington, D.C.: U.S. Government Printing Office, February.

————. 1985. *Medicare's Prospective Payment System: Strategies for Evaluating Cost, Quality and Medical Technology.* Washington, D.C.: U.S. Government Printing Office, October.

Office of the President. 1992a. *Budget of the United States Government, Fiscal Year 1993.* Washington D.C.: U.S. Government Printing Office.

————. 1992b. *Economic Report of the President.* Washington, D.C.: U.S. Government Printing Office.

————. 1991. *Budget of the United States Government, Fiscal Year 1992.* Washington D.C.: U.S. Government Printing Office.

————. 1986. *Economic Report of the President.* Washington, D.C.: U.S. Government Printing Office.

Omenn, Gilbert. 1990. "Prevention and the Elderly: Appropriate Policies." *Health Affairs* (Summer): 80–93.

Palmer, R.M., Saywell R.M., T.W. Zollinger, B.K.Erner, A.D. LaBov, D.A. Freund, J.E. Garber, G.W. Misamore, and F.B. Throop. 1989. "The Impact of the Prospective Payment System on the Treatment of Hip Fractures in the Elderly." *Archives of Internal Medicine* 149(10): 2237–2241.

Pearman, William A., and Philip Starr. 1988. *Medicare: A Handbook on the History and Issues of Health Care Services for the Elderly.* New York: Garland Publishing.

Pepper Commission (U.S. Bipartisan Commission on Comprehensive Health Care). 1990. *A Call for Action.* Washington, D.C.: U.S. Government Printing Office.

Physician Payment Review Commission. 1992. "Monitoring the Financial Liability of Medicare Beneficiaries." Report 92-3. Washington, D.C.: Author. Photocopy.

————. 1989. *Annual Report to Congress.* Washington, D.C.: U.S. Government Printing Office, March.

————. 1987. *Medicare Physician Payment: An Agenda for Reform.* Annual Report to Congress. Washington, D.C.: U.S. Government Printing Office, March.

Plotnick, Robert, and Felicity Skidmore. 1976. *Progress Against Poverty: A Review of the 1964–1974 Decade.* New York: Academic Press.

Poterba, James, and Lawrence Summers. 1985. "Public Policy Implications of

Declining Old-Age Mortality." Paper presented to the Brookings Institution Conference on Retirement and Aging, May 2, 1985. Washington, D.C. Revised.

ProPAC. See Prospective Payment Assessment Commission.

Prospective Payment Assessment Commission. 1991. *Medicare and the American Health Care System—Report to the Congress.* Washington, D.C.: Author.

_____. 1990. *Medicare Prospective Payment and the American Health Care System: Report to the Congress.* Washington, D.C.: Author, June.

_____. 1986. *Technical Appendixes to the Report and Recommendations to the Secretary, U.S. Department of Health and Human Services.* Washington, D.C.: U.S. Government Printing Office, April 1.

Radner, Daniel. 1987. "Money Incomes of Aged and Nonaged Family Units, 1967–84." *Social Security Bulletin* 50 (August): 9–28.

Rettig, Richard. 1982. "The Federal Government and Social Planning for End-Stage Renal Disease: Past, Present, and Future." *Seminars in Nephrology* 2 (June): 111–133.

_____. 1976. "The Policy Debate on Patient Care Financing for Victims of End-Stage Renal Disease." *Law and Contemporary Problems* 40 (Autumn): 196–230.

Rich, Spencer. 1988. "Provisions of 'Catastophic' Insurance Act." *Washington Post,* July 1: A21.

_____. 1987. " 'Catastrophic' Bill's Cost Raises New Doubt." *Washington Post* September 14, 1987: A4.

Rivlin, Alice, and Joshua Wiener. 1988. *Caring for the Disabled Elderly.* Washington, D.C.: Brookings Institution.

Rizzo, John A. 1990. *Financially Distressed Hospitals: A Profile of Behavior before and after PPS.* DHHS Pub. No. (PHS) 90-3467. Hospital Studies Program Research Note 14, Agency for Health Care Policy and Research. Rockville, Md.: U.S. Public Health Service.

Ross, Christine, Sheldon Danziger, and Eugene Smolensky. 1987. "Interpreting Changes in the Economic Status of the Elderly, 1949–1979." *Contemporary Policy Issues* 5: 98–112.

Ruggles, Patricia. 1990. *Drawing the Line: Alternative Poverty Measures and Their Implications for Public Policy.* Washington, D.C.: Urban Institute Press.

Ruggles, Patricia, and Paul Cullinan. 1985. "The Contribution of Transfer Payments to the Incomes of the Elderly." Washington, D.C.: Urban Institute. Photocopy.

Ruggles, Patricia, and Roberton Williams. 1989. "Longitudinal Measures of Poverty: The Role of Assets." *Review of Income and Wealth* 35 (September): 225–244.

Russell, Louise B. 1989. *Medicare's New Hospital Payment System: Is It Working?* Washington, D.C.: Brookings Institution.

Scitovsky, Anne. 1984. "The High Cost of Dying: What Do the Data Show?" *Milbank Memorial Fund Quarterly* 62: 610–15.

Sheingold, Steven. 1986. "Unintended Results of Medicare's National Prospective Payment Rates." *Health Affairs* 5 (Winter): 5–21.

Shikles, Janet L. 1990. "Medigap Insurance: Premiums and Regulatory Changes after Repeal of the Medicare Catastrophic Coverage Act and 1988 Loss Ratio Data." Statement before the Subcommittee on Health, House Committee on Ways and Means, One Hundred First Congress, Second Session March 13. Pub. No. GAO/T-HRD-90-16. Washington, D.C.: U.S. General Accounting Office.

Showstack, Jonathan A., Bart D. Blumberg, Judy Schwartz, and Steven A. Schroeder. 1979. "Fee-for-Service Physician Payment: Analysis of Current Methods and Their Development." *Inquiry* 16 (Fall): 230–246.

Silverman, H. A. 1991. "Medicare-Covered Skilled Nursing Facility Services, 1967–1988." *Health Care Financing Review* 12(3): 103–108.

Simon, Matt. 1989. "Flimflam: The National Committee and Its Pitch to Seniors." *Union* (April/May): 13–16.

Skidmore, Max J. 1970. *Medicare and the American Rhetoric of Reconciliation.* University, Ala.: University of Alabama Press.

Sloan, Frank, M.A. Morrisey, and J. Valvona. 1988. "Medicare Prospective Payment and the Use of Medical Technologies in Hospitals." *Medical Care* 26(9): 837–53.

Smeeding Timothy. 1986. "Nonmoney Income and the Elderly: The Case of the 'Tweeners.' " *Journal of Policy Analysis and Management,* 5 (Summer): 707–24.

———. 1982. *Alternative Methods for Valuing In-Kind Transfer Benefits and Measuring Their Impact on Poverty.* Technical Report 50, U.S. Bureau of the Census. Washington, D.C.: U.S. Government Printing Office.

Smits, Helen, Judith Feder, and William Scanlon. 1982. "Medicare's Nursing-Home Benefit: Variations in Interpretation." *New England Journal of Medicine* 307 (Sept. 30): 855–62.

Somers, Herman M., and Anne R. Somers. 1967. *Medicare and the Hospitals: Issues and Prospects.* Washington, D.C.: Brookings Institution.

Soumerai, Stephen B., and Dennis Ross-Degnan. 1990. "Experience of State Drug Benefit Programs." *Health Affairs* 9 (Fall): 36–54.

Soumerai, Stephen B., Dennis Ross-Degnan, Jerry Avorn, Thomas McLaughlin, and Igor Choodnovskiy. 1991. "Effects of Medicaid Drug-Payment Limits on Admission to Hospitals and Nursing Homes." *New England Journal of Medicine* 326 (Oct. 10): 1072–77.

Starr, Paul. 1982. *The Social Transformation of American Medicine.* New York: Basic Books.

Sullivan, Cynthia and Tom Rice. 1991. "The Health Insurance Picture in 1990." *Health Affairs* 10 (Summer): 104–115.

Sulvetta, Margaret B. 1992. "Achieving Cost Control in the Hospital Outpatient Setting." *Health Care Financing Review* (1991 Annual Supplement) (March): 95–106.

Torres-Gil, Fernando. 1989. "The Politics of Catastrophic and Long-Term Care Coverage." *Journal of Aging and Social Policy* 12: 61–86.

U.S. Bureau of the Census. 1991a. *Money Income of Households, Families, and Persons in the United States: 1990. Current Population Reports,* ser. P-60, no. 174. Washington, D.C.: U.S. Government Printing Office.

_____. 1991b. *Poverty in the United States: 1990. Current Population Reports,* ser. P-60, no. 175. Washington, D.C.: U.S. Government Printing Office.

_____. 1986. *Money Income of Households, Families, and Persons in the United States: 1985. Current Population Reports,* ser. P-60, no. 156. Washington, D.C.: U.S. Government Printing Office.

_____. 1990. *Trends in Income By Selected Characteristics.* Series P-60, #167. Washington, D.C.: U.S. Government Printing Office, April.

U.S. Congress. House Committee on Ways and Means. 1992. *1992 Green Book: Background Material and Data on Programs within the Jurisdiction of the Committee on Ways and Means.* Washington, D.C.: U.S. Government Printing Office, June.

_____. 1991. *1991 Green Book: Background Material and Data on Programs within the Jurisdiction of the Committee on Ways and Means.* Washington,D.C.: U.S. Government Printing Office, June.

_____. 1990. *1990 Green Book: Background Material and Data on Programs within the Jurisdiction of the Committee on Ways and Means.* Washington, D.C.: U.S. Government Printing Office.

_____. 1988. *Background Material and Data on Programs within the Jurisdiction of the Committee on Ways and Means.* U.S. House of Representatives. Washington,D.C.: U.S. Government Printing Office, May.

_____. 1985. *Background Material and Data on Programs within the Jurisdiction of the Committee on Ways and Means.* U.S. House of Representatives. Washington,D.C.: U.S. Government Printing Office, May.

_____. Select Committee on Aging. 1985. *America's Elderly at Risk.* 99th Cong 1st Session Committee Print 99–508. Washington, D.C.: U.S. Government Printing Office, July.

_____. Senate. Special Committee on Aging. 1982. *Health Care Expenditures for the Elderly: How Much Protection Does Medicare Provide?* 97th Congress, 2d Session Committee Print. 92–225 Washington, D.C.: U.S. Government Printing Office, April.

U.S. Department of Health and Human Services. Social Security Administration. 1990. *Social Security Bulletin: Annual Statistical Supplement, 1990.* Washington, D.C.: U.S. Governmental Printing Office.

_____. Health Care Financing Administration. 1987. *Report to Congress:*

Impact of the Medicare Hospital Prospective Payment System—1985 Annual Report. HCFA Pub. No. 03251. Washington, D.C.: Author.

————. 1986. *Catastrophic Illness Expenses.* Report to the President. Washington, D.C.: Author, November.

U.S. Department of Health, Education, & Welfare. Health Resources Administration. 1973. *Expenditures for Personal Health Services: National Trends and Variations, 1953–1970.* DHEW Pub. No. (HRA) 74-3105. Washington, D.C.: U.S. Government Printing Office.

————. Health Services and Mental Health Administration. 1972. *Health Service Use: National Trends and Variations.* DHEW Pub. No. (HSM) 73-3004. Washington, D.C.: U.S. Government Printing Office.

U.S. General Accounting Office. 1991a. *Medicare: HCFA Needs to Take Stronger Actions Against HMOs Violating Federal Standards.* Pub. No. HRD-92-11. Washington, D.C.: Author, November.

————. 1991b. *Medigap Insurance: Better Consumer Protection Should Result from 1990 Changes to Baucus Amendment.* Pub. No. HRD-91-49. Washington, D.C. Author, March.

U.S. Public Health Service. 1990. *Health United States, 1990.* U.S. Department of Health and Human Services. Washington, D.C.: U.S. Government Printing Office.

U.S. Social Security Administration. 1991. *Social Security Bulletin, Annual Statistical Supplement.* Washington, D.C.: U.S. Government Printing Office.

Varner, Theresa. 1987. "Catastrophic Health Care Costs for Older Americans: The Issue and Its Implications for Policy Development." Paper 8702. Washington, D.C.: American Association of Retired Persons, June.

Waldo, Daniel, Sally Sonnefeld, David McKusick, and Ross Arnett. 1989. "Health Expenditures by Age Group, 1977 and 1987." *Health Care Financing Review* 10 (Summer): 111–120.

Ways and Means. *See* U.S. Congress. House. Committee on Ways and Means.

Welch, W. Pete. 1991. "HMO Market Share and Its Effect on Local Medicare Costs." Urban Institute Project Report 3840–01. Washington, D.C.: Urban Institute, March.

Wiener, Janet. 1990. "Medicare at 25." *Perspectives* (Suppl. to *Medicine & Health*) (Aug. 6).

Wilensky, Gail, Peter Neumann, and Linda Blumberg. 1987. "The Medicare Catastrophic Drug Benefit: An Analysis of the Cost Estimates." Washington, D.C.: Project HOPE, Sept. 9.

Winslow, C. M., D. H. Solomon, Mark Chassin, Jacqueline Kosecoff, Nancy Merrick, and Robert Brook. 1988. "The Appropriateness of Carotid Endarterectomy." *New England Journal of Medicine* 318: 721–27.

Wolff, Edward. 1987. "Estimate of Household Wealth Inequality in the U.S., 1962–1983." *Review of Income and Wealth* 33 (September): 231–56.

Wood, Juanita B., and Carroll L. Estes. 1990. "The Impact of DRGs on Community-Based Service Providers: Implications for the Elderly." *American Journal of Public Health* 80(7): 840–43.

Wyszewianski, Leon. 1986. "Financially Catastrophic and High-Cost Cases: Definitions, Distinctions, and Their Implications for Policy Formulation." *Inquiry* 23 (Winter): 382–94.

Yeas, Martynas, and Susan Grad. 1987. "Income of Retirement Aged Persons in the United States." *Social Security Bulletin* 50: 5–14.

Zedlewski, Sheila, Robert Barnes, Martha Burt, Timothy McBride, and Jack Meyer. 1990. *The Needs of the Elderly in the 21st Century.* Urban Institute Report 90-5. Washington, D.C.: Urban Institute.

Zuckerman, Stephen, and John Holahan. 1992. "Measuring Growth in the Volume and Intensity of Medicare Physician Services: 1985– 1989." Urban Institute Working Paper, #4708 Washington, D.C.: Urban Institute, May.

Zuckerman, Stephen, W. Pete Welch, and Gregory Pope. 1990. "A Geographic Index of Physician Practice Costs." *Journal of Health Economics* 9 (June): 39–69.

INDEX

ABOUT THE AUTHOR

Marilyn Moon is currently a senior research associate with the Health Policy Center of the Urban Institute. She has written extensively on health policy, policy for the elderly, and income distribution. Her current work focuses on health system reform and financing. She recently wrote, with John Holahan, W. Pete Welch, and Stephen Zuckerman, an Urban Institute Report entitled *Balancing Access, Costs, and Politics: The American Context for Health System Reform*. Recent articles include "Medicare's Future: Increasing Pressure for Radical Reform," "An American Approach to Health System Reform," and "What Should Be the Role of States in Health Care Reform?"

Marilyn Moon has also served as director of the Public Policy Institute of the American Association of Retired Persons. She has worked as a senior analyst in the Human Resources and Community Development Division of the Congressional Budget Office, and associate professor of economics at the University of Wisconsin-Milwaukee. Recently, she has served as a consultant to the U.S. Bipartisan Commission for Comprehensive Health Care (the Pepper Commission) and as a committee member for a two-year Institute of Medicine study on the quality of care in Medicare.

DATE DUE

~~SEP~~		~~MAY~~
~~NOV 16 1996~~		
~~MAR 1~~		
~~APR 2 5 2001~~		

Demco, Inc. 38-293

LIBRARY
N.Y.